D1042232

DISCARDED

PRAISE FOR ROBERT GARFIELD AND
BREAKING THE MALE CODE

"Dr. Garfield explains why emotional intimacy is a rare quality in male friendships and offers a clear road map for men to forge deeper connections. His style is warm, engaging, and user-friendly. I suspect that countless wives will put this book on their husband's bedside table."

— **Harriet Lerner, PhD**, author of
The Dance of Anger and *Marriage Rules*

"Rob Garfield knows that the cure for what ails men is intimacy—connection to themselves and others. With compassion and wit, he shows men, step by step, how to move beyond the strictures of Male Code into the richness of an open heart. Both practical and moving, *Breaking the Male Code* belongs on the shelf of every man wanting to grow and every clinician dedicated to helping."

— **Terrence Real**, author of *I Don't Want to Talk About It*

"In this wonderfully readable book, Dr. Robert Garfield brings his extensive knowledge and rich experience to show how men think and feel about their relationships with other men. *Breaking the Male Code* delivers a powerful and hopeful message, one that provides men of all ages with the skills necessary to enjoy deep and fulfilling relationships with one another. This book has the potential to dramatically improve *all* the important relationships in men's lives!"

— **Constance Ahrons, PhD**, professor emerita at the
University of Southern California and author of
The Good Divorce and *We're Still Family*

"A compelling book that goes to the heart of male loneliness and points the way toward deeper and more fulfilling friendships in men's lives."

— **Samuel Osherson**, author of *Finding Our Fathers*
and *The Stethoscope Cure*

"Remember how Thoreau said that men 'lead lives of quiet desperation'? If only he'd read Rob Garfield's book! He'd understand not only why they're desperate but also how to address their needs. A vital message about men's emotional needs, offered with care, thought, and great compassion."

—**Michael Kimmel**, author of *Guyland* and executive director
for the Center for the Study of Men and Masculinities
at Stony Brook University

"With warmth and empathy, Rob Garfield takes on the task of helping us to overcome our stereotypes about maleness and our often incomplete definition of friendship so that men can relate to one another in an intimate way."

—**Donald N. Bersoff, PhD, JD**, former president of the
American Psychological Association

"Garfield does a superb job of revealing the obstacles to intimacy in men's friendships as well as providing a detailed guide on how to build such friendships. Linking the theoretical with the practical, this book will be extremely useful for men everywhere."

—**Niobe Way, EdD**, professor of Developmental Psychology at
New York University and author of *Deep Secrets: Boys'
Friendships and the Crisis of Connection*

"*Breaking the Male Code* is a book that will change lives. Garfield's broad and deep knowledge of men, their struggles, doubts, and perseverance, coupled with their often unfulfilled wish to connect with other men is evident on every page. His sage direction will enable men to relish life more fully."

—**Evan Imber-Black, PhD**, program director for Marriage
and Family Therapy at Mercy College and author of
The Secret Life of Families and *Rituals for Our Times*

"*Breaking the Male Code* has the potential to be among every therapist's best friend in terms of what they'll want to recommend to their male clients. A valuable resource for males of all ages and for the women who love them."

—**Robert Heasley, PhD, CMF**, former president of
the American Men's Studies Association and professor of
sociology at Indiana University of Pennsylvania

BREAKING THE
MALE CODE

UNLOCKING THE
POWER OF FRIENDSHIP:

OVERCOMING MALE ISOLATION
FOR A LONGER, HAPPIER LIFE

ROBERT GARFIELD, MD

GOTHAM BOOKS

YUMA COUNTY LIBRARY
2951 S. 21st Dr.
Yuma. AZ. 85364

**GOTHAM
BOOKS**

Gotham Books, an imprint of Penguin Random House
375 Hudson Street
New York, New York 10014

Copyright © 2015 by Robert Garfield

Penguin supports copyright. Copyright fuels creativity, encourages diverse voices, promotes free speech, and creates a vibrant culture. Thank you for buying an authorized edition of this book and for complying with copyright laws by not reproducing, scanning, or distributing any part of it in any form without permission. You are supporting writers and allowing Penguin to continue to publish books for every reader.

Gotham Books and the skyscraper logo are trademarks of Penguin Random House LLC.

LIBRARY OF CONGRESS CATALOGING-IN-PUBLICATION DATA

Garfield, Robert (Physician)

Breaking the male code : unlocking the power of friendship, overcoming male isolation for a longer, happier life / Robert Garfield, M.D.

pages cm

Includes bibliographical references.

ISBN 978-1-592-40904-4 (hardcover)

1. Men—Psychology.   2. Masculinity.   3. Male friendship—Sociological aspects.
4. Men—Family relationships.   I. Title.

HQ1090.G358 2015

155.3'3224—dc23   2014043844

Printed in the United States of America

1   3   5   7   9   10   8   6   4   2

Book Design by Elke Sigal

While the author has made every effort to provide accurate telephone numbers, Internet addresses, and other contact information at the time of publication, neither the publisher nor the author assumes any responsibility for errors or for changes that occur after publication. Further, the publisher does not have any control over and does not assume any responsibility for author or third-party websites or their content.

None of the names of any individuals mentioned in my stories, other than those of family or friends, correspond to any actual persons living or dead. The stories are composites and are used to illustrate particular dynamics that commonly occur in men's relationships.

For
Milt and Harriet Garfield, my parents,
who blessed our friendships.

Sandy Whipple, my wife, who encouraged
me to write this book and backed it up
with unflagging support.

Jake Kriger, my best friend, an awesome
man, who taught me how to be a best friend.

CONTENTS

PART 1
MEN'S FRIENDSHIPS TODAY

PART 2
FRIENDSHIP FUNDAMENTALS

PART 3
SPREADING THE WEALTH

PART 1

MEN'S FRIENDSHIPS TODAY

CHAPTER 1

Men in Transition

A quiet settled over the room as the seven men present realized that the pleasantries, initial joking, and munching on veggies and pretzels had come to a close. We were going to talk about why they were here, why they'd come to our men's group.

There was a sense of awkwardness, as there usually is when men recognize they're about to speak openly with one another. The silence deepened.

"Who wants to start us off?" Jake Kriger, my co-therapist, looked around the room. "Briefly. Let us know why you're here."

I expelled a deep breath. The saying "And so it begins again" ran through my mind. I was fastening my emotional seat belt, readying myself for the takeoff of this new group.

Randy, a fifty-two-year-old high school teacher, cleared his throat. "I'm here because I got laid off from my job. I'm a teacher, and I've worked at my school for twenty-five years. They just canned me," he said, the hurt clearly visible in his face. "I've been out of work for eight months. I guess I'm depressed, and I haven't been able to shake it." He flicked his head back, as though trying to toss off this mood.

Heads bobbed in sympathy. Randy fell quiet, signaling that was all he had to say.

Jake and I looked around the circle. "Who wants to go next?" he asked.

Mark, a fifty-five-year-old hand surgeon, leaned forward. "I'm not really sure why I'm here," he said, with a small shrug. He looked tired, as though he hadn't slept well for several nights. "My wife and my couples therapist thought it would do me good. Our therapist told me that coming here might help my relationship with Sally."

He hesitated. "She's talking about leaving."

The mood in the room plummeted. Mark tried to barrel on in a descriptive mode, but his voice began to quaver, and he slowed down. "Obviously, I'm shook up," he said. "I don't want to lose her. I didn't know things were this bad. She says if I think that, I haven't been paying attention."

He paused and looked around the room. "I don't have anyone to talk with about this. I mean I *have* friends, but I don't talk with them. Not about this."

The head-bobbing from the other guys had slowed, morphing into looks of sadness and concern for Mark. He'd just delivered a heavy emotional package, and I wondered how the men would handle it.

Allen, a forty-eight-year-old contractor, jumped in. "Well,

things with Shelly, my wife, aren't so bad. My problem's more about my son. He won't listen to me, and I get, well, pissed off. Lately, I walk out of situations so I won't explode."

Hastily, he added, "Not that I hit people or break things, nothing like that." He smiled uncomfortably. Allen was a large, imposing guy with a soft, controlled voice. You could imagine him knocking things over if he stood up suddenly.

The TV character Tony Soprano flashed through my mind. I wondered if Allen had a more volatile side that he wasn't copping to.

When things start to get uncomfortable or feel out of control in our groups, members typically try to rescue the mood, divert attention from issues that they can't readily explain or fix.

As though he'd read my mind, Allen swiveled his head toward Mark. "And what can you *do* about these things? Sometimes I think it's better to just shut up. You just don't know how people are going to take things, you know?" He looked around, inviting a response from the other guys.

Allen was raising an important question. How safe is it to share vulnerable feelings with others, both inside and outside the group? Men often decide not to open up because they expect their feelings to be dismissed or that the other person will feel burdened listening to them. The group members seemed interested in his remark.

Sensing an opportunity to establish some direction with the group, I leaned in.

"The things you're all talking about here are hard for *anyone* to bring up," I said. "It takes a lot of courage, and skills as well, to share this kind of stuff, especially for guys. We really struggle to talk about these kinds of feelings." I looked around the room at everyone. "That's what we're here for. We're going to help each other figure out and say what we're feeling, and support each other.

So you can better deal with the problems that are going on outside in your lives as well."

I hesitated, and raised my hands out to them. "Look. You guys have already started."

Everyone had perked up, listening attentively.

"How does that sound to you?" I asked.

Many heads jiggled affirmatively. Some men looked hopeful. Others seemed thoughtful, as though they were reflecting on how this venture of getting real with other guys might actually happen.

Jake and I looked at each other across the circle, as we often do, communicating with our eyes and barely perceptible nods. The look said, "Good! Some connection is happening here."

I breathed out. The train was starting to move.

The men I describe above share common problems, goals, and desires: They want to feel more open and emotionally connected with others. They want more authentic and satisfying relationships. And they want support to help them better connect with their partners, their children, and their colleagues. As a psychotherapist and a teacher for the past forty years, now in the Department of Psychiatry at the University of Pennsylvania, I've helped thousands of men with similar struggles—men who are in pain, who want to open up and connect with others but for a variety of reasons feel they can't.

CONFRONTING THE EMOTIONAL CHALLENGES

A lot has changed since I started my career in the mid-1970s. Over the past several decades, we've experienced an ongoing sexual revolution, an explosion in dual-career families, changes in family structure due to divorce and remarriage, and an increasingly un-certain economic environment.

In the 1980s, psychologist Harriet Lerner wrote, "Men seldom become scholars on the subject of changing their intimate relation-ships, because they do not yet need to." The challenges that face men today, however, suggest that we now need to look harder at how we struggle with intimacy if we want to feel fulfilled and have satisfying relationships.

Among other things, we've been called upon to share our emo-tions more openly, respond to women differently in the workplace, revamp our roles as husbands and breadwinners in our families, and involve ourselves more in parenting and day-to-day housework. *We've been called upon, in short, to revise our conception of what it means to be men.*

The women in our lives play an important role in this equation as well. While they've gained more opportunities for education, better-paid positions, and increased power in the workforce, they're encountering their own new challenges. Women are now called upon to negotiate more responsibilities and make more life-altering decisions than ever before. Having been responsible for carrying the lion's share of domestic work and child care as well as handling everyone's feelings, women are now asking the men in their lives to participate more fully in both the practical *and* emo-tional aspects of family life.

Men seem to be adapting well to some of these challenges. A Pew Research report from 2012 showed that with dual-career married or cohabiting partners, fathers are spending three times as many hours with their children (7.3 hours per week) and twice as many hours doing housework (9.0 hours per week) as they did in 1965. Dads' and moms' traditional roles are converging regarding time spent on paid work versus housework and child care, though neither has overtaken the other. In 1965, the ratio of time spent on paid work versus housework and child care was 85–15 percent for men, and the inverse, 15–85 percent, for women. Today this ratio is about 70–30 percent for men and 40–60 percent for women.

THE EMOTIONAL INTIMACY DILEMMA

Guys still struggle in the feelings department, however. This is not new news. Men have long demonstrated difficulty in dealing with their emotions in close relationships with both women and men in the practice of what we call *emotional intimacy*. Emotional intimacy is the experience of being deeply connected to another person who knows and understands your most important feelings and who shares his or her own with you. It is primarily a connection of the heart.

If there were a label for this problem in the *Diagnostic and Statistical Manual of Mental Disorders*, it might read something like *"Emotional Intimacy Deficiency*—a problem characterized by a sense of shallowness in one's relationships with others, associated with a failure to recognize or express feelings, to reveal personal details about oneself, to be vulnerable or let anyone help you, to comfortably share attention or let go of control, and to listen without having to solve a problem." Guys who struggle with emotional intimacy are more likely to withdraw and isolate themselves during times of stress, when they most need help.

There is no such diagnosis, of course, but the problem is nonetheless real and its consequences are sobering. Men who have trouble communicating feelings or having close relationships with others are at risk for a number of problems. They take longer to recover from minor illnesses, have lower resistance levels, and have reduced survival times when diagnosed with terminal illness. They are 50 percent more likely to have a first-time heart attack, and twice as likely to die from it, than men with strong social ties. When depressed, these men have significantly lower rates of recovery than those who have close relationships.

Psychologist Niobe Way tells us that when adolescent boys stop sharing their intimate feelings with their peers, we see an alarming increase in their rates of depression and suicide. Wives who cite their husband's "emotional unavailability" as the primary cause of divorce initiate two out of every three divorces today. At the far end of the life cycle, older men without close relationships have 20 percent lower ten-year survival rates compared with those who do. You get the idea.

The struggle with expressing feelings and forming intimate connections afflicts guys from all socioeconomic strata, ethnicities, races, and sexual orientations. A gay friend of mine who knew I was writing this book said to me, "Charles [his partner] is so impossibly uptight when he's feeling upset. He just won't talk to me. Does this count as an example of how guys struggle with feelings?"

"Oh, yes," I told him.

While there is diversity in the way men both within and between different cultural groups express their emotions, our society's dominant rules regarding how men should behave—otherwise known as Male Code—affect men from *all* backgrounds. For men to lead emotionally open and, as a result, healthier lives, we must first acknowledge the impact Male Code has on all of us. I will describe this more fully in the next chapter.

For men to succeed in today's world, we need to expand our

definition of healthy masculinity to include emotional intimacy (EI) skills along with traditional male behaviors. The important words here are *expand* and *include*. This book's purpose is not to denigrate traditional masculine behaviors or insist that one model or set of behaviors supplants another. My purpose is to help men learn about and embrace their own rich and complex emotional natures, and honor the enormous range of ways we express ourselves as men.

THIS IS NOT YOUR FATHER'S MEN'S MOVEMENT

The changes in men's attitudes about masculinity and emotional intimacy that I'm describing here are of no less consequence for men today than those Betty Friedan described for women fifty years ago in *The Feminine Mystique*. They have the potential to transform men's lives and the world around us in equally momentous ways.

When people have asked me about the "men's movement" today, I've joked that "it's a very quiet revolution" because of the social stigma associated with men expressing their feelings openly, and their resultant aversion to admitting that they want more emotional connection in their lives. For many men, however, I believe that this desire for closer, more authentic relationships resonates with core values that they hold regarding equality, compassion, and respectful engagement with all individuals.

The men's movement (originally called the men's liberation movement) in this country started in the 1960s. I think of it as having evolved, roughly, in three stages: *corrective*, *reflective*, and now, *connective*.

Initially, in the 1960s and 1970s, some men aligned themselves with the egalitarian goals of feminism, attempting to redress gender-based inequalities, as well as those of other marginalized groups, including Blacks, gays and lesbians, and Native Americans. Other men chose to address laws and social policies that discriminated against men, particularly concerning fathers' rights. Still others, many of whom were involved in religious and community-based groups, provided mentoring and counseling to men about issues of violence, abuse, and addiction.

A second, reflective phase emerged in the early 1990s, introduced by the poet Robert Bly (*Iron John*) and psychologists Michael Meade and Robert Moore, who formed the "mythopoetic men's movement." Here, men were encouraged to connect with their "deeper masculine natures," to find renewed emotional energy in their relationships with other men, as well as to overcome what was seen as a passive response to feminism. This approach was based on archetypal elements drawn from Jungian psychology and Native American rituals.

Today, the key focus of the men's movement is exploring and changing the ways men connect with each other and with important others in their lives. Over the past two decades, authors and researchers including Terrence Real (*I Don't Want to Talk About It*), Samuel Osherson (*Finding Our Fathers*), and Michael Kimmel (*Guyland*) have powerfully shown that society's expectations about how "real men" should act seriously constrict men from relating in openhearted and humane ways. The recurring themes in their writings underscore the importance of men forming healthy relational bonds with others, the pain of loss when these are broken, and pathways for repair and healing.

LEARNING EMOTIONAL INTIMACY (EI) SKILLS

When I arrived in Philadelphia in 1974 to begin my career in psychiatry, my life was in turmoil. My marriage was falling apart, I was in a new city, and I didn't know anyone with whom I felt comfortable talking. I remember walking around in my clinic on Green Street in a daze as the new medical director. I was depressed, not sleeping well. I couldn't remember having felt this bad—or disconnected—before. And I wasn't talking with anyone about any of this.

I was, in effect, a poster child for the kind of problem I've been describing—the guy who was suffering and couldn't admit it because he was ashamed and embarrassed to feel so vulnerable. Over time, I did manage to overcome these challenges, to heal and come out feeling better and stronger.

During these early years, however, I gained a strong understanding of how my male patients might be experiencing their own travails. I was struck by how allergic many guys seemed walking into my office, alone or with their wives, looking as if they'd rather be anywhere else, say, chained in a stockade rather than have to talk with me about their problems. I got it.

Over time, I came to realize that our traditional system of psychotherapy, based on focusing on emotionally sensitive material, underestimated how difficult this was for most men. Even those who are in desperate pain and who need help often lack the skills to talk about their feelings in a constructive way. It's not perceived as a manly thing to do, and so they've never been taught how to do it.

I remember speaking with Tom, an engineer in his mid-forties, who was recovering from a heart attack. He had become depressed and withdrawn to the point that his wife, Marge, threatened to separate unless he would get help with her. "I told her that I don't believe in psychotherapy," he said, his eyes downcast, looking resigned.

We normally don't think of psychotherapy as a religion, something that we "believe in" or not, but hearing these kinds of comments routinely from men caused me to wonder whether we were providing men with the right kind of help, with therapy that could feel more accessible to them.

HELPING MEN TO BETTER CONNECT

Over the next two decades, I worked with men in mental health clinics, as a teacher and training director of a family therapy program, as well as in private practice. During this time, I discovered some key principles, often ignored in traditional therapy approaches, that were vital in helping men to open up, better express their emotions, and connect with others, and to form a strong alliance in therapy.

1   *Acknowledging the Goodness of Men and of Traditional Masculine Values*

When men struggle in their lives, they feel down on themselves. They present to their loved ones in a variety of ways, by becoming depressed and withdrawn or, conversely, defensive, controlling, arrogant, and sometimes even threatening. Underneath, however, feelings of shame and humiliation usually predominate.

In the therapist's office, men often feel at a disadvantage, deficient in what Priscilla Blanton and Maria Vandergriff-Avery called relational power. Even in situations where they emotionally flounder, however, they need to be reminded, to remind themselves, that they bring something positive to the table, that they're worthwhile, even if not at their best.

I saw this in a touching exchange between a Hispanic couple with whom I worked at my mental health clinic during my early days in Philadelphia. Angel, a forty-eight-year-old elementary school teacher's aide, and his wife, Maria, saw me because Angel had become depressed and withdrawn after his mother had died four months before in Puerto Rico.

"He's a macho guy. Not much of a talker. But he's a good dad, and he works hard. I know he's going to be OK," said Maria, sitting close to Angel. She turned to him, lovingly, and punched him in the arm. He looked up and smiled. We spent the rest of the hour talking about the impressive sacrifices Angel had made over the past year, traveling to San Juan, sending money for his mother's care, while scraping to support Maria and their three kids. He agreed to talk a little more about how sad he was about his mom's death, and to take some medication. True to Maria's prediction, as Angel began to talk about his sadness, his mood began to lift over the next couple of months.

2   Presenting EI Skills as Behaviors That Men Can Learn

Cultural messages about how men are supposed to act, the rules of Male Code that I mentioned before, are so strong, and often invisible, that men frequently assume they can't or shouldn't behave in any other way. They think being a man necessarily means operating under a prescribed set of "masculine" behaviors, those that include solitude, strength, and independence and shun intimacy, asking for help, or expressing emotion. These rules often interfere with men addressing their emotional problems in therapy.

Throughout my career, I've taken an interest in how individual psychological, familial, and cultural forces, as well as biological factors, collectively influence our gender behaviors. I've studied the research and the arguments about what accounts for "masculine and feminine traits." My analysis to date: There's no real evidence that EI skills are "hardwired" into the brain, or that if we dig down far enough we'll discover an "essential" maleness or femaleness deep in our cores.

Men and women do not strictly conform to any one particular model, any one specific set of traits or behaviors that define their gender. Thus, as author Harry Brod suggests, we live in a culture of "masculinities" (or "femininities") in which each person expresses their gender in a unique way, as a blend of mainstream traits along with alternative features or behaviors that give their maleness or femaleness its own unique character. Moreover, expectations about masculine (and feminine) behavior vary across cultures, over an individual's life cycle, and, as mentioned earlier, over history as well. I elaborate on these issues in chapters 2 and 3. In short, we revise our gender behaviors as we go along and as we need to.

When men hear this, they usually feel hopeful and relieved. It's comforting for them to know that they can learn EI skills, albeit with some work, and that these can become valuable additions to their emotional repertoires—new "tools in their emotional backpacks," as I'm fond of describing them.

Tom, the engineer I mentioned above, routinely fought with his wife, Marge, about grocery shopping. He'd check the fridge to see what was needed, then go out to buy food, and later, she'd end up criticizing him for forgetting important items or not checking in with her beforehand. He was stuck on how unappreciative of his efforts she was and how she "emasculated" him. I asked him if he thought it was "unmanly" for him to check in with her, to ask for help on the grocery list. He hadn't thought about this. I continued, suggesting that possibly being manly isn't always about knowing everything in advance and being right all the time. I told him that maybe *not* knowing and checking as needed was OK, that it might even make him a *better* man. Tom agreed to try this out (to Marge's delight) and upon being thanked by her, reported back to me, "It seems that there's more than one way to be a man, correct?"

3   Appreciating the Power Men Have to Support Each Other

Toward the mid-1990s, my best friend and colleague, Jake Kriger, and I recognized in our discussions that there was a hole, a missing piece in the existing approaches to psychotherapy with men. Many "gender aware" therapists—Richard Meth and Robert Pasick (*Men in Therapy*) and others—were beginning to describe individual approaches for working with men in therapy that addressed the resistances about which I spoke earlier. This was progress.

Jake and I sensed that there was an untapped potential in the group experience for men, however. Author Samuel Osherson (*Finding Our Fathers*) alludes to this when he describes the deep desire in men for intimate contact with each other and for creating more openhearted emotional bonds. We also recognized the unique feelings of identification that could arise and empower men to open up and support each other in their important relationships outside of the group.

Jake and I had participated in men's consciousness-raising and support groups in the 1970s and 1980s. These were groups to help men become aware of how social stereotypes affected their behaviors and attitudes toward women. We'd found these models to be initially promising, but ultimately disappointing in their failure to create deeper bonds of intimacy among the men in the groups. Some of their limitations were structural—lack of focus on EI skills, lack of clearly defined goals or of firm leadership. There were often undercurrents of competition (e.g., Who's the most gender-sensitive man in the group?) or negative feelings between members that weren't addressed and ultimately interfered with the men forming a solid nucleus of a group.

With these pitfalls in mind, we set out to explore and develop a therapeutic group experience for guys that might harness the positive energies of group therapy to create strong bonding experiences for men that could further support their developing EI skills.

THERAPEUTIC MEN'S GROUPS

In the fall of 1995, we began to run our therapeutic men's groups, which we later named Friendship Labs. These groups involved elements of support, education, and personal growth for men. They focused on the development of EI skills, encouraging the men to express themselves in openhearted ways and provide empathic feedback for each other. We think of our groups as laboratories or emotional think tanks where men can try out new ways of thinking, feeling, and interacting. I've written about and presented this model extensively in local and national workshops and conferences.

Our groups focus on helping men develop emotional competencies—the Four C's, we call them—which include learning how to make good *connections* in close relationships, share heartfelt *communication*, develop a strong practice of *commitment*, and manage *conflict*. We guide our men in developing these skills, utilizing their direct engagement with each other as well as exercises and mini workshops throughout the year. We encourage their contact with each other outside of the group and, later, after they leave the group.

Creating an atmosphere of safety and respect is important. In the middle section of this book, I describe how these intimacy skills can be applied in your own friendships with other guys, but that to do so, you must first create a relationship of trust. For example, men often joke around with each other to diffuse awkward or difficult conversations, but this behavior makes real communication difficult. Letting your friends know you take their problems and concerns seriously and being willing to open up to them as well is important. Nothing demonstrates trustworthiness more than trusting someone else.

Over the years, we've helped hundreds of men in our groups develop closer relationships with each other and, as a result, with their families and others who are important to them. I've become impressed with how much guys can empower each other to become more emotionally open and to help other guys find joy and healing in their relationships outside.

Ralph, a sixty-seven-year-old retired university administrator who'd been in the group for over a year, showed up at a meeting worried and complaining that he'd had chest pain for the past three days. He hadn't called his doctor, despite his wife Sarah's advice. The other men in the group practically jumped out of their seats. Some were alarmed and asked him why he didn't call or go for help.

"What were you thinking, not listening to Sarah? Isn't she a family practice doctor, for God's sake?" Andy, one of the guys, was incredulous.

"I thought it would go away and didn't want to call unnecessary attention to myself," Ralph answered, embarrassed. Everyone groaned. Even Ralph knew that was a lame answer.

Two of the men offered to drive Ralph to a nearby emergency room after the group. It was fortunate they did, because his EKG showed an irregular heartbeat. There was no sign of a heart attack, but the ER doctor was concerned enough to call his wife and keep him overnight in the hospital.

The next morning, Ralph called me. He told me he was fine and at home. The guys had waited with him until Sarah showed up. He had called them that morning, clearly touched, and reflected about his behavior over the previous days.

"I felt like an idiot. I just couldn't accept the help from Sarah. I was scared and too proud to admit it." He hesitated. "I told her that last night. Really apologized. Told her that I appreciated her so much and that I wouldn't do this again."

"What did she say?" I asked.

He chuckled. "She said, 'If your guys can make that stick, I'm sending a large batch of chocolate chip cookies with you to the next group.'"

PROMOTING INTIMACY
THROUGH MEN'S FRIENDSHIPS

As our groups progressed, we were pleased with the advances our men made with their individual problems, depression and anxiety, marital struggles, and issues with their kids and work. We were getting positive feedback from their therapists, with whom we were collaborating about their increased emotional openness in therapy.

One issue, however, was beginning to stand out like a sore thumb in our group sessions—our guys' relationships with other men. While our men, like most fellows, had male friends, they were still reluctant to open up with them as they were doing with the guys in the group and with their close family members. They wanted relationships with other guys where they could do this.

Jake and I took notice. We certainly recognized the incredible love and support we had developed in our own friendship, and with other men as well. I think we assumed that, because our men were learning EI skills in the group and translating this into their own family systems, these skills would automatically spill into and strengthen their male friendships outside of the group. When I inquired about this with other male patients, they just stared at me blankly. Apparently, the good therapy work we were doing wasn't making much of an emotional dent in their guy friendships.

I was curious and began to research the issue of men's friendships. I discovered studies going back forty years that identified men's desire for close male friendships, their valuing of these, including their capacity to recognize and participate in emotionally intimate exchanges with other men. While guys were able to share openly in protected research settings, their willingness to do so petered out when they were back in the outside world.

Sociologist Ray Pahl states that friendships today are based primarily on trust and emotional intimacy. If you talk with men, they'll agree that this is true *in principle*, but it has not yet fully translated for them into *practice*. As sociologist Beverley Fehr summarized, men, while capable of opening up, have chosen to tamp down their male friendships and share their vulnerable feelings primarily with women, to whom they find it easier to talk, while *complaining about this situation at the same time.*

REEVALUATING THE ROLE
OF MEN'S FRIENDSHIPS

As Jake and I looked at this trend more closely, we realized that men today, including our own patients, were missing out on an important resource—friendships with other guys—for experiencing and sharing emotional intimacy and for gaining support in other aspects of their lives. We decided to do two things about this.

The first step involved paying more attention to this issue in our clinical work. This has paid off in spades: We began asking guys about their male friendships (most have them) and how much they shared with their guy friends about personal feelings (most not nearly enough). We encouraged them to develop deeper relationships with these guys, both by sharing their feelings and by asking for and offering them support. For most of our men, the results were immediate and positive. Apparently, there is a world full of guys out there, many of whom you already know, who want a closer relationship with you. You'll read about how to orchestrate and nurture these connections in the middle section of this book.

A few years ago, we also renamed our psychotherapy groups Friendship Labs to emphasize the important role close male relationships play in promoting EI skills in men's lives.

The second step was to initiate our own research on the status of emotional intimacy in men's friendships today. I wanted to get a sense of how accurate our perceptions were about this issue outside of our own more narrow personal and clinical domains.

We recruited a larger group of professionals for help, and in 2012, we launched the Men's Friendship and Emotional Intimacy (MFEI) Survey. We surveyed a representative sample of 381 men across the country, online, about their friendships. We asked them what the friendships were like, the level of "closeness" or emotional intimacy they experienced, what intimacy behaviors existed in their friendships, what they valued or wanted to change, and how much they relied on them for support in their other important relationships.

Our results showed that the men felt some things were working well in their friendships, and that they also wished for changes. For example, most men were satisfied with the number of friends they had and greatly valued them. While most already had some emotional intimacy in these relationships, the majority wanted even more. Oddly enough, the men who reported higher emotional intimacy scores were more likely to say they wanted more.

Different from those in the past, men reported they were now *as or more emotionally expressive* with their guy friends as they were with female friends. They also expressed awareness of vulnerability in their friendships, noting techniques they employed to protect them. The men who reported the highest levels of intimacy in their friendships got the most support with their marriage, their kids, and their work relationships.

Overall, these results validated the work we'd been doing with men in our Friendship Labs, highlighting the importance of their learning EI skills and encouraging them to actively develop these within their male friendships.

A detailed summary of the study and our first published findings is presented in the Appendix of this book. Relevant findings are included throughout the various chapters.

DEVELOPING YOUR OWN MALE FRIENDSHIPS

A man's friendships may be one of his most valuable—and underutilized—resources for helping him experience and learn how to be close to others.

This book is written to help men better appreciate and realize this potential in their male friendships. It presents a game plan for how they can accomplish this.

I begin by observing how male friendships reflect our culture's view of masculinity and men's roles in society. Part 1, titled "Men's Friendships Today," helps us appreciate the importance of emotional intimacy in men's lives. In this first chapter, I've described the dilemma guys have with emotional intimacy in their health and relationships, in therapy, and finally, in their friendships. Chapters 2–4 address the cultural challenges of Male Code and psychological obstacles to developing close male friendships; the history and evolution of male friendships and how these compare today with women's friendships; and, finally, how men's friendships support the development of emotional intimacy behaviors over their lifetime.

Part 2, titled "Friendship Fundamentals," describes the important skills men need to build intimate friendships. Here I introduce guidelines and exercises drawn from our Friendship Labs that enhance men's emotional intimacy skills. Case illustrations from our groups, along with personal examples and stories, flesh out how men can empower their friendships. In these chapters, 5–8, I explain how you can forge strong initial connections with male friends, have emotionally meaningful "conversations from the heart," keep your close friendships in good repair, and, finally, manage conflict in your friendships when it arises.

The three chapters of the final section, Part 3, "Spreading the Wealth," cover how close guy friendships can powerfully help you in your marriage or partnership, in parenting your kids, and in navigating the complicated waters of the workplace.

There should be enough information here for guys to deepen and strengthen their male friendships, even ones they've had for a while. If you don't yet have positive male connections in your life, the book can help you begin to make some good ones. If you're a woman, a spouse, or a man's partner and want to support your guy in developing ways he can be closer to others, this book is a great way to support him. My hope is that male readers will find encouragement in these pages to more fully enjoy themselves with other men, to support each other in opening up to be more authentic and responsive human beings, and to be closer with the important others in their lives.

CHAPTER 2

Breaking the Male Code

Hidden Obstacles to Close Male Connections

As I mentioned in Chapter 1, when I first started out in my career, I was going through a rough time—starting a new job, with no friends, and going through a divorce, all at the same time. During this stressful period, I knew I needed to talk to people about what I was going through. I'd never before felt so powerful a need to open up, to get support, but the whole prospect of doing so seemed daunting to me.

Marty, a psychiatrist who worked at my clinic, seemed like a down-to-earth and likable guy, so I screwed up my courage and gave him a call. I told him I wanted to get together to play racquetball, but underneath, I was hoping to talk with him about some of my personal concerns.

When Marty returned my calls, however, something strange

happened: I kept putting off getting back to him. I finally returned his call, weeks later, and we made a date to get together.

When we met at the club, he was genuinely perplexed. "What took you so long to get back to me? Are you OK?" he asked me directly.

I cringe now when I think about what came out of my mouth that day: In a fake, casual manner, I responded, "Nah. I'm good." Then I added, very sincerely, "I'm sorry, man. I let it slip away. I've been really busy." I flashed him an I-know-you-understand smile. He hesitated for a second, giving me a look that said he wasn't buying it, but I was uncomfortable and hurried us onto the court before he had a chance to challenge me. I wanted this whole thing to disappear. I knew my response was lame and dishonest. In truth, I didn't know what to say to him.

Eventually, this upset did blow over, though I never did share with Marty why I wanted to get together in the first place. We continued to play racquetball, but our conversations remained superficial, never extending beyond the time we spent together bashing balls around the court.

Why is it that men so often run away from what we most deeply desire and need? Some of you guy readers may be able to identify with my botched effort at connecting with Marty. In retrospect, I was ashamed of feeling vulnerable and wanting to open up with him. In the moment, I couldn't imagine that he—or anyone, for that matter—could really understand what it felt like to be *that* lonely and so in need of emotional support. The prospect of exposing my feelings—and potentially being judged for them—terrified me.

I was also blown away by how completely I'd shut down with Marty, even when it seemed he might be really open to listening to me. I needed to better understand the powerful, bewildering force that had stopped me from taking that risk with him.

MALE CODE

I now understand what happened to me that day, and what happens to many men when they feel emotionally vulnerable. We encounter a resistance inside, one triggered by societal expectations, both spoken and unspoken, about how men are supposed to behave. I call these guidelines or set of expectations Male Code. These rules for men have been in serious practice for the past two hundred years in the United States and other Western nations, and they haven't changed very much over this time period.

Male Code endorses a set of behaviors that include emotional restraint, withholding personal information, defending our position, controlling our and others' behaviors, sustaining ourselves without assistance, acting independently, competing, commanding attention, and being physically tough.

Training camp for these rules begins for boys early in their lives, as early as three years of age. They learn from their parents, and through contact with other institutions (nursery, day care, schools, the playground), what psychologist William Pollack (*Real Boys*) calls Boy Code, social guidelines that encourage boys to move away from their emotional, expressive natures. Sociologist Michael Kimmel (*Guyland*) says that these guidelines intensify as boys move through adolescence into their young adult years. He describes the attributes of Guy Code, expanding on boys' earlier behaviors and three distinct sets of cultural dynamics—entitlement, silence, and protection—that reinforce these behaviors. I use the term *Male Code* to emphasize how these rules discourage emotional intimacy behavior in men and how this affects their health and relationships with others.

Sociologist George Mosse states that our modern views of masculine behavior date back to the late eighteenth century in Europe, following the chivalric traditions of the Middle Ages, through the Enlightenment. At this time, the Greek ideal of the human body came to represent the manly qualities of selflessness, chastity, fearlessness, and patriotism. Kimmel describes the simultaneous emergence of the "self-made man" in early nineteenth-century America, who defined his manhood through self-control, separating himself both from the comforts of city life and the personal sphere of home and women.

Social scientist Robert Brannon's well-known four rules of masculinity—No sissy stuff. Be a big wheel. Be a sturdy oak. Give 'em hell—have, according to many scholars, consistently represented the values our society expects from men over the past century.

WHY MALE CODE HAS SUCH A LONG SHELF LIFE

While many of the guidelines of Male Code seem outmoded, limited, even a little silly in today's world, it's still a tough protocol to walk away from. It has endured because of a powerful system of rewards and punishments, a "carrot and stick" model that has developed over time.

On one hand, adherence to traditional male behaviors has for generations allowed guys to acquire positions of privilege, prestige, and power. A young man in his twenties recently reported to me that he'd gotten a promotion to junior manager in his food distribution company. "I showed my boss [a man] that I could hold my ground: I don't flinch when there's a conflict. I can carry projects by myself, and I 'win the points' when I negotiate with other colleagues and with clients."

He neglected to say whether his coworkers liked him or felt respected by him, or whether he was a good listener. Apparently, these items didn't come up all that much when he and his boss discussed his promotion. Kimmel observes that privilege has often made men blind to the harmful aspects of Male Code because of the rewards it has provided.

Rigid adherence to Male Code, nonetheless, has caused and continues to cause problems for men. Some are small, day-to-day discomforts that guys try to hide or are embarrassed about.

Think about the last time you pretended that something was in your eye when you felt like crying. (It might have been pretty recently.)

When you're lost, can't figure something out, or find yourself home alone for a few days while your partner is away on a business trip, you might be tempted to pick up the phone and call a guy friend for dinner and some good conversation. But do you?

Male Code is particularly destructive when it forces us into an either-or position that doesn't allow flexibility, compromise, or the opportunity for our own or another person's point of view to be heard. It is harmful when it operates as an unspoken, yet strictly enforced, social policy that decides whether or not you're a "real man."

Kimmel speaks of "gender policing," the tendency of men and boys in our society to closely monitor each other to make sure that guys are acting "up to code." When they aren't, the masculinity squad may mete out harsh consequences, from bullying in the school yard or online, to passing over a man for membership in a club or for a promotion.

In more extreme situations, not living up to Male Code can result in men's becoming victims and/or perpetrators of violence. Gay beatings and school shootings are examples.

To be clear, the problem with Male Code does not lie in any of the particular traits, behaviors, or attitudes that it endorses. For example, emotional restraint is critical at times, such as when you're trying to have a productive conversation with your boss and she's pushing your buttons. Likewise, you may need to defend your position (or your ideas, or someone else) to show you possess the necessary strength or courage to get a job done well.

As we shall see, such traditional "male" behaviors, applied in a context of respect and compassion, can be quite wonderful. The problem is when our masculine ideology is recruited to shut down another person's, or our own, humanity.

LIVING BETWEEN TWO WORLDS

Male Code has been particularly inhospitable to emotional intimacy (EI) behaviors in men. George Mosse tells us that from the early days of this new masculine ideology, countervailing views that promoted softer, more intimate ways for men to behave sustained little support. So powerful was this new masculine ideal in Europe, for example, that "the first and longest lived homosexual periodical in German, *Der Eigene*, frequently lamented the effeminacy of modern society and called for a return to militant masculinity."

Trying to hop between two separate emotional landscapes— traditional masculine ideology and the "brave new world" that includes practicing EI skills—creates tremendous stress for many men today. Psychologist Joseph Pleck labeled this dilemma gender role strain, pointing out that slavish adherence to traditional male standards often creates problems for men's health and their relationships.

Take a look at the lists below. Contrast the behaviors on the left side, which are associated with Male Code, with those directly to their right. The latter traits are associated with emotional intimacy, the traits we need to successfully manage and enjoy close relationships. Allowing our eyes to wander back and forth across the aisle between these columns gives us a sense of the dilemma men face on a day-to-day basis. We struggle to live between what we've been told are two incompatible worlds, one for "real men" and another for everyone else.

TRADITIONALLY MASCULINE BEHAVIORS	EMOTIONAL INTIMACY BEHAVIORS
Emotionally Restrained	Emotionally Expressive
Withholds Information	Self-Discloses
Defends Position	Shows Vulnerability
Takes Control	Lets Go of Control
Self-Sustaining	Gives and Gets Support
Competitive	Cooperative
Independent	Reciprocal
Commands Attention	Listens and Empathizes
Physically Tough	Physically Affectionate

THE REAL COSTS OF MALE CODE

When men attempt to live in an emotionally split world, they pay a high price. I discuss in Chapter 1 the stress-related health problems, both physical and emotional, as well as marital and parenting troubles that arise when men aren't able to openly express their emotions or develop close relationships with others.

Let's look at some other problems: Rigid adherence to Male Code, with the expectations of physical toughness and going it alone, can cause men to ignore their own health needs and fail to seek attention for their medical problems. American men make 134.5 million fewer physician visits than American women each year. A quarter of the men who are forty-five to sixty do not have a personal physician. Many have decided they don't need to have annual physicals and don't visit physicians.

When asked why, they admit to feelings of fear, denial, embarrassment, and a dislike of situations out of their control. They decide that health visits are not worth the time or cost. This reluctance has serious consequences, and contributes to their receiving late diagnoses and experiencing more complications when they do get treatment, including early death.

Male Code also figures in when we examine how risk-taking behavior ("Give 'em hell") and the excessive need to control situations play out in everyday tragedies in our society. In alcohol-related driving fatalities, for example, while the driver crash rate per miles driven is higher for women, men as drivers are more likely to cause deaths in their accidents. Guys behind the wheel die more often as well, even when their blood alcohol levels are comparable to women's, because of their higher-risk driving behavior.

The excessive need to control situations, to resort to force, and to avoid expressing vulnerable emotions have been correlated with men's high incidence of initiating domestic violence and child abuse and their falling into depression and suicide.

These same features also prevent men from developing positive emotional connections with their children. They forfeit the opportunity to provide real support, set positive examples, and provide a healthy sense of protection for their kids. These children are more prone to depression and anxiety, and to becoming victims and/or perpetrators of bullying and child sexual abuse.

OUR FRIENDSHIP "DEMENTORS"

Nowhere has Male Code held tighter control over EI behavior for men than in their male friendships. While guys have always had and, for the most part, enjoyed their male friendships, the "gender police" are always hanging around, watching closely and whispering on occasion:

"Don't show too much emotion, do not cry. Act like things are in control. Don't reveal information about your close relationships that might cause your friend to think you're weak. Also watch those hugs, don't hug too long, and don't show too much affection or admiration for him. He'll think you're fatuous, sucking up to him." I could go on.

Can you identify any of those voices in your head? Have you ever found yourself reacting to these cautions? Many guys, under the spell of Male Code, often feel too ashamed to expose their vulnerabilities to their buddies, even when their problems are spiraling out of control and they could really use the support.

While our research suggests that this trend is changing, I thought it would be best to discuss what guys are up against now, the negative internalized stereotypes that block us from pursuing closer relationships, before I introduce our guidelines for developing EI behaviors in Part 2. Forewarned is forearmed.

Male Code generates several common forms of resistance that arise when men are challenged to relate in more openhearted, intimate ways. You may recognize several or all of these as I describe them. But because they are often held unconsciously, they can emerge in our behaviors at unexpected times, creating problems. The embarrassing incident with my friend Marty that I described earlier in this chapter was an example of this.

I've found it useful to identify these resistances so that men can identify and confront them in their efforts to get closer to others.

Let's take a look at the most common roadblocks to emotional intimacy in men's relationships. I call these, with affection and some humor, friendship dementors. The name evokes those shadowy creatures in J. K. Rowling's Harry Potter books, who drain the happiness out of people and fill the empty spaces with depression and despair. For our purposes, *dementors* refers to frequently held beliefs by and about men and emotional intimacy that distort the truth, suck the joy out of us, and force us into play-acting rather than living our lives.

While friendship dementors wreak havoc on our close male friendships, it doesn't help to try to simply banish these wayward creatures. They represent aspects of ourselves that we need to face and integrate, rather than ignore. Once we get to know these negative biases—up close and personal—our close relationships will have a much better shot at success.

First, let's identify these disruptors of emotional intimacy and observe how they work to subvert close male relationships.

MACHISMO

The first dementor, Machismo, represents our ingrained beliefs about the qualities that define a "real man." These include tendencies toward isolation, emotional restraint, control, indifference, and competition.

The term *machismo* has become synonymous with *hypermasculinity*, an overemphasis on traditional masculine traits. This overvaluation of "hard guy" traits can skewer and distort relationships when not balanced with softer qualities like compassion and emotional honesty.

The Machismo Dementor shows up from time to time when a guy feels threatened and insecure and is compensating by presenting himself as unaffected and indifferent. When a man is entirely ruled by this dementor, he hardens himself like a fossil, losing his ability to connect openly with others. In this state, he hardly seems like a person with whom you could have a close friendship.

Mick, a forty-five-year-old real estate developer, joined our group complaining of headaches, arguments with his sixteen-year-old son, and trouble working with his contractors. He was a serious, driven guy from a working-class family in South Philadelphia. When he spoke, there was an edgy, arrogant tone in his voice, one that communicated, "I know better than anyone else." "No one listens to me, that's the problem," he complained. He told the guys in the group that he didn't have any close friends. I wasn't surprised to hear this.

At the beginning of a session, a group member, Aidan, limped in on crutches, wearing a leg cast and looking like he was in a lot of pain. He'd slipped on the ice while walking to work, and in trying to keep his balance had twisted his leg so that it broke. Everyone winced at the story.

Mick immediately jumped in, regaling the group with a long-winded account of how, as a teenager, he had fallen off a bicycle at night and had broken his hip. He'd had to crawl almost a mile to make it back to his house. "Now, *that* was a bad break," he chortled. He seemed quite impressed by his own story, unaware of his impact on the men, who were just staring at him in disbelief.

I asked Aidan how Mick's comment made him feel.

He took a deep breath. "Horrible," he finally said. "Like he wasn't really listening and just wanted to tell his story, to hear himself talk." He hesitated, and then turned to Mick, still obviously hurt. "You know, man, if you talk like this with your son and your workers, I can see why you're having problems."

Around the room, some guys were nodding.

Mick's face went pale. I had the feeling he'd gotten responses like this one before. Would this sink in? I wondered.

"I'm sorry, man. I should've known not to say that." Mick looked embarrassed, shook his head, genuinely frustrated with himself. "Your leg looks bad. I feel bad for you."

I jumped in. "Why didn't you say *that*?" I asked him.

He looked at me, puzzled, and shook his head. "I don't know exactly. I just kept thinking what my dad said to me after my bike accident. He didn't ask me if I was OK but told me even worse stories about what'd happened to him when he was a kid. I thought his message was 'If you tell someone how much worse your suffering was than theirs, how much worse it could've been, it'll make them a stronger man, better able to handle adversity.' Something like that." While describing his father's theory, however, he didn't seem all that convinced of it.

My co-therapist quickly responded, "How'd that message work for you? How's it working with your son and coworkers?"

"Not too well, I guess," Mick conceded sheepishly. The edge had started to come out of Mr. Know-It-All's voice, making him feel a little more accessible to us.

Mick realized at this point he was going to have to learn to speak more from his heart, to remain open to his own vulnerable feelings and those of others (to dial back his Machismo Dementor), if he was going to be able to improve his relationships with his son, his employees, and others, including the guys in his Friendship Lab.

HOMOPHOBO

The second dementor, Homophobo, represents our fear of homosexuality and/or anyone who is perceived or identified as gay, lesbian, bisexual, or transgendered. This dementor often leads the pack in scaring men away from close male friendships. Homophobo discourages guys from acting too interested, caring, or emotionally open with other men for fear of being seen as sexually attracted to them. He torments gay as well as straight men.

While this dementor seems to derive his strength from our internal fears about sexuality and masculinity, institutionalized forms of antigay prejudice—organizational, religious, and state-sponsored—also contribute to this fearmongering.

In the United States, laws discriminating against LGBT persons, for example concerning gay marriage and gay rights, remain in force in many communities. Religious organizations also, particularly the more extreme, such as the one led by the late

Baptist pastor Fred Phelps, continue to exclude gay men and the practice of homosexuality. Overseas, at least seventy-six countries (mostly in Africa, Asia, the Middle East, and Oceana) currently consider homosexual behavior a criminal offense, and six of these have declared gay sex punishable by death.

When Homophobo takes over a man, he finds himself running away from strong or vulnerable feelings, especially positive ones toward another man, because he believes these feelings will be misinterpreted or criticized by the recipient and/or others. In some, this dementor evokes feelings of intense shame, contempt, and even hatred for themselves and/or the other man.

Today, most guys are able to tamp down the Homophobo Dementor through some combination of education, self-reflection, and emotional support. Sometimes, unanticipated life situations, such as working with a gay colleague, can help a man become aware of and resolve homophobic attitudes. An extreme example was Ron Woodroof, depicted in the film *Dallas Buyers Club*, who was a virulently antigay man and had to go through a life-threatening struggle with AIDS and work closely with other victims of the virus before he could finally shrug off his Homophobo and embrace close relationships with both gay and straight men.

It turns out that Homophobo is an "equal opportunity" tyrant: He troubles gay men in their friendships with each other as well as with straight guys, through a process psychologists call internalized homophobia. Here, gay men turn Homophobo's prohibition of positive feelings for other men, particularly straight guys, against themselves.

I was educated about these internalized restrictions by my friend David, an openly gay colleague. We were preparing a workshop together on gay-straight relationships for an organization to which we both belong. Munching on sandwiches, we mulled over our views on the topic. "Here's a contradiction," I said, poking a little fun at him. "You're the gay guy and I'm the straight guy. But when you hug me, your hugs are so stiff." I squinched up my face in mock distaste. "What's that about?"

"Well, think about it," David countered, not missing a beat. "When a gay man is around a straight guy, especially a guy he likes, he's also thinking, 'I don't want to scare him off. I don't want him thinking that I'm coming on to him, or to be viewed as a predator.' So, yeah, I'm probably careful with my hugs. Does that make sense to you?"

I was somewhat taken aback, not really expecting such a candid response. I was also saddened to hear that my friend instinctively stifled his hugs to protect me, and himself, from what I felt was a stupid societal prejudice that had nothing to do with the reality of our friendship.

"Yeah, I get it," I said. "Thanks."

I hesitated, and then added, "You know you don't have to worry about that stuff with me, right?" He gave me a reassuring nod. Still, I appreciated my friend's willingness to educate me about what it was like for him to be on "the other side" of a close gay-straight friendship. And, while I might be hallucinating, I think talking about this has contributed to our having warmer, more relaxed hugs since then.

DUMBO

The third dementor, Dumbo, represents our naiveté and insecurity when dealing with emotions in our relationships. Of all of the dementors, Dumbo is the one most responsible for men's general ineptness in sustaining and protecting their close male friendships.

Dumbo promotes confusion, laziness, and lack of interest in men about their own feelings and those of others. He trades on our wishes for simplicity in relationships without regard for the thought and effort required to make them work.

Dumbo's idea is that guys are essentially simple creatures, unaffected by and without need for the richness and complexity of emotional connection in life. He draws his power from social stereotypes, both literary and scientific, that highlight male emotional shallowness and ineptitude.

The television cartoon dad Homer Simpson might be today's Dumbo poster hero. Albeit a lovable character, Homer is portrayed as a bumbler who, when not stuffing his face with donuts at work, is either at Moe's Tavern drinking with his buddies or at home on the couch with a Duff beer. In his relationship with his wife, Marge, he's usually screwing things up. In several episodes, he manages to lose his baby, Maggie. In all these situations, Marge has to come to his rescue and bail him out.

Psychological and scientific data have been oversimplified to suggest that men have an "innate" inability to identify, express, and process emotional information. However, both Anne Fausto-Sterling and Cordelia Fine (the former a neuroscience researcher, the latter a psychologist) have pointed out that while men's and women's brains demonstrate some structural, physiological, and hormonal differences, there is a huge diversity and overlap within and between the sexes in our abilities to process and communicate emotions.

Moreover, these differences don't prevent either sex from functioning at high levels in relationships. For example, neuroradiologist Michael Phillips has shown that men and women recruit their listening skills differently—men from their left hemisphere, women from both hemispheres. At the same time, psychologist Kittie Watson, who evaluated men's and women's listening skills, found no measurable differences in how well each sex is able to listen in conversations!

Additionally, we are learning that our brains have a marvelous capacity to grow and rewire themselves through experience, a feature known as neuroplasticity. Recent radiographic studies of the brain have shown that structural changes can occur over time as a result of therapeutic interventions such as cognitive behavior therapy (CBT) and meditation.

This suggests that learning plays a critical role in a person's developing EI skills. If a man has poor listening or communicating habits, he can learn to improve these *if he chooses to*, and his brain will cooperate.

Our Dumbo Dementor simply dismisses the importance of men developing emotional skills. Dumbo's message that this is all "touchy-feely baloney" encourages guys into shallow, progressively lonely relationships with other guys.

To nourish their close relationships, men are discovering that they have to bring more energy and attention to the process. They're not going to be able to curl up and take an "emotional snooze" on the couch with Dumbo and expect that they can just wake up and find that their important relationships have sustained themselves on their own.

Charlie was a fifty-two-year-old man who owned a large hardware store in suburban Philadelphia that had been run as a family business for several generations. A broad-shouldered, husky fellow, he told us that he had joined the group at his doctor's urging because he was having problems with his "ticker"—irregular heartbeats. His son, Dale, had recently left home for college. "I don't know how this all figures in," he said, grinning and shrugging his shoulders.

His wife, Adele, had mentioned to me that Charlie had been unusually glum lately, pacing around the house, muttering words about "the end of the family business." He had been sleeping poorly and was becoming "bad company," she said.

The men in the room stared at him blankly. There was a tiresome naive quality in Charlie that people found irritating. He'd throw out feelings, and then sit and wait for others to make sense out of them—essentially, to do his homework.

Sensing this feeling toward Charlie arising from the men, Jake said, "Let's take a step back." He turned to Charlie and said, "Tell us why you've come to this group, Charlie. Really. Can you say?" The other men seemed relieved by this question.

Charlie met Jake's gaze like a deer in the headlights. Silent for what seemed an eternity, he answered, "I don't know. I really don't." Moments like this challenge the facade that a man has erected between himself and others, the mask behind which he hides complex emotions that make him uncomfortable, or even evoke feelings of dread.

Stephen, a longtime group member, shook his head and spoke up. "You know, Charlie, think about it. You've got heart problems. Your son's going off to college. You're continuing to run your father's business, with no one in your family to continue the legacy. You've got to have feelings about these things." Stephen looked frustrated. "What do you tell your buddies, the guys at work?"

Charlie responded, dismally, "I don't talk to those guys about this stuff. My wife says I don't have any real friends. I think of her as my best friend, but she says I don't really talk with her, either."

"OK," I offered, "suppose we think of friends as people we can really talk to about what's in our heart." I patted my own heart and looked at Charlie. "Maybe your 'ticker' would like to communicate something. Why don't you start with us?"

Charlie hesitated, as though he was debating inside. Without knowing what would happen next, he'd have to risk speaking openly about his feelings. As he began to speak, his patented look of confusion began to fade, revealing some genuine emotions. He began to discuss his sadness about Dale leaving home. He also said he felt like a failure, angry with himself that he hadn't produced offspring for his father, now retired, who would continue the family business. When he finished talking, he took a deep breath, clearly relieved that he'd survived this ordeal.

"How was that?" I asked him.

He seemed genuinely uncomfortable. "I feel guilty, like I'm breaking the rules." He looked at me and explained that his father would never talk about personal feelings in this way. Not just with other men, but with him as well. There was a long pause. Then he took a deep breath and added, "Guess I've got to learn to do more of this." There was a round of nodding heads in the room.

Charlie took it in. He was starting to wrestle with his Dumbo Dementor and rousing himself from a long emotional siesta.

MISOGYNO

This fourth dementor represents our feelings, sometimes hidden, of mistrust, fear, or dislike of women. These feelings, especially when they go unrecognized, can disrupt a friendship. They can also undermine a guy's relationship with his female partner.

Misogyno prevents a man from being open and vulnerable

with women because he feels threatened by them. This fear can show itself as aloofness and indifference, or more aggressively as contempt and disrespect.

Misogyno also encourages men with Peter Pan–like qualities, aimed at disarming women through boyish charm and emotional expressiveness, while he avoids acting as a responsible grown-up in the relationship. This dementor believes that any woman's demands for reciprocity should be taken as a warning sign, and that a man worth his salt should be on the alert, ready to jump ship or find a ready alternative if his woman shows any sign of unavailability.

Misogyno is a pretender when it comes to supporting close male friendships. This dementor encourages men to enlist each other in running away from or, alternately, demeaning women, and calls this friendship. We see this with men who are constantly badgering their guy friends to go off and hang with the boys, without any concern for their family obligations. A warning sign here is when this "buddy" spends all of his time with you ragging about or putting down his wife or the women he's dating.

Misogyno encourages a guy to enthusiastically side with his friend's complaint against his wife, ignoring his friend's contribution to the problem. He uses the friendship to "grind his own ax," projecting his own frustrations onto women rather than helping his friend effectively sort out the problem. In extreme situations, this dementor will drive a man to excessive controlling or stalking behavior, even violence, to secure his needs. Men in this state are delusional, having convinced themselves that this behavior will stabilize love in their relationship.

Misogyno draws his power from the long history of oppression and prejudice against women. Presumptions about women's inferiority and the dangers they pose for men have been staples of religious texts, mythology, scientific writings, literature, and philosophy for centuries. In his *Nichomachean Ethics*, for example, Aristotle asserted that women simply didn't possess the strength of character required for high-quality friendships. Some men still believe this, ignoring that in today's world it's usually women who are the strongest advocates for emotionally close friendships.

Bick was a forty-five-year-old music teacher who came to see me when his wife, Rene, and friends told him he needed to get therapy for his temper. Bick started out complaining about how his wife was constantly criticizing him for being irresponsible, not including her in decisions he made or letting her know when he'd be back from meetings in the evening. He dropped the hint that during some of these evenings, he was at strip clubs.

He admitted that he was raising his voice with his wife, threatening her more frequently these days. But he was skeptical about whether *he* really needed help. "You know," he said with sincere self-pity, "she was so much more positive when I married her. It seems that after ten years of marriage, she's lost any appreciation of the things I do for her." I discovered that his parents had had a fractious relationship. His dad was harsh, verbally abusive, and his mom, for her part, was withdrawn and depressed until she overdosed with sleeping pills when Bick was twelve. He'd never gotten over this and had never forgiven her for abandoning him and the family.

He confessed that he finally sought therapy because his close friend Roger wasn't speaking with him. "I had a fight with Rene and right after that I called him and asked him to go with me to the Gentlemen's Club, y'know, just to blow off some steam. He didn't call me back after we talked. I figured something was wrong." He truly had no clue, not just about his own role in his marital problems, but also about why his friend would be angry with him.

I figured that Roger might be the best person to get the ball rolling with Bick, so I urged him to get together with his friend, to get an honest answer from him about what happened.

He came back humbled from their encounter. "Roger said he was insulted that I would try to drag him into my fight with Rene." He added, still stunned, "He also slammed me for treating her with 'such disrespect.' He said, 'No wonder she's lost interest in you. You treat her like dirt.'" Bick seemed dazed. "I wasn't ready for that."

His friend had called Bick out on his Misogyno Dementor, and Bick was having to take heed, maybe for the first time.

Then he looked up at me cautiously and asked, "What do you think?"

I wouldn't have passed on that opportunity for anything. "I'd have to agree with your friend," I said slowly and gently. "What he said is worth thinking about." He was silent for a while then. During that time, I remember thinking, "Isn't it great when your client's best friend functions as your co-therapist?"

IDENTIFYING YOUR OWN
FRIENDSHIP DEMENTORS

This might be a good time to pause and reflect a bit on your own friendship dementors. Nearly all of us have at least one, and many of us have several. Not to worry—these obstreperous characters usually respond to firm limit-setting and will stand down once you call them on their bad behavior. Answering the questions below is a good first step toward sending these friendship nemeses packing.

If you find any of the questions particularly relevant to your own friendships, take a few notes. These ideas will come in handy when you proceed to Part 2 of the book, "Friendship Funda-mentals." They'll help you more easily adopt the recommendations from these chapters and open your mind to your healthy, inner "friendship mentors" in doing so.

1 *Machismo:* Do I tend to isolate myself, stay emotionally "cool," try to control situations and conversations, and/or behave competitively on a regular basis? How do these qualities affect my ability to get close to other men?

2 *Homophobo:* Does my fear of being perceived (or recog-nized) as gay sometimes keep me from opening up with other men? How does that reticence affect my life?

3 *Dumbo:* Do I tend to avoid awareness of my own and others' emotions—especially when they might cause conflict? How might more awareness of my feelings affect my friend-ships with other men?

4 *Misogyno:* Do negative feelings about women ever threaten my guy friendships? Alternatively, do these friendships ever undermine my relationship with my own partner? If so, how?

CHAPTER 3

A Brief History of Male Friendship

On a winter evening in 1840, in a small second-floor room over the store that Abraham Lincoln shared with his best friend, Joshua Speed, a heated conversation took place. Lincoln told Speed that he planned to break off his engagement with Mary Todd. He'd composed a formal letter to send her, explaining why he wasn't ready to get married.

Speed knew that Lincoln deeply loved and respected Mary, but also that he wrestled with doubts in matters of the heart. He was angry that his friend would consider breaking up with his fiancée in such a distant and disrespectful manner. He argued that Lincoln should speak with her face-to-face, honestly but kindly. Essentially, he was telling Lincoln to "man up" in his most intimate relationship.

Lincoln argued back but eventually relented, agreeing to do what he knew in his heart was right. At that moment of decision, Speed grabbed the letter out of his friend's hand, ripped it up, and threw it into the fireplace. Shortly afterward Speed moved back to Kentucky to take over his family's farm.

Abe and Mary closed the distance between them and eventually got married. They lived quietly in Springfield for many years until moving to Washington, DC, in 1861 to become the country's premier political couple—president and first lady of the United States.

Despite their geographical distance, Abe and Joshua continued to be best friends, regularly expressing their affection for each other in letters and brief visits. Through the years, they supported each other unstintingly in their life choices and buoyed up the other in times of desperate self-doubt.

At one point, Lincoln wrote, "You know my desire to befriend you is everlasting—that I will never cease, while I know how to do any thing."

Even in the face of their most deeply held difference—the emancipation of slaves—Speed managed to remain supportive of Lincoln throughout his presidency. After Lincoln's assassination, Speed wrote in sorrow: "Our friendship and intimacy closed only with his life."

Speed and Lincoln's friendship was not unique in its time. Literary critic Caleb Crain observes that throughout the eighteenth and much of the nineteenth centuries, European and American men were able to "express emotions to each other with a fervor and openness." During this period, a new sense of freedom celebrating reason and the emotional well-being of individuals had emerged: Intensely felt same-sex friendships between both men and women flourished. The poet Walt Whitman wrote in 1871: "Many will say it is a dream ... but I confidently expect a time when there will be seen ... running ... through ... America, threads of manly friendship, fond and loving, pure and sweet, strong and life-long, carried to degrees hitherto unknown."

MALE EMOTIONAL INTIMACY THROUGH HISTORY

When we look around us today, only 150 years after Lincoln's death, it's hard to find much evidence of this kind of openhearted expression between men in the United States. As I discuss in Chapter 2, "Breaking the Male Code," the social rules that govern how men are supposed to behave have resulted in guys today severely restricting their emotions and readiness to share personal information with each other.

There is a tendency to assume that what we see in men's relationships today reflects some essential truth about men's nature, biological or otherwise. A review of history, however, exposes this notion as groundless. In fact, men have shown a deep interest in, and capacity for, emotionally rich and closely bonded friendships since the beginning of recorded history.

Let's take a brief tour.

Classical literature, including the Bible and Greek and Roman mythology and philosophy, is filled with stories of close male friendships. The stories of David and Jonathan in the Old Testament, Achilles and Patroclus in the *Iliad*, and Damon and Pythias in Cicero's *De Officiis* are a few examples. These are all about men who were deeply, emotionally bonded and devoted to each other, to the point of being willing to sacrifice their lives for their friend.

In Homer's *Iliad*, Hector, the leader of the Trojans, killed

Achilles's dearest friend, Patroclus. Patroclus returned as a spirit, pleading with Achilles to bury his bones with his own so that they could be together in death. The great warrior grieved inconsolably because he was unable to embrace his friend one last time. He had refused to fight for the Greeks, who struggled, but he now agreed to join their battle in order to avenge his friend's death. The war turned on this friendship, and the Greeks prevailed. Achilles slayed Hector, but afterward, tragically, lost his own life.

Aristotle believed that men bonded for pleasure and "utility" (commerce). Most important, though, their friendships brought out the best in each other. Cicero found a spiritual sense of reciprocity in friendship: "two souls seeking to become one," or uniting for each other's benefit.

These sentiments were echoed in literary works and letters from the Middle Ages through the Renaissance. In the year 1071, Saint Anselm penned a note to his fellow monk, Gundulf: "Since thy spirit and mine can never bear to be absent from each other, but unceasingly are intertwined . . . why should I depict to thee on paper my affection, since thou dost carefully keep its exact image in the cell of thy heart? For what is thy love for me but the image of mine for thee?"

Love letters like this between clergy seem excessively flowery to us today. Most historical scholars, however, explain that these men expressed their love and affection for each other far more openly than modern men do.

Over the following centuries, in both Europe and America, the emotional bonds in men's friendships began to be tested in love triangles with women. As heterosexual relationships began to achieve more status in the social order, male-male loyalty struggled to sustain its former primacy. Later, particularly in America, a new vision of manhood emerged, in which men would prove their masculinity by removing themselves from modern civilization, testing their strength in the wilderness, away from the comforts of hearth and home. They sought to revive their male friendships in what author Leslie Fiedler described as "an Eden devoid of women." Ishmael's friendship with Queequeg in *Moby-Dick* and Tom Sawyer's bond with Huck Finn are examples in literature of this trend.

But the attempt to foster a kind of male bonding free from civilized life, one that could transcend race and religion, never gained traction in late nineteenth-century Europe and America. A period of "romantic friendship" that celebrated close same-sex relationships prevailed briefly during the nineteenth century in Europe. This trend, however, was quickly swept away with the advent of the Victorian period and its powerful insistence on marriage, heterosexism, and a reenergized form of homophobia arising in the culture. This ultimately contributed to the further weakening of the adhesive bonds and emotional intimacy in men's relationships.

THE VICTORIAN INFLUENCE

While many in his era shared Whitman's vision of a more openhearted kind of "manly friendship," by the end of the nineteenth century, this dream seemed more like a fading memory. Victorian moral concerns, scientific writings, and a changing economy had begun to redefine the roles and relationships between men and women in more restrictive ways.

Two new social paradigms, the "doctrine of separate spheres" and the "companionate marriage," became defining guidelines for men and women in Europe and America. The first paradigm promoted rigid complementary roles for both men and women. In their "sphere," women were expected to spend most of their time inside their homes, functioning as spiritual and emotional guides for their families. Men, on the other hand, were encouraged to range beyond the hearth and embrace the role of economic provider, leaving the responsibility for their emotional relationships and domestic responsibilities to their wives. They were also expected to avoid showing strong or vulnerable emotions, which might be interpreted as weakness.

The "companionate marriage" focused on romantic love and exclusivity, in effect discouraging couples from enjoying same-sex friendships. According to sociologist Stacey Oliker, however, women's friendships with other women were preserved in order to provide collective support for their families and their marriages. Men, on the other hand, were discouraged from pursuing close relationships outside of their families.

During the second half of the twentieth century, some of these rigid prescriptions—for example, that women should stay safely at home and not be "tainted" by the workplace—were challenged by both feminism and a sexual revolution. Other social rules, however, particularly restrictions on male emotional expression, persisted in the form of Male Code and continue to strongly affect men's willingness to share feelings with same-sex friends well into the twenty-first century.

MEN'S FRIENDSHIPS TODAY

When we reflect on changes during the past century in how men view masculinity and emotional intimacy, we can better appreciate why mainstream guys' friendships today may seem shallow or lackluster. The sense of dedication and commitment that we find in Lincoln and Speed's relationship, or in loving friendships between other men further back in history, seem to have faded away, or at least been ignored.

For a lot of men today, friendship is a kind of afterthought, subordinated to other life priorities. Spending time with a friend is something you might do after you complete your job duties, spend some quality time with your wife and kids, squeeze in a few regular visits to the gym, and enjoy a little time to chill with yourself. By the time you accidentally run into some guy who might be a friend, the conversation is likely to be hasty and awkward.

"Hey, man, we'll have to get together sometime."

"Yeah, *absolutely!*"

If a tad more honesty creeps into the conversation, one of you might admit, "Sorry, I just haven't had time to call."

When pressed, most men will acknowledge that friendships with other men are important to them, but they also confess that they don't put enough time or energy into them. Nor do they have a convincing explanation for their MIA tendencies. While "I'm really busy" is the most common response, it is often accompanied by an uncomfortable don't-ask-me-to-explain shrug. A cloud of ambivalence seems to hang over the topic.

Male friendships, I believe, are smack in the middle of an identity crisis. Our society no longer insists on an old-school model of masculinity that requires men to be perpetually cool, emotionally restrained, and in control. Men are now allowed to have *some* connection to their emotions, but nobody seems sure about how much, when, and with whom. We are a society that is no longer sure who men are or should be.

Pop psychology has moved in quickly to try to reassure us about the nature of male identity. Pick your favorite archetype: Mars? Iron John? The Caveman? If discomfort persists, television and movies rush in to distract us with comical stereotypes that depict men and their friendships as naive and tactless, alcohol and party driven, or competitive, sexually preoccupied, and power hungry. We scratch our heads, laugh, or groan but don't find much in these images to help us feel more real and connected in our friendships with other men.

The 2009 film *I Love You, Man* shows a bit of progress in its willingness to present male friendship as more than an occasion for hilarity. Here, we get a rare look at the real feelings of a man in search of a close male friend. When Peter Klaven (Paul Rudd) sets out to find a male friend, he encounters a stunning set of obstacles, including homophobia, rejection, and humiliation. When he ultimately does find "best friend material" in Sydney Fife (Jason Segel), he has to confront his own fear of guy-to-guy emotional commitment before he can enjoy the rewards of close friendship.

Humor (and there's plenty of it in this movie) seems to provide some anesthesia for our anxiety and uncertainty about what "real masculinity" is and how men can go about getting close to each other. It also pokes fun at the absurdities and contradictory expectations that surround this topic in our culture.

To resolve these contradictions, I believe we men need to take a leap of courage. We need to risk moving beyond stereotypical, socially acceptable male behavior and try to connect with each other in ways that are, well, a little more real.

THE MALE STATUS REPORT:
SHOULDER-TO-SHOULDER FRIENDSHIPS

At this point, you may be thinking, "How is this my issue? I'm a guy and I've got plenty of friends." Most men *do* have friendships with other men. In fact, research shows that men tend to have as many same-sex friends as women do. Certainly, the men in our MFEI Survey indicated that they were happy with the number of male friends they had. What they wanted was to have *closer relationships* with these guy friends.

The common form of friendship between men today is what sociologist Geoff Greif describes as shoulder-to-shoulder style. Picture two guys standing next to each other, looking outward. If they're talking, they're usually expressing their thoughts and opinions about what's going on "out there"—in sports, politics, work—rather than about their own or each other's feelings. These relationships include feelings of warmth and loyalty for the other man, but rarely involve sharing detailed personal information or offering deep emotional support. Shoulder-to-shoulder friendships present an awkward portrait of men today: They desire contact and, at the same time, avoid uncomfortable emotional exposure.

A shoulder-to-shoulder friendship is a bond that you have with a guy in your life whom you like and hang out with on occasion. You might work out regularly with this guy, or watch athletic events together. Maybe you both work in the same location and regularly share a beer together after work. Alternatively, he might be a man with whom you connect as part of a couple, when you and your partner go out socially. Perhaps he shares neighborhood carpool responsibilities with you or helps you with physical projects like building a patio or moving. Or he might be someone you've known a long time, a person from childhood or college whom you may see infrequently but whose company you continue to enjoy.

There's no question shoulder-to-shoulder friendships are important to men. They give us a feeling of connection and membership within a community that is progressively harder to find in today's world. There's plenty of loyalty and fun in these relationships. Staying power, too. For some men, these relationships go back decades.

George, an engineer in his late fifties, describes an annual get-together in Canada that he and six other men, former college friends, have been attending for twenty-five years. Their reunions take place in a rustic lakeside cabin, sparsely furnished with cots, mattresses, and a wood stove. For the men, used to easy comforts in their everyday lives, the place is perfect: It's rugged, low maintenance, and declares, "We're self-sufficient!"

"Really, nothing of great significance happens on these trips," George says. "We hang out and we fish. Sometimes we throw the fish back in. We talk, though not about anything very deep. I watch myself getting older with these guys. It's a little depressing, but it's also comforting."

He then goes on to tell me how he thinks about each of these men during the year, particularly when he feels lonely. This past fall, he and his wife had sent their youngest daughter off to college. The house was very quiet. He'd thought about calling some of the guys, but he didn't.

Maybe, he says, he'll bring it up with them next summer.

What George describes is pretty typical of shoulder-to-shoulder friendships—a shared sense of loyalty, enjoyment in activities, and comfort within a predictable routine. Yet, at a deeper level, George feels a sense of unease about not fully connecting with these men. He and his buddies don't share much detailed emotional information with each other, nor do they ask for, or offer, much emotional support. Time goes by, feelings are left unspoken, and impulses to connect are suppressed and then forgotten. When bits of important information are exchanged between these men, they are often downplayed or shrugged off. "Sally's pretty stressed out these days" could easily mean "Sally told me last night she's planning to leave me." The guys go home for the evening, never suspecting that their friend might need extra support.

Men are typecast as being incapable of expressing their feelings or responding authentically to those of others. According to social research, however, they actually *choose* to act this way, conforming to what they believe is acceptable masculine behavior. Compliance with these norms, they presume, comes with an emotional "get out of jail free" card, a belief that if they avoid acknowledging feelings, they will be immune to hurts or disappointments that arise in their relationships. The image that comes to mind here is the ludicrous scene in *Monty Python and the Holy Grail* in which the Black Knight, after losing both arms in battle, continues to stubbornly proclaim, "It's just a flesh wound!"

A well-known TV sports commentator, observing the disappointing loss of a nationally ranked football team to a less talented rival, stated that the favored team "had been playing *not to lose*, rather than playing to win." How often do we see teams lose at the end of a contest after they've been ahead, when they pull back to protect themselves rather than continue to invest their full energy in the game?

This kind of emotional withholding occurs routinely on the

playing field of men's friendships, and the consequences can be quite damaging. When men don't talk about their feelings or listen to those of a buddy, they may never clearly communicate their caring for a friend, even to themselves. This keep-your-distance policy can make it difficult to repair a frayed friendship. And, if the bond is disrupted or lost, it can make grieving all but impossible.

BUDDY, WHERE ART THOU?

John and Al were workout buddies who had met at a local gym. They bonded when they discovered they were both old-school guys who liked to lift free weights and hated exercise machines. Al was in his mid-sixties and ran a pool maintenance service, while John, in his early forties, practiced law in a large firm. They had been meeting weekly for several years on Wednesday afternoons, regularly spotting each other while they lifted weights. As the gym became more upscale, they joked that they were now each other's "fitness trainer." While the men felt warmly toward each other, they never socialized outside the gym, nor had they met each other's wives.

When Al failed to appear at the gym for a few weeks, John assumed he was away on vacation and had forgotten to tell him. A couple of weeks later, John inquired about his friend at the front desk and was told by the clerk that Al's wife had canceled his membership. "He died of a heart attack two weeks ago," the clerk reported.

Apparently, Al had had a chronic heart condition he'd never mentioned to John.

John was shocked and deeply saddened. He felt he had lost a

close friend in Al, without ever knowing something as fundamental as the man's serious, ongoing health condition. He asked
for Al's address and phone number so he could send his condolences to his wife, but he wondered if she would even know who he
was. He was angry and sad, for himself as well as for Al. How was
it that he didn't know about Al's illness? His own wife probably
wouldn't understand either, since he'd hardly ever mentioned Al to
her. John felt horribly alone in his grief.

The trauma of Al's death was heightened for John by what
psychologist Pauline Boss calls ambiguous loss. This happens
when a person doesn't have enough information about the lost
person to allow them to make sense of the loss and emotionally
heal from it. Families of soldiers missing in action frequently suffer
from this condition, leaving family members depressed, confused,
and sometimes reluctant to commit themselves emotionally in
other relationships.

Men can also suffer ambiguous loss if a family member or friend
decides to drop out of a relationship without clarifying the reasons
for the disruption. In many shoulder-to-shoulder friendships, men
haven't developed the habits of emotionally intimate communication, so they don't know where they truly stand with each other.
When conflicts arise, they're clueless about how to resolve them.
Left in a state of emotional limbo, they often try to quell or ignore
their painful feelings and find themselves unable to heal.

REDESIGNING OUR FRIENDSHIP AGENDA

We've seen that men have experienced emotionally close friendships in earlier periods of history, and that there is a missing

dimension of emotional intimacy in our current model of male friendship today.

Before we move ahead to discuss how this dimension can be restored, however, we must first acknowledge that male friendships in the past have supported different social agendas or values from our own, some of which feel out of place today.

In order to foster meaningful friendships with other men, we need to clarify our own goals and values, the agenda that we want our friendships to support. A good list—one consistent with the world we live in now—might include: 1) equality and inclusiveness in our relationships; 2) acceptance of our own vulnerability and our need for strong emotional connections; and finally 3) respect for our differences with others and curiosity about what we can learn from these differences.

Let's first look at some of the agendas or values from past eras that close male friendships have supported. How might we change some of these in order to best support values that are important and relevant to us today?

Bonding for Exclusion and Dominance

In Aristotle's time, "high friendship," or friendship that supported admirable or virtuous behavior, was seen as an option *only* for men, since women were viewed by men as lacking sufficient character to be able to sustain close friendships. As noble and satisfying as close male friendships may have been, the reality is that they served for many centuries to support the segregation of the sexes and the dominance of men over women.

By contrast, most men today are looking for more equal and shared connections with their spouses and partners. In our MFEI Survey, men reported wanting support from their close friends to help them achieve this equality and connectedness. Our survey showed that the more intimate a man's friendship, the more help he was likely to receive from his guy friend in trying to understand and enhance his partner relationship.

Bonding to Prove You're a Real Man

Many men still carry in their heads a prototype of what sociologist Jan Yager calls the heroic friendship, an idealized endeavor in which a man proves his worthiness through acts of extreme courage, self-sacrifice, and even a willingness to put himself in harm's way to demonstrate his commitment to a friend.

From antiquity to modern times, many stories of close male friendship take place on the battlefield or, in some cases, on the playing field. These settings often provide a dramatic plotline, opportunities for heroism and an adrenaline rush in the service of overcoming an adversary. Battling a common opponent, and/or participating in a cause "larger than oneself," is a central feature of what I call the wartime friendship.

This kind of longing runs deep in many men.

Yet guys today can't, nor should they need to, rely solely on being in extremis in order to demonstrate their commitment to their friendships. Nor should they be looking to their buddies for opportunities to prove their manhood. Men would be better served by looking to their guy friends for deeper connection and emotional support.

For this, we need more open, compelling models for "peacetime friendship," ones that provide men the opportunity to connect with each other in openhearted ways and to demonstrate their loyalty in the course of everyday life. In Chapter 7, I introduce some ideas and examples of how guys might do this. Hearing about this, a colleague of mine offered, "You mean you don't have to slay a dragon—you could just regularly check in, pay attention, and show up for your friend?" That didn't quite have the cachet of Achilles avenging Patroclus's death, but . . .

"Yes," I replied.

Bonding for Uniformity and Agreement

Our current Male Code attempts to define how all men *should* act, feel, and think. It insists that if you follow the rules (described in Chapter 2) you're "in," you're acceptable, you can qualify for love, affection, power, and privilege. And if you don't, well, you're in trouble.

This attitude often intimidates men from culturally diverse backgrounds, whether racial, ethnic, sexual, or socioeconomic, from expressing themselves openly. Sociologist Theodore Cohen observed that working-class white males had an easier time expressing themselves with each other in their friendships than did their middle-class counterparts. Similarly, sociologist Clyde Franklin discovered that working-class African American male friends also had an easier time with each other than their upscale middle-class counterparts.

The old saw "It's lonely at the top" seems to have some truth to it. As men, particularly those from more marginalized backgrounds, achieve more economic success, power, and prestige in society, they often begin to restrict themselves emotionally. Even when they are lonely and unhappy, they may avoid EI behaviors because they don't fit into the dominant success scheme of our culture.

Author Peter Nardi also points out that gay men's friendships may find protection in their distance from mainstream male values. In *Men's Friendships*, he states that while gay men often follow the traditional masculine path of pursuing sex as a means to intimacy, when these relationships do not develop as primary love interests, gay men are often more easily able to continue them as emotionally intimate friendships.

While homophobia and antigay sentiment have been rampant in various societies and certain historical periods, this prejudice and persecution have by no means been a steady state throughout history. Historical records indicate that same-sex erotic activity has occurred in most countries, not only in ancient Greece and Rome but also in Europe, China and Japan, and South America as well as in native tribes, including Native Americans. Our current kerfuffle over "who's gay and who's not" hasn't always been such a public obsession resulting in men feeling judged about having emotionally close relationships with each other, and often avoiding intimate relationships (both nonsexual and sexual) with other men because of this concern.

If we can continue taking steps toward accepting differences in men's (and women's) sexual preferences, we allow more leeway in *everyone's* desires to establish more openhearted relationships. In our survey, there was no distinction between gay and straight men in their desire for close male friendships—both wanted more emotional intimacy in their friendships with other guys.

WOMEN'S FRIENDSHIPS: THE BENEFITS OF "SWEAT EQUITY"

Men have a lot to learn from women about how to manage their friendships well. While women today also struggle with maintaining close relationships, their friendships continue to be more durable and emotionally accessible than men's. Friendships between women have long functioned to support women, providing both personal emotional support and help in their roles as caretakers of their marriage and families as well as organizers of their relational networks.

Women also seem to have a better appreciation of what goes into sustaining close friendships. They will fight for—and in—their friendships to preserve them, and they suffer hard when a friendship falters or fails. Recent literature reflects the sense of urgency that women feel about this relationship. Within the past five years, more than seven books by women about their own friendships—with titles like *Friendships Don't Just Happen!*, *When Friendship Hurts*, and *The Friendship Fix*—underscore the importance women place on keeping their female friendships in good working order.

As a result, women today are better motivated and more adept than men at reaching out to others. Reflecting on the competency gap between men and women in establishing close bonds, psychologist Harry Reis once quipped, "The only thing that seems to be required for an intimate discussion is a woman."

Like men, many women retain old friendships from childhood. However, as adults, most women also develop a group of "second tier" or "third tier" friendships that emerge from their neighborhoods or child-centered activities. These friendships provide individual support as well as sustenance for their marriages and families. In Part 3 of this book, two chapters are devoted to ways that close male friendships, similarly, can enrich men's relationships with their partners and kids.

The notion that women's aptitude for close friendship is a biological imperative, that women are somehow "hormone-ized" for friendship, has emerged in the ongoing research on neuroscience and gender. In her study on oxytocin, sex hormones, and stress reduction, Shelley Taylor points out that women will *tend to* (their children) and *befriend* (other women) rather than simply fight or flee, the typical male responses in the face of stressful stimuli.

In reading this fascinating research, I would only suggest that we not underestimate the hard work that goes into making and sustaining good friendships based on sweat equity, not hormones alone. Just as men do, women have to struggle to make and keep good friendships. Doing so today, in the face of dual careers and other time and energy suckers, is harder for *everyone.*

When the men in our groups succeed in building closer friendships and better communication skills—achievements they've previously dismissed as "women's work"—their female partners are often the first to give them credit.

One of my patients, Claude, a fifty-five-year-old pharmaceutical researcher, told me that he had set up a date for coffee with a close friend, Franck. When Claude told his wife, Jeannie, about the planned meeting, she was taken aback. "Not just because she likes Franck—she thinks he's a good guy," he told me, "but because *I* called him, on my own, to get together." He reported their inter-action verbatim:

"'You really called him?' she asked me. Her eyes were open wide."

"'I did,' I told her."

"And she told me, 'Wow, good for you!'"

Claude added his own interpretation for me. "She was really saying, 'It's about time, you slacker, that you took some responsi-bility for that relationship.'

"I took this as a big compliment." He smiled. "Jeannie's really serious about her friends."

In today's world, the issues confronting men in forming in-timate relationships are at once less controversial and carry a greater sense of urgency than ever before. As we move forward, it's helpful to recognize how close male friendships help men at *all* stages of development in the life cycle. We'll look at these stages in the next chapter. You'll have the opportunity to identify where you are among these stages, how your male friendships are working, and, if the situation calls for it, what you and your friends can do to better support each other.

CHAPTER 4

The Seasons of a Man's Friendships

The guys are sitting outside. It's a sunny afternoon. We're eating chips and sandwiches, drinking beer on the adobe deck of the Bell Tower restaurant overlooking downtown Santa Fe. Several of us are wearing black T-shirts, the logo reading GEEZER—A PERSON. NOT YOUNG. NOT DEAD. SOMEWHERE IN BETWEEN. Barry, a health care consultant and a frequent organizer of our reunions, has brought the shirts from Sarasota for us.

The Geezers are a group of seven guys, all 1963 graduates of Evanston Township High School. We have been getting together now for twelve years. We meet each year in different places around the country. Don't ask me about the name Geezers. It wasn't my idea.

On the deck, Jeff, a busy Wilmington lawyer, tells me there is no way he'd miss these get-togethers. He says they're "highlight" experiences for him. For me, too.

The conversation is animated. We're talking about our kids, our grandchildren, and retirement. We decide to call Joel, a small business owner in Indiana, who couldn't make the reunion this year. He tells us he's OK, that he misses us. He'll join us next year.

We mosey around to that edgy topic—health. Johnny, a retired photographer, looks energetic, having recovered from an exhausting battle with stomach cancer two years ago. That's a relief: It was a scary two years for us all.

The conversation leaps back and forth, crossing decades in seconds. We recall things for each other. Corky, a high school teacher, reminds me of a job he and I had, stacking lingerie catalogues on a conveyer belt at the RR Donnelley plant in Chicago during our last summer in high school. Oh my God! Yes, I remember that.

I think of these old friendships as a loving memory trust. They bring me back to times when I was young and unknowing. They remind me about what's good about my "essential" self. We affirm for each other how we've all grown and changed, endured and overcome, even triumphed over the years. These friendships are faithful companions, even through periods of silence. They ride shotgun and cover our backs.

Bob, also a business owner, and I are bantering about religion. I can't help myself and burst into laughter. I'm feeling relaxed, now that I'm with my friends, lighter than I can remember for a long time. Another great benefit of old friendships, perhaps the most important, is that they allow us to laugh.

Psychologists Erik Erikson and Daniel Levinson have shown

that each person, no matter how old, needs to master specific, age-related challenges in order to feel fulfilled. A man's close male friends can help him navigate these turning points in ways that profoundly affect his health and relationships. In this chapter, we'll take a close look at men's friendships over the life cycle. At each stage, we'll cover the key emotional challenges that men face and how their friendships can help them successfully master these challenges.

As you read this chapter, take the opportunity to reflect on your own male friendships today. Can you identify the life stage you're in? Ask yourself whether your friendships are providing the kind of experiences you want and need. If not, you'll get some ideas about how to "upgrade" these connections so that they better meet your emotional needs.

BOYS' FRIENDSHIPS

From preschool through middle and high school, boys travel through a whirlwind of rapidly shifting developmental challenges. These involve learning to trust others, developing independence and initiative, and later, a sense of identity.

From the beginning, boys' abilities to develop strong friendships predict how well they will perform in school, develop social skills, and handle stress and transitions in family life, as well as how they will fare in future adult relationships. A powerful capacity, indeed.

According to developmental researchers Michael Thompson and Catherine O'Neill Grace, children begin to form friendships earlier than we might think. As soon as infants can crawl, they begin to seek out other little kids. By age three, most boys have begun to gravitate to other boys as playmates, while girls seek out other girls.

From the preschool years through middle school, guy (as well as girl) friends learn important social and cognitive skills while playing together. These include sharing, resolving conflicts, and basic empathy skills. These skills are necessary for children to form what psychiatrist Harry Stack Sullivan called chumships.

By age seven, boys are well versed in the rules of Boy Code, a precursor of Male Code that elaborates how young males are supposed to behave in society. They vigorously debate these rules with each other and levy judgments about whether they or other boys are living up to standards—who should be called out (and possibly tormented) and who gets a pass.

All kids do this, Thompson and Grace explain, as a way of establishing and negotiating gender behavioral guidelines for themselves. Close friends help each other navigate this complicated maze of boyhood expectations, providing each other with guidance as well as protection, both emotional and physical. How well boys fare in this evaluation has deeper implications for their self-esteem than we like to think.

FRIENDSHIP SAFETY ALERT

Boys in general are not naturally violent. They exhibit higher levels of aggression in childhood than girls, according to psychologist Lloyd deMause, but not because of testosterone (boys and girls have equal levels during their early years). Rather, deMause suggests, boys are more aggressive because they are routinely nurtured (held, cuddled, and talked to) less than girls in their early years. Our Male Code fosters a denial of boys' needs for tender nurturance and, as a result, they receive less stimulation to certain areas of the brain, including the corpus callosum (relatively smaller in boys than in girls to begin with), that help them manage their emotions and impulses.

Thus, our habit of reducing nurturance and affection in rearing young boys actually inhibits their development of emotional independence and the ability to control their impulses. This exaggerates boys' hunger for acceptance and recognition, their desire to be admired by or belong to a group, to feel special, or, alternatively, to avoid shame and humiliation. Bullying thrives in a culture that promotes boys' use of violence as a "manly art," an acceptable way to achieve these ends.

There are strong links between bullying, youth violence, homicide, and suicide, so we should be paying attention to these phenomena. We should not consider violence and aggression part of normal developmental behavior in boys. Harassment and bullying have been linked to 75 percent of school shooting incidents.

With no friends or connection to a group, boys feel vulnerable and unprotected, and indeed, when isolated, are at greater risk for being bullied.

I lived with this kind of terror every day for six straight months during third grade. During my walk home alone from Stewart Elementary School in Chicago every afternoon, a tall fifth grader named Donald Jennings would step out of the shadows from nowhere, it seemed, onto the sidewalk. He would catch up

to me, walk alongside me, and start punching, pushing, and taunting me. Sometimes there would be other kids with him, sometimes not.

"Here you are again, little boy," he would whisper, a sinister
chuckle echoing in my ear. "Where do you think you're going?"

He seemed to know just where to find me, like a wasp heading
to its nest. If I were carrying books, he'd make it a point to knock
them out of my hands onto the ground. I had no idea of why he was
picking on *me*. I had no relationship with him in or out of school,
except as his target. I was stunned, confused, terrified.

And I told no one.

I'm not comparing my story to many far more horrific ones
that I hear in my office. But when I listen to men who were bullied
or abused as kids, I understand why many never spoke up. Doing
so would have meant violating a section of Male Code that goes
something like this: 1) If you express fear or become visibly upset
about being pushed around or abused, it means you're a wimp or a
coward; 2) A guy should be able to dispose of his rivals by himself,
even when he can't; and 3) If you snitch on your tormentor, you
may be punished worse.

In our Friendship Labs and workshops, many men reveal episodes of boyhood abuse for the first time, things they've never
shared with anyone. "The priest used to rub up against me, from
behind, when no one else was around." "Whenever I walked into
the dining hall, there was a chorus, 'Here comes Mr. Lukewarm.'"
"He'd spit on me, laugh, and call me a fag." Their silence had
deepened their wounds and left many emotionally scarred with relationship problems, depression, even drug and alcohol addictions.
Sharing these experiences with other guys was the first step for
many in their healing process.

I got lucky with Donald Jennings. One of my friends who saw him terrorizing me urged me to tell my parents. Reluctantly, I did. They promptly made a beeline to the school principal. Shortly afterward, to my huge relief, Donald stopped emerging from the shadows on my walks home. I could breathe again.

The torment ended, but the feelings from the experience never really did. When my family moved from the city to the more "genteel" suburb of Evanston, I made some good friends. Among them was a stronger, muscular kid named Randy Johnson, who went to a neighboring elementary school. When kids from rougher neighborhoods invaded our playground, I tried to make sure that Randy (who had a killer headlock that left your head ringing for hours) was in the vicinity. He used to wear a ring that left an impression on the foreheads of several nasty fellows who tried to harass me and my other friends. Life felt a lot safer with Randy around.

Years later, I learned that Randy was killed in Vietnam. I get sad and feel grateful at the same time when I think about him. He never sought out violence, but he would put himself in harm's way to protect his friends, people he cared about. He was a saving "bodyguard" for me during my middle childhood.

BOYZ TO MEN

As boys move into their middle and late teens, an important shift occurs. Up until this point, they've been able to bond with each other more personally, sharing intimate feelings. In her research on middle school boys, psychologist Niobe Way observes, "Boys want 'deep depth' friendships with other boys in which secrets are shared, trust is total, and they have the confidence that their friend will not betray them or laugh at them when they are feeling vulnerable." By their late teenage years, her research suggests, they've already started to move away from this intimate kind of sharing, adopting instead a more hardscrabble, distant way of relating to each other, one dictated by the rules of Male Code.

Girls come into the picture, bodies harden, hormones surge, competition flourishes, and boys' friendships begin to morph into the kind of shoulder-to-shoulder relationships we discuss in Chapter 3. Most boys manage to adapt to this change. They reconfigure their ways of relating to each other in order to preserve their loyalties and enjoy their friendships.

There is an unspoken emotional cost for boys going through this transition, however. "Boys know that there is a problem," Dr. Way states. "[They speak] about the pressures at home and in school to 'man up,' be independent and keep their problems to themselves. . . . At the ages of sixteen and seventeen years old, when the suicide rate among boys in the United States increases to five times the rate of girls, boys [speak] of losing their close relationships and feeling increasingly isolated. . . . We need to allow them to express their vulnerabilities and not make these vulnerabilities a matter of manliness, maturity or sexuality."

It's important to take a fresh look at how our Male Code affects young men's friendships as they move from boyhood into manhood. Boys are instructed to "put away childish things," and it seems that human feelings and vulnerability have been tossed onto this pile.

We have to ask ourselves if this guideline is one we want to continue promoting for today's young men and their friendships.

YOUNG ADULT FRIENDSHIP

From their late teens until age thirty, young men are beginning to establish their identities as adults. This usually involves leaving home, separating from and negotiating changes in their relationships with parents, then pursuing higher education, military service, or moving out into the work world. During this phase, tasks such as emotional separation, living independently, bonding with other guys, further independence with study skills, or, alternatively, mastering entry skills in the work world, dominate their landscapes.

Some of these challenges are delayed or extended for economic reasons. Thirty-four percent of today's youth will stay home after high school or move back in for a period of time between the ages of eighteen and thirty-one, as a "backup" until they can support themselves independently. Guys are also expected during this time to develop rudimentary EI skills that prepare them for having close relationships, marriage, and a family in the future.

When today's young men are forced to confront the prospects for their futures, many find themselves confused and adrift. The economic environment, the task of sorting out a career or job path, can seem daunting. Thinking about major life changes, such as marriage, family, and career can feel overwhelming. Many guys living on their own for the first time, and no longer under the jurisdiction of their parents, are disconcerted by how complex these decisions are, and yet are reluctant to seek guidance and support about their questions.

The message they get from home, from their parents, particularly their fathers, is often, "You're on your own. You've had the advantages. You should be ready to handle the big responsibilities." The pressure doesn't help for many young men. Nascent voices of their Machismo and Dumbo dementors, reinforced by Male Code, often encourage them to blow off or avoid dealing with their emotional fears, rather than admit to these and seek support.

In his research, Michael Kimmel observed that many of his male, college-age subjects, contrasted with women of this generation, had no Plan B in mind, no thought-through ideas about what they would do if college and their notions about how life was supposed to go didn't work out as planned. Many were living in a bubble, avoiding the hard questions about their futures.

An older generation of mentors may be failing to respond adequately to young men today, a topic I discuss further in Chapter 10 on parenting. But many young men, in an effort to look confident, also struggle with how honest they can be with *themselves and each other* about their personal life challenges.

GETTING REAL WITH YOUR BROS

Close friendships seem as if they should be an obvious source of support for guys who are navigating the new challenges of independent living. Our own and other research shows that males during this life stage report having plenty of friends with whom they spend time. When they are connecting with each other, openly and vulnerably, they can really help each other.

Tony and Connell lived together as friends in a community house in West Philadelphia for several years while they were in college. "We talked about everything," Tony told me. "When Connell and Annie [the woman Connell eventually married] were first together, she was opposed to his watching porn. She felt it was destructive and demeaning to women. We all argued about it. Connell and I thought that was stupid, no big deal. We talked about him and Annie, though. After a while, we both decided she was right. It really did change the way I thought about women—forever."

Are there advantages to having close friends here? Sure. If there's an open channel between you two, your friend can probably understand exactly what you're struggling with. He's probably thinking about the same things and may have even come up with some ideas or tried out some solutions that have worked. The beauty here is that no one needs to have an absolute answer; there's help just in being able to *voice* your feelings and thoughts to a guy you trust.

For young men, these kinds of talks are generally more reliable and honest when they occur one-on-one with a buddy rather than with a group of guy friends at a bar or another setting in which the focus is on other things. The important feelings often get left out or tamped down in this environment.

OR . . . FAKING IT

Some men in their twenties have already adapted the postures of cool reserve that characterize familiar shoulder-to-shoulder friendships, and in the process deprive themselves and their friendships of the kind of emotional enrichment Tony and Connell were able to have. They've bought into the "go it alone" model, backing themselves into an emotional corner and become symptomatic.

Our MFEI Survey revealed an enlightening finding about

young men and their friendships during this life stage: While most young men have plenty of friends that they spend time with, the level of intimacy in their friendships drops more precipitously at this time than at any other life stage. While they are maintaining and developing new friendships, the pressure to *look as if* they know what they're doing, to *portray* that they're following a smooth, unruffled course into manhood, often results in their adopting postures of confidence that hide the truth. They're bonded with their guy friends, but they're not necessarily sharing the most vulnerable feelings and questions, sometimes with painful consequences.

LEGAL SUBTERFUGE

One day, Jonah, a twenty-two-year-old patient, came in with a grim look on his face. He looked pale and haggard. I'd been working with Jonah to resolve some of his symptoms of anxiety and panic, as well as stress in his relationship with his father. He'd made good progress over the past four months.

"I couldn't sleep last night," he said. A junior in college, he'd just returned to his apartment after celebrating Thanksgiving with his family. He looked wound as tight as a drum.

"I just can't do it." He hesitated. "I don't want to do it."

"What?" I asked.

"Take the LSATs. I don't think I want to be a lawyer." A moment of comic relief flickered through my brain. The kid looked as if he were at death's door over taking a graduate school aptitude test. Yet I knew this was not funny for Jonah.

"Do you have to?" I asked.

He looked at me angrily. "Well, what am I supposed to do? My dad's a big-shot lawyer. I have the grades. All my friends are going to professional schools. I got rave reviews at my clerkship in my dad's friends' law firm."

"Do you know what you want to do after you graduate?" I asked.

He looked desperate, as if he were at gunpoint. He shook his head no, but didn't say a word. My heart went out to him. He looked so sad.

I breathed. "Have you talked to anyone about this? How about your friends? They must be going through the same questioning now." Jonah had some good guy friends.

He rolled his eyes and looked at me as if I were an idiot.

"Clearly, you don't get it," he said. "My friends think I'm a legal whiz—big man on the debate team, all of that. How am I going to tell *them* that I have no idea what I want to do? They're just not the kind of people you talk to about those kinds of things."

"Really?" I said, with exaggerated curiosity. "You talk to me about these things."

"Yeah, well, you're a shrink. Guys my age don't get into this stuff. We like to keep it light."

I hesitated, pushed back slowly. "I get it. But think about this. These guys are your *friends*. They look up to you. You've told me so. They count on you to tell it like it is. If you're not sure you want to go to law school, do you really think they want you to lead them on, to blow smoke in their face? Are you really trusting them if you can't share a question that matters to you?" I was pressing him hard, playing the "man up" integrity card here.

I pulled back a little for him. "Look, you're not going to announce this over the PA system in your frat house, but what about just talking to George about it?" George was his best friend. "Find out what he thinks?"

I might have just as well offered him a glass of sour milk, and he shook his head. Then he breathed. "I guess I've got to do something about this."

The next session, Jonah returned, looking a bit more chipper.

"So," he started, "I brought this stuff up with George. He just listened, didn't say anything for a long time. I have to admit, I was amazed at how much better I felt, just talking to him. Then after a while, he told me he thought I was an amazing guy, and he was confident I'd figure this out."

Jonah looked up at me with grudging acknowledgment. "You were right. There was no judgment."

Then, his mood shifted and, with incredulity, he added, "And get this. Unbelievable. Out of the blue, George tells me he had to leave high school for an entire year, before he came to Penn. He was in a residential treatment center for depression! I can't believe I didn't know that. He never told me."

"How was that to hear?" I asked.

"I felt sad for him, really. But it made me feel closer to him. Our sharing this stuff with each other." He looked softer than I'd seen him before.

"Anything else?" I asked.

He expelled a long, deep breath. "Yeah. We talked about my dad. I'm gonna have to tell him about me and law school. I just don't know what he's going to say. But I'll find out." He shrugged.

I thought he was going to be OK. Jonah had taken a big step. I shook my head affirmatively.

"Yeah, so, shrink"—he regained his cool—"I guess I need to open up more with people, right?"

I recalibrated and mustered my best it's-up-to-you shrug. "Yeah, well, let's see, right?" I said.

He was cool with that.

THE MIDDLE YEARS

Most men do eventually figure out their "quarter life" crises, manage to live on their own, find a career path, and meet a partner. Entering the next phase of early midlife, however, between ages thirty-five and fifty, can feel like an emotional whirlwind. It's a period of intense multitasking, especially at first. Men in this stage are trying to achieve close bonding with spouses or partners, establishing themselves in jobs and careers, and becoming first-time parents, all at the same time. Many guys confess to being exhausted during the early part.

Erik Erikson identified emotional *intimacy* (establishing close bonds with others) and, later, *generativity* (nurturing and passing on the fruits of our labors, including wisdom, to others) as the key development tasks of this stage.

Stress arises for both men and women now, not just because of increased time demands but in adjusting to changing role expectations as well. For example, in a recent Pew Research Center survey, it was discovered that while today's fathers are spending three times as many hours per week with their children as they did in 1965, they are twice as likely as their wives to say that it's not enough and feel bad about this. For both dads and moms, changing gender role expectations contribute an additional degree of uncertainty during this stage.

PRESERVING YOUR LIFELINES

This may be the most vulnerable stage in the life cycle for men because of the sheer volume of new emotional challenges they face. The go-it-alone, I-can-solve-it-myself attitude reinforced by traditional Male Code adds to their stress. A 2013 "State of Friendship" survey by Lifeboat: Friends at Their Best found that the early years of marriage and parenting were less satisfying than any other stage in the life cycle for *both men and women*. Both sexes said this took a toll on their outside friendships. The drop-off in friendship support for men, however, is higher because women are still better at preserving friendships, as well as making new ones, when the situation calls for it.

In our own MFEI Survey, we found that, for men, the number of close friends and the amount of time spent with them dropped most significantly during the period after their children were born. This is a huge lost opportunity for guys, and at a time when they can most use the support. Men often complain, with justification, that their old friendships don't feel emotionally responsive to the new wave of responsibility they are experiencing.

The answer here, plain and simple, is that in order to survive and thrive during this life stage, men need guy friends more than ever. It's important to be intentional about this as a goal. Reintegrating old friends, making some new ones, addressing the transitional nature of your life, and retooling your emotional friendship skills (discussed in Chapter 6, "Conversations from the Heart") can all help!

BRIDGING THE GAP

After Connell moved out of the community house with his partner, Annie, he and Tony struggled with their friendship. Tony hadn't imagined how much he'd be affected when Connell moved out. He was shell-shocked at first, and felt abandoned by Connell. They'd never really talked about this.

The men struggled to stay in contact over the next few years. For his part, Connell was caught up in a swirl of activities—moving out, buying a house, getting married, and dealing with Annie's family.

Then they had a baby. Most recently, Connell found himself and Annie sharing parenting responsibilities for their six-month-old son, Luke, while Connell worked from home. His days were jam-packed, filled with emotional highs and lows, focused on work, his kid, and his marriage. The days of hanging out in the community house, with lots of time to chat, felt remote to him.

It hit Connell one morning when he woke up tired and sad, looking over at the other side of the bed and seeing Annie fast asleep. They'd argued late into the night about a trip he had to take for his business, his having to be away from her and Luke. Seeing her there, he suddenly felt very alone.

The thought flew into his head. "This is exactly what I'd be talking with Tony about." He and his friend had been in contact only sparingly over the last few years, mostly because of how busy Connell had been. Tony had been more flexible. He'd moved out of the community house and was living with his girlfriend, Sharon. Connell had told himself he didn't have the time to reboot his relationship with Tony, but at that moment, the truth settled hard on him: He hadn't *made* the time.

He shook his head, climbed out of bed, and, walking into his study, picked up his cell and dialed.

When Tony answered, Connell opened with, "Hey, man. Someone told me you're good with kids." Tony was a Waldorf preschool teacher.

There was an awkward silence. Connell continued, "You have time to babysit?"

Picking up on the humor, Tony flipped back: "I don't think Luke can afford my rates." They couldn't see each other doing this, but both guys smiled.

"Not him, idiot," Connell shot back. "Me. I need your services."

Tony didn't miss a beat. "That kind of help is beyond your pay grade, my friend," he said gently. "This would have to be pro bono."

"I'll take it," Connell said. He felt relieved, and happy.

The guys met in the park that weekend and walked with Luke in the stroller. They got around to talking about how they needed to connect more regularly. Too much was going on, and they were missing out on each other's lives. Tony shared that he'd been hurt by Connell's rapid exit into his new life, that he'd felt left behind. Connell apologized and said it had been a scary transition for him over the past several years. He hadn't yet figured how to balance all these new situations. He'd been "holing up" in his new life. He loved his wife and Luke, but, he said, "It gets hard sometimes." Tony noticed that he looked sad as he said this.

They walked in silence for a while. Finally, Tony said, "Tell you what. How's about Sharon and I cook you and Annie dinner next Sunday. You'll come over early with Luke, so you can get home early. We'll take care of the food and cooking. You just bring your bodies. Think you guys can handle that?"

Connell looked hard at his friend, and shook his head, as if he were just waking up and shaking off the cobwebs. "That makes way too much sense," he laughed. "Absolutely. Let's do it."

BOOMERS AS LATE BLOOMERS

The years of establishing a career, marriage or partnership, and family life fly by quickly, more quickly than most men imagine. During the later middle years, between the ages of fifty and seventy today, men watch their children leave home. Their jobs or careers are peaking or have plateaued, and their marriages have stabilized, become comfortable, enjoyable—or not.

During these years, men are reviewing the developmental tasks of their middle years that Erik Erikson identified: Have they been generative or productive, achieved what they wanted? Do they still feel relevant in their work and personal life? Have they established intimacy in their relationships, closeness in their marriage and with their children? And are they avoiding stagnation?

As an early member of the Baby Boomer generation, I find these questions easy to identify with. My generation grew up in an era of idealism, the belief that the world is a perfectible place, and that working hard and staying true to your ideals get you what you want. At this stage, guys are hoping for some closure on these questions, yet many are finding that life feels anything but settled for them.

A recent study showed that while most Boomer men are happier than their younger counterparts (about their compensation) in the workplace today, they're also *more stressed out* (uncertain of their futures). Similarly, as divorce rates for the general population have stabilized over the past several decades, they have *doubled* for guys over fifty. In 1990, fewer than one in ten people who divorced were fifty or older. In 2009, that figure rose to one in four.

Many of the men in our Friendship Labs haven't spoken much at all about these troubling questions. They confess to wanting to have deeper connections with other guys, but they haven't done much about this. The Lifeboat "State of Friendship" survey indicated that many guys at this stage were disappointed with the quality of their friendships. At this life stage, retirement and divorce are two of the most difficult issues for men to discuss.

Raj, a sixty-year-old radiologist, confessed that he was continuing to push himself to do surgery, aggravating a chronic herniated lumbar disc in the process, because he couldn't face the prospects of losing the respect of his colleagues if he stopped. "I don't even need the money," he said, frustrated. "And I'm not interested in doing surgery anymore." He hesitated. "I just can't get it out of my head, thinking, 'What will my colleagues think?' An 'old guy, over the hill' is what keeps coming up for me."

In another group, Daniel, a fifty-three-year-old small business owner who had agreed to a divorce two years earlier after a long, painful marriage, found himself enraged and depressed when his two teenage children refused to see or visit him. He'd recently invited his new girlfriend to move into his apartment. "After years of misery, trying to make things work, I agree to divorce. I continue to financially support everyone. Now, when a little happiness comes into my life, my kids and my ex decide to punish me!" he complained.

In both situations, there were other men in the groups who had gone through midlife divorces in which children were involved, men who'd retired or were thinking about it, and some men who were struggling with health issues. These guys readily jumped in with their own experiences, providing comfort to each other, giving and receiving support. Most of our guys discover that there are men out there, even some whom they already know, who are willing and eager to listen—if they give them a chance.

THE NOT-QUITE-SO-SILENT GENERATION

Older men, affectionately known as seniors, tend to be more enthusiastic about their friendships. These men, over age seventy, are the fastest-growing segment of our population, mostly due to advances in health care and better information about nutrition, exercise, and lifestyle. Also, younger generations are producing fewer offspring, and later. With better health and more time on their hands, senior men are looking to connect more deeply with other guys.

Developmental psychologists have suggested that our later adult years are most valuable in allowing us to reflect upon and appreciate the meaning of our lives. Erikson identified the goal of this life stage as resolving the problem of *integrity versus despair.* This third phase also encourages us to care for ourselves and direct our remaining energies in ways that we feel are important to us and to others.

In our Friendship Labs, older men talk about health, their vitality, their sexual, physical, and mental fitness, their relationships, their grandchildren, and the future. They also talk about illness, loss, and death, including that of people who have been dear to them, and their own mortality. As one fellow in a group recently described it, "We cover the big-ticket items."

While this generation of men has a reputation for being reticent to talk about deeply personal feelings and more apt to follow traditional lines of authority, they also come with certain advantages, ones that make them strong candidates for close friendships. These include economic security, more free time, and (for some) good emotional skills from their years of parenting and marriage. Also, lack of tech savvy (generally a sore point for these guys) can work in their favor: They're not apt to want to spend time hiding behind electronic devices.

Aging can add barriers for men in their friendships. Some have lost dear friends and need to make new ones. Others need to upgrade their friendship skills, learn to speak more openly, and reach out to other men. Health issues can interfere with mobility and make getting out with friends more difficult. Guys who aren't actively addressing these issues are vulnerable and prone to withdrawal, isolation, and depression.

SOMETIMES A WALKER IS JUST . . .

Bernard, an eighty-year-old retired psychology professor, teetered into my office. He looked back into the waiting room and pointed to his walker, which he'd left in the corner. He scowled. "That's the damn problem, the walker!" He was miffed. "I can't get around with it. It's too slow and clunky."

Bernard was a well-respected teacher and author at the University of Pennsylvania. His wife, Betsy, said he had become withdrawn and depressed following his hip replacement surgery six months prior. He'd dropped out of contact with his friends and wasn't returning their calls.

"Even with all this physical therapy, I just can't walk steadily anymore. I'm a damn cripple!" Bernard had been an avid walker, born in the Cotswolds in England. He'd been a long-distance runner into his seventies.

"You're mad at your walker?" I asked.

He looked desperate and fixed his gaze on me. "Look, Doctor, I just can't do this anymore. I love my wife, but I'm sitting around all day and she's fussing over me, reminding me to use my walker all the time."

I'd seen this before. You deprive a man of his mobility, and he becomes despondent, irritable, and frustrated. I was going to have to help Bernard calm himself down first so he could adjust to his loss, strengthen what he could salvage, and recapture his self-esteem—a tall order for a proud guy like this.

I decided to take an academic approach. I reviewed with the professor the literature on aging, injury, depression, and recovery. I especially emphasized the material on friendship and health improvement.

Bernard's two best friends, Lenny and Mortimer, also retired academics, lived in his neighborhood. Since his surgery, they'd offered to pick him up and drive to Rittenhouse Square, where the three of them regularly walked. Bernard had been declining their calls.

After reviewing the literature, however, he grudgingly agreed to call them. "They're not going to like what they hear from me," he warned, referring to his opinions about doctors, hip replacements, and walkers. I coaxed him to give it a try.

Over the next couple of months, the guys walked together. Bernard's mood lifted. The walks on the flat pavement in Rittenhouse Square Park, tea and discussions with his friends, along with some slow progress in physical therapy, all seemed to be helping. Betsy reported that he was more chipper. She felt relief, although she believed he was still cheating on his walker when she wasn't around.

"They"—referring to Lenny and Mortimer—"don't seem to be bothered by this contraption," he said, pointing to the walker, which he was now bringing into my office. I noticed some clips attached to the handle. "Mort gave me these," he explained. "That's so we can carry water bottles on a hot day." There was also a brightly colored decal, wrapped around a side rail, that read PSY-CHOLOGISTS ARE MORE STABLE. Lenny's grandson had printed it up. He shrugged. "I can never deny the lad."

He added, "Funny thing also. When I walk with my chaps, Lenny is now talking about having prostate surgery, and Mortimer about his heart medications." He squinched up his face. "What's becoming of us!" he exclaimed.

"It's normal talk between older guys," I reassured him. "I call it the Organ Recital—a way we comfort ourselves about how our bodies age and change, how we need to take care of ourselves. Maybe even"—I raised my eyebrows—"an entrée into . . . discussing mortality." He caught my drift and relaxed.

A silence ensued. I looked over at his walker. "So, Bernard, do you still hate this machine?" I asked. He looked over at it and thought awhile. "Well, you should know, I'm not a Freudian, but at this point I think I can comfortably say, 'Sometimes a walker's just a walker!'" He chortled at his joke. I groaned, and we grinned at each other.

If you've identified your own life stage and understand how close friendships can support you during this period, you're ready to tackle Part 2 of this book, the skills section. If you're currently short on guy friends, you can learn how to make some great new ones. Learning new communication skills also never hurts when it comes to deepening the male friendships you already have.

Two frequently overlooked areas, how we can maintain and protect our close male friendships, are included in the following chapters. You don't want to just *have* friendships, you want them to *thrive* and *grow* from the challenges that close friendships inevitably encounter.

PART 2

FRIENDSHIP FUNDAMENTALS

CHAPTER 5

At the Starting Gate

Making Connections That Matter

No modern writer has better described both the desire and the frustrations involved in setting out to make a close male friend than Stuart Miller. In the 1980s, Miller, a professor of literature at UC Berkeley, spent several years in Europe and the United States trying to make close male friends, while reflecting upon and writing about his experience. What he discovered and shares in his book, *Men and Friendship*, is profound and moving.

At the beginning of his journey, he read the author Willie Morris and quotes him: "You can train someone to kick a football or to take out an appendix but some things cannot be learned. If there is an aesthetic to friendship, it exists in the reality and not in the effort. As with most of the complex achievements of life . . .

friendship may even be God-given, and in this sense it is also a creature of accident and hence a rare blessing."

I resonated with Miller in his response to Morris's writing. This was exactly what I had to wrestle with in the episode with my friend Marty, which I describe in Chapter 2. If developing close male friendships is a "complex achievement"—and it is—then do we leave it to Divine Providence to bring our friendships to us? Do we think of them as random accidents of nature? Can we lie back, breathe deeply, and imagine that a friend will materialize from our openhearted meditative states?

Miller considered this question and recognized the temptation to abort his mission. But he decided instead to strike out into the unknown. "Enough had happened in my life that I had to make a try. It was an accumulation of problems and awareness . . . something deeper, a sense that a closeness with one or a few other men, like the friendships I had had in college, but more adult, had finally to be put back into my life. I found myself too deeply alone; starved, in a way. The time had come to find true friendship with other grown-up men."

Like Miller, most of us men have to plow ahead on our own, exploring ways to discover close male friends as well as the capacity within ourselves to *have* these relationships. Miller's journey did eventually lead to his finding some deep and lasting male friendships.

CEREMONIES AND RESPECTS

As mysterious and wondrous as friendships are, I've found it necessary and useful to follow certain guidelines that allow us to approach these relationships in ways that give them an optimal chance to develop and thrive. Ralph Waldo Emerson instructs us to surround our friendships "with ceremonies and respects," to approach them thoughtfully, so that they are well founded at first and well cared for over time.

In preparing for your journey to seek out a close male friendship or deepen one you already have, it's really helpful to do some mental prep work before you jump in. First, start by reflecting upon what has worked for you in the past, your expectations, and what you've learned from both your failures and successes. Next, take the time to consider the following five questions: What? Who? When? Where? How? From my own experience and work with other men, carefully addressing each of these—no speed musing here—will go a long way toward helping you develop friendships that really work for you.

THE "WHAT": EXAMINING YOUR EXPECTATIONS ABOUT FRIENDSHIPS WITH MEN

The first step is to ask yourself: "What are my expectations for a close guy friendship?" "What needs of mine do I hope to fulfill?" "What am *I* willing to contribute to the relationship?" Your responses to these questions will clarify your mission so you can embark on it with a healthy mix of optimism and realism.

We may have thoughts and feelings on this subject that we weren't totally aware of. At one level, we may simply want a male companion, a guy we can hang out with, share interests with, and trade information with about day-to-day life. At a deeper level, though, we may hope for a friend who will fill a hole in our lives and help us feel less lonely. We may want a soul mate, a friend who understands us, to whom we can open up, and who loyally "watches our back" no matter what.

In addition, we may want a person who will help us fill in some gaps in our own "male competencies." He might be a man who is particularly successful professionally, or who has a strong relationship with his wife and children, or who is readily able to stand up for himself—someone, as Aristotle said, who can offer us a model of a "better self." We may also want a friend who will admire us, find in us what we believe is valuable, and whom we can help and positively influence in genuine ways.

When we pause to reflect on our motivations for friendship, we may also discover less altruistic reasons. Friends can provide financial connections, entrance to business opportunities, and other professional perks. Friendships of "utility" are common between men. But ask yourself: Is this what I truly want? What features of a friendship will be most fulfilling to me in the long run?

We need to be realistic and flexible in our expectations about friendships. Several years ago, Ben, a friend I don't see as often as I'd like, told me, "I need to warn you. I like you very much. I think of you as one of my best friends. But I don't reach out much. I don't like to disappoint people and I'm not good at getting together a lot. I don't seem to need a lot from my friendships."

At first, I thought that Ben would "get over it," that he'd be so charmed by my companionship he'd become more active in our friendship. But over time, I discovered he was just being honest. No matter how good a time we had together, it would be months before he contacted me again. Over the years, I've continued to consider Ben a good friend, but our relationship is more limited in contact and sharing than with my other friends.

BREAKING THE MALE CODE

Reaching out for your *ideal* of friendship is admirable and courageous. But if the connection you hope for doesn't develop seamlessly or, as I address in chapters 7 and 8, if bumps occur along the way, don't give up on your guy friends too quickly. These relationships may rest quietly in the background for extended periods, needing time to stretch and breathe. But they can also reemerge in poignant, meaningful moments over the course of your lifetime. If you're like many men, you'll be glad you kept them.

THE "WHO": CHOOSING GUY FRIENDS

Timothy, a successful catalogue publisher and a patient of mine, struggled painfully to imagine a man he might consider as a close friend. All his experiences so far, he said, had been unsatisfying. The men he knew were either too intellectual, too dull, too banal, or too "locker room." It was clear he really was lonely and wanted a friend, but so far, none of the men he knew met his lofty standards.

After this "not good enough" rant had been going on for some months, I asked Timothy, "Is there *any* man you've met that you like?" He thought for a moment and replied, "Well, there is a guy. He's a fellow on my board. He seems nice. And he comes up with hilarious retorts when other board members act like prigs at our meetings. He's been extremely helpful to me and, yeah, I've enjoyed my contacts with him—even though they don't happen very often."

"It sounds like you like him," I ventured.

"Yes," Timothy replied, and then went quiet. When I asked him if he'd ever considered inviting the fellow to lunch or to his club to play squash, he hesitated and then said, "Well, I think I might be uncomfortable doing that. He might not like me."

In exploring Timothy's insecurities, I wondered how often fears of rejection stop men from taking the initiative with men they already know. As you think about whom you might like to have as a close friend, you might start by asking yourself, "Are there men I already know and like with whom I could become closer?" New best friends don't always require an around-the-world fact-finding mission! They may be guys you see in your day-to-day life—at work, in the gym, or in church—but to whom you haven't yet reached out further. Think about it.

A new close friend might also emerge from your past, a person with whom you shared important experiences in childhood, college, or young adulthood. Men, particularly those middle-aged or older, often find that these male relationships resurface at reunions, at conferences, or even on Facebook. The experiences shared earlier in life can serve as a springboard for rekindling, and possibly advancing, an old friendship.

John and I reconnected twelve years ago when our group of high school male friends reconvened as the Geezers at the Delaware shore home of another of our old friends. John and I had played in a high school folksinging trio and had been on the wrestling team together. He'd been a good friend in high school. I was the better student and he was the better wrestler, which in high school seemed about equally important. We had one small tiff over a girl we'd both dated, but it was minor. There had been mutual respect and affection—the stuff of friendship.

Driving home from the shore after our reunion, I recalled to John an incident I'd never forgotten. During my sophomore year, when I had to sit out because of a broken leg, he and I had been caught eating donuts by our wrestling coach at a basketball game. The coach, a "make weight" fanatic, had flown into a rage and ordered John at the next Monday's practice to go across the street to a diner, eat two pieces of banana cream pie, and then wrestle every guy on the varsity team, from ninety-five pounds to heavyweight.

Finding John in the bathroom after that practice, retching his guts out, deeply upset me. I was disgusted and angry with the coach. My friend certainly did not deserve that kind of treatment. I also felt guilty, since he was the one who'd suffered the coach's wrath. The incident contributed to my dropping out of wrestling that year. No one on the team, including me, ever brought up this episode. John continued to wrestle successfully on the team, making his way to the state championship competition his senior year.

As I concluded my recollection, I turned toward John in the passenger seat. "Can you believe that happened?" I asked. There was a brief silence. Then John said, "I didn't think anyone remembered that day." And then added quickly, "You know, I still hate that guy. I actually have dreams of running into him somewhere and punching his face in. He humiliated me so badly, and there was no reason, no reason at all, for him to do that to me."

I replied, "I should have said something—we all should have said something." Sitting there in the ensuing quiet, I felt as though a weight had been lifted. I'd been able to raise an important and painful experience for both of us, one that had lain dormant for decades. When I think of that exchange, it seems that it jump-started my feeling of connection to John and helped to renew a friendship that has continued during recent reunions.

While making a close friend is sometimes a matter of deepening a connection we already have, other times it's about striking out anew. Often, friend hunting requires us to expand our territory, place ourselves in new settings that give us a better opportunity to meet men we might like.

Andrew, a divorced man in one of our Friendship Labs, reported that he spent long hours in his office devising actuarial strategies for his clients. He said he worried that he was "devolving into hermit status." Andrew's children were grown and out of the house. He avoided dating and suffered from prostate problems, which his family doctor told him were exacerbated by his sedentary lifestyle. His urologist was more blunt. "The organ is telling you to 'use it or lose it.'" Andrew admitted that he was not yet ready to date, but was lonely and wouldn't mind having some male friends.

Though he was shy, Andrew was liked by the other men in his group. When another group member asked if he did anything for fun, he said, "I sail." The group promptly charged him with organizing a sailing trip for them, which he did—and which went splendidly. On the boat, Andrew seemed to come to life. He engaged confidently as captain of the ship and reportedly smiled for the first time that anyone could remember. Three weeks later, he declared he had put his name on the list at a local sailing club and had gotten three calls from other men who wanted to sail with him. Grinning, he said with shy humor, "They were falling all over themselves to be with me!"

It is important to pay attention to the "chemistry" we feel in the relationship when we're first getting to know another man. Social science research tells us that attractions between people— including friendship attraction—arise out of a sense of familiarity, shared values and attitudes, physical attributes or personality traits we admire, and the feeling that we are appreciated by the other person. When a man communicates traits we enjoy—for example, warmth, a sense of humor, intellectual curiosity, athleticism, a sense of reserve, or passion for his work—we may find ourselves thinking, "This is a guy I enjoy being with. Yeah, I might want to spend more time with him."

It may seem odd here to use the word *chemistry*, a word typically used more narrowly to describe a romantic and/or sexual connection. But there's no doubt that spontaneous reactions of warmth, interest, and mutual admiration play an important role in drawing guy friends to each other. It is important for men to honor these feelings. They help us to clarify what we're looking for, what energizes us, and what can serve as a solid foundation for a close friendship.

I recently spent time with an old college friend, Jackson. When we got together, I felt an instant, edgy excitement that I remembered feeling frequently when we were friends in earlier years. Jackson is a musician and an author. He is passionately involved in political activities and lobbies on behalf of underserved minorities in the Southwest. He has a charming, and often disarming, way of challenging social convention. When I'm with him, I find that I give myself permission to express a more rebellious or blunt side of myself—which, after forty years of practicing psychotherapy, I've worked hard, probably too hard, to control. I really appreciate the chemistry of this friendship. Being around Jackson can be challenging, but I always feel enlivened after we've spent time together.

THE "WHEN": MAKING TIME TO CONNECT

"Friendship requires more time than poor busy men can usually command," observed Ralph Waldo Emerson. Men cite lack of time as a major reason for not connecting with other men. Many admit, with embarrassment, that they don't take the time to reach out to other men with whom they might become closer. These same men also claim that they can see their best friends every few months, or even every few years, and "pick right up where we left off."

In my experience, however, intimate friendship requires "dirt time," sufficient time spent together to allow the relationship the comfort and safety to develop at an easy pace. Speed relationships give us plenty of information, but not intimacy. Fathers of teenagers know that the most personal communications often take place on the ordinary morning car ride to school or the weekend walk to the grocery store, where the conversation is neither planned nor anticipated.

The failure to maintain close male friendships or establish new ones is a critical loss for men at any age. But for men in their late twenties and thirties, old friendships may be particularly likely to be pushed into the background as the burgeoning demands of work, marriage, and parenting clamor for attention. In our groups, men often lament the loss of these friendships. It feels ironic to them that these connections are no longer there when they most need support in dealing with the new challenges of their adult lives.

Matt, a man in his early thirties, burst into my office his first session, bounded into a chair, and began rattling off a string of problems. He was a successful fellow, by most standards, who'd inherited his father's business. Of course, he loved his wife, without question, but she made demands on him that were too much. Likewise, he admitted, being the parent of two young children was wearing him down. On top of this, the economic pressures of running his father's business were fierce. He felt he couldn't talk with his wife or family about any of these things. After his nonstop litany of complaints, all I could think to say was "Oy!" and that we'd talk more about this at our next session.

At the next meeting, I asked Matt if he had any friends. He looked at me blankly. "Well, yes, I do. But when would I have any time for these people?" Like many men, he thought of friendship as one more responsibility on his to-do list. But I reminded him of his struggles with his wife, children, and colleagues, none of whom he could talk with about his needs. "So who *do* you talk to about this stuff?" I asked. He looked blank again, and then said, "You?"

"Me?" I echoed. "That's it?" He was silent for a while, looked up and said, "I guess I could use a friend."

A week later, Matt strode proudly into my office, looking as if he'd just bagged a bull elephant on a hunting trip. "I went through my contact list and tracked down my old friend Jerry," he said. Jerry had been his best friend in college, with whom he'd lived, shared his most personal thoughts—and hadn't spoken to for years. "We just lost touch with each other," he said wistfully. "Fortunately, he's still in Philly, and we got together. He's still single, but . . . we talked about all my woes. His, too. Like we used to. We didn't come up with any great revelations, but the funny thing was that when I went home that day, I was feeling a *lot* better." He glanced at me and chuckled softly. "Pretty crazy, right?"

THE "WHERE": FINDING PLACES TO CONNECT

Once you've committed to spending time with friends, the next important question to consider is: Where?

Guy hangouts are harder to find than they used to be. In a lovely illustrated book, *Where Men Hide*, James Twitchell describes the steep decline over the past century of "sacred spaces" in which men have privately convened to relax, converse, and sometimes raise hell. A century ago, nearly a third of men in the United States were members of some fraternal order, such as the Masons or the Elks. Today, membership stands at 7 percent.

Today's men, of course, continue to seek places where they can connect with each other. For a "guy fix," we head for Friday night poker games, the local bar, weekend business retreats, or outdoors for sporting events, fishing expeditions, or a friendly game of tennis. Privately, however, many men report feeling uncomfortable "being real" with other men in these settings. What's a guy supposed to do? Slam a tennis ball down the baseline and then shout, "So, guys, time out! I need to talk about how I might get laid off next month!" The fact is, there are no rules of the road to guide today's men to safe places that might help them to grow friendships.

In our Friendship Labs, we encourage men to discover places where they can get together with other men to share what is really going on in their lives. We recommend starting out with an activity you already enjoy and think the other man might as well. Working out, doing sports, bicycling, or fishing are activities that many men relate to and can easily convene for.

The trick here, however, is to make sure you set aside some private, one-on-one time and space for talking before, during, or after these activities. For example, going to a sporting event to-gether could work just fine as long as you make some time be-forehand (for a meal, perhaps) or afterward (for a drink or dessert). The idea is to share a good time *and* create an opportunity to get to know each other better.

Meals or a drink can be opportunities in themselves, or they can be tied to an event. If you are interested in music, theater, or political rallies, or have a particular hobby that the other man has shown interest in—computers, woodworking, cars, you name it—you can suggest getting together to share one of these interests. What's important is choosing an activity in a place that's com-fortable and interesting for both of you. The aforesaid requires a bit of thinking, about both yourself and the other person.

Lest you think this approach sounds a little like preparing for a date—it is. Making successful friendships with men may require you to hang out a little beyond your comfort zone. But think about it: How would you feel about getting a call from a guy you like who has tickets to a concert featuring your all-time favorite band, the Who? Or who knows you like Egyptian art and has scored passes to an exclusive opening at your local art museum? (If Pete Towns-hend or the gold mask of King Tut don't do it for you, fill in your own activity of choice.) For most of us, it would feel pretty good. Here's a person who wants to spend time with you and has not just his interests in mind, but yours, too.

Sometimes, finding a good place to meet with a friend involves some guesswork and the willingness to take risks. The first time I invited my friend Doug to get together, I felt a bit awkward about where to go with him. Doug seemed like a really "cool" guy. He's a university professor who is a favorite with his students—creative, witty, and insightful. Walking in the city with Doug takes two to three times longer than it ordinarily would because you can't go down a block without his stopping to talk to someone he knows. Doug also has opinions about just about everything: movies, restaurants, politics, and (possibly because he's originally from New York City) he doesn't mind arguing about any of these. I personally love these things about him.

I decided to invite Doug to walk with me in Philadelphia's Fairmount Park, in a section known as the Wissahickon Gorge. I felt a little nervous, since the gorge can be a deceptively challenging terrain, with steep trails and paths that aren't always clear-cut.

Hiking is my thing. I enjoy meandering in the woods and generally don't worry about getting lost because I always manage to find my way back. But Doug, though fit and lean, didn't do a lot of hiking. I didn't know how he was going to respond to the uncertainty, both physical and directional, of my proposed adventure. He seemed to be a guy who liked to know where he was going— and I wasn't offering him the option of a known path. Would my choice of venue kill off a barely born friendship?

While a safer choice might have been to have a meal or see a movie together, my instinct was to go for it: First, I knew Doug liked adventure. Second, I've found that hiking allows you to talk in a relaxed, easy way, where conversation can develop naturally.

When we entered the park and got to the main trail near the creek, I pointed to several possible side trails we could climb. "Where would you like to go?" I asked him. Doug looked at me, totally at ease and without a clue, and said, "You choose, I'll follow. You're the mountain guy." Without hesitation, I said, "Let's try this trail, to the left. I've never done this one before."

With that I strode forward, trudging uphill, with Doug following. We spent the next few hours wandering along these paths in seamless conversation, stopping along the way to take in some of the hidden beauties of the wooded setting. As we walked, I could see that he was feeling at ease and I began to relax more myself.

At one point, we encountered a side trail that went steeply down, and we had to decide whether to follow it, using branches and roots as hand- and footholds to the bottom—or simply turn back and retrace our steps to our starting point. I looked down. The ground was dry and the vegetation seemed sturdy. I looked at Doug and said, "Want to try it?" He raised his eyebrows at me, implying he wasn't sure we could do this.

My rational self didn't really think the trail was that difficult, and I trusted that Doug could handle it. "Follow me, bud," I said. "We'll go slow. Watch where my feet and hands go." With me leading, we descended, actually rather quickly, together. When we finally returned to our cars, he looked pleased and admitted, "I guess you know how to get around in the woods."

Twelve years later, Doug and I still walk in the Wissahickon. Our initial get-together was fortuitous because we discovered that wilderness was a good venue in which we could connect personally. When I visit him at his house in Maine, he always makes sure we have a good mountain hike or two during which we can talk privately.

Our dynamic hasn't changed. Even when we walk in Center City around where Doug lives, he still wants me to choose which way we go.

"What, you don't know your way around your own neighborhood?" I ask him.

"No, I do," he says. "But it's more of an adventure when you choose the path. I already know my own directions."

I can't really argue with that logic, and there's something I enjoy about Doug's trusting me to lead the way. I also think he enjoys letting me know whether he thinks I'm doing a good job.

THE "HOW": ASKING A GUY TO GET TOGETHER

Inviting a man to get together to explore a possible friendship almost always involves some anxiety. This makes sense: An invitation is not a business call. It's not a request to borrow a ladder or to get the phone number of a plumber. Underlying this invitation is an unspoken statement: "You're someone I'd like to spend time with and get to know better, and I'm hoping you'll feel the same way."

No question, reaching out like this takes courage. You wonder: Will the guy be interested? Will I be blown off politely—or not so politely? Even if he's somewhat open, will he already be so overloaded with work projects and family responsibilities that he'll put me off forever? Or maybe he thinks he already has enough friends? Such scenarios for disappointment can make a man ready to sprint for the exit before he even arrives at the starting gate.

In our men's groups, we've seen how this anxiety can play out. When we have given guys the assignment to call each other during the week to check in and share a personal feeling, many of them still feel they have to start with an apology ("Hi, sorry; I'm calling about the assignment") or a man cliché ("How about those Phillies?"). Guys often laugh about how lame their comments sound to them when they first make these personal contacts.

Reaching out to another man to share something "real" often feels unmanly to men. In our groups, we promote the idea that wanting to be close to other men is a *good* thing—it's what being masculine is all about. We also remind our guys how good it feels to be called and invited to share and connect with other men. Doing so is a form of cultural rewiring, one that strengthens both our sense of self and the experience of being part of a tribe. Being proactive emotionally and overcoming fears about reaching out to other men is a challenge worth tackling.

Invitation Skills

When you're reaching out to make a new friend, always remember the following three things: Clear the necessary space and time to meet. Communicate positively. And be patient and persistent in arranging a get-together. Mastering these skills substantially increases the odds that your friendship invitation will be successful.

Clearing Space

Frank, a new member of one of our groups, was almost always late for meetings. When another member confronted him about this, he groused: "It's my wife's fault. She never lets me go out. When I want to get together with other guys, she's always telling me I don't do enough at home for her and the kids." It turned out that he was coming late because he invariably got into a fight with his wife when he was supposed to be leaving for the group.

The men listened silently. Finally, a guy named Mark asked, "Do you have a problem letting your wife know about your plans in advance? Or in following through with your agreements about household stuff, or the kids?" Mark looked at Frank straight on. "Because if you do, she's going to be very pissed off with you and not be very supportive of your having friends, or even going to this group."

Frank was stunned by the retort. After a moment, he confessed that he'd never before gotten such a direct challenge about his behavior at home. That he'd gotten this feedback from another man also helped him swallow a bitter pill: the awareness that taking on new activities, including new relationships with other men, doesn't exist in a vacuum, and that clearing these plans in advance with one's partner and/or other family members is an important prerequisite for receiving their support.

Over the next few weeks, Frank reported back to the group that he'd gotten better at giving his wife a heads-up about his plans. "She seemed surprised, a little suspicious at first," he said. "When she asked me why I was doing this, I told her that the guys in the group kicked my butt because I hadn't cleared the time with her." He grinned. "Now she scoots me out the door every Tuesday night to make sure I get to the meeting."

Positive Communication

When you invite a man to get together, be specific about what you want to do and communicate some real warmth. Make it clear that you really want *his* company on this outing. This clears away any misconceptions that the call is a work "add-on" or some vague, unserious pleasantry ("Yeah, bro, we've *really* got to get together sometime!"). Share why you want to do this particular activity with him: "I've been wanting to see this movie, and it sounds like your kind of film" or "I usually do this bike route on my own, but it would be nice to ride with another hard-core rider." You might try an even more direct approach: "I need a break from [spread-sheets, my three-year-old, my in-laws visiting for the week]. Have you got an hour to take a walk? I could use a friendly ear and the chance to catch up with you as well." You're much more likely to get a positive response if you suggest a concrete activity and do so in a way that makes the other guy feel valued.

Patience and Persistence

When we extend an invitation to a potential friend, we'd all like to hear "Terrific! Let's do it. See you then." Instead, more often we get "Sounds interesting. Let me check [with my wife, my calendar, my travel schedule, my daughter's soccer practice times] and I'll get back to you, OK?"

Stay flexible and be prepared to negotiate. This man is busy, like you. He may want to get together, but he's got his own commitments to rearrange. Be prepared to work with him, to revise and renegotiate time and activities if necessary: "Great. Can you get back to me by Friday so we can plan?" Or "Since you're pressed for time, maybe we could do lunch nearby, say for an hour and a half, rather than driving all the way into town." Staying loose is a part of making a new friendship. Being patient and persistent communicates that you're willing to be flexible to make the connection happen.

Sometimes, life circumstances can put a new connection on hold. When this happens, do your best to let it be. People are often squeezed by projects, relationships, losses, or family involvements and simply don't have the time or energy to take on new commitments at the moment. Try not to let these inevitable realities foreclose the possibility of starting up a good friendship sometime in the future.

Gary, a busy colleague, once told me that Stan, a fellow in his running group whom he liked very much, had been calling him for about six months to get together socially. Gary really didn't have a moment to spare, but he didn't know how to say this to Stan. After months of putting off his running buddy, he finally told him that he really liked his company but he just didn't have time for a new friend in his life now. Gary girded himself for Stan's annoyed response. Instead, Stan looked at him for a moment, and then gave him a big hug. "I knew at that moment, this guy was going to be my friend!" Gary told me.

Sometimes, the other person may not respond to your invitation at all. No matter how well crafted or effectively delivered your invitation, it may seem as though it's fallen into a black hole. Don't beat yourself up about it. The reasons for the nonresponse may be multifaceted and not readily understandable. Sometimes, it's OK to just let a mystery be. Whether or not you decide to resend this invitation in the future, you should feel proud that you extended yourself to this guy. Keep the faith. Move forward on your journey to make good male friendships.

Steps to Take Now

Envisioning Your Friendship
Imagine you're taking an enjoyable trip, working on an important personal project, or, alternatively, going through a rough emotional patch. What kind of man would you want to share these experiences with you?

- List the three qualities most important to you in a good male friend. *listening responsiveness, ability to laugh*

- What do you imagine a good friend would ask from you in these situations?

- Are you ready to pursue, as well as deliver, this kind of commitment?

Your Friendship Posse

- Make a list of men, past and present in your life, whom you consider to be your friends. Whom do you need to re-connect with in order to reenergize the friendship?

- Write the names of other men you know whom you'd like to add to your friendship list. Think about men whose company you enjoy, who show an interest in you, and who are available for fun as well as help. Also think about men you've extended yourself to and who've let you know they value your presence in their lives.

- Whom in this group would you be willing to reach out to in order to get to know them better? Write down their names.

Make a Friendship Date

The purpose of a friendship date is to get to know another man better, to explore whether you want to become closer friends, and to get a sense of whether he shares a similar interest.

■ Plan your invitation: Write down the reasons you want to get to know this man as a friend. Clarify the times you're available to meet with him and possible places to meet, taking into account what you know about his situation, interests, and time constraints. Tell your wife or partner about your interest and get support to go ahead with this plan.

■ Make the contact: Connect in a way that's comfortable for you—face-to-face or by phone, e-mail, or text. Be direct and tell your friend-to-be why you want to get together with him. Communicate warmth and a genuine interest in the meeting. Be patient with his response and flexible in negotiating an agreement about time and place to get together. If you get off to the right start, the meeting is well worth waiting for.

CHAPTER 6

Conversations from the Heart

Conversations between men often consist of small talk, information trading, and problem solving, with the unspoken goal of keeping things light. But for men's friendships to really grow and develop, guys need to dive a little deeper. They need to share what's personally important in their lives and offer each other genuine listening and support. I call these kinds of exchanges conversations from the heart.

Our MFEI Survey found that close friendships between men were linked with "heart" behaviors such as emotional expressiveness, self-disclosure, vulnerability, reciprocity, and emotional support. We also found that the majority of the men wanted more intimacy in their male friendships, whether they already had some or not.

WHY I LOVE SUPERFICIAL GUY TALK

You may feel skeptical that male friends need to upgrade their conversations. You may recognize, as I do, that we men have our own ways of communicating that don't always conform to the rules that apply in, say, couples therapy textbooks. Perhaps you can identify with the following example:

On any given day when I enter my fitness club, Alan, a senior staff person and consistently calming force in our bustling facility, tosses a comment my way. "Hey, Rob, I just saw *Argo*. I thought it was really good, whaddaya think?" I'm moving at the speed of light, in a hurry to get in my workout. Barely turning my head, I reply, "Way overrated. You gotta see *The Sessions. It's* amazing." If this exchange sounds a bit minimalist, it is. But Alan and I both know that this routine creates a connection between us. I think about his impressions when I see movies, and he picks up on my suggestions and gets back to me on them.

As I dump my bag and clothes in the locker, Big Jack is at the end of my aisle. He's an incredibly fit, muscular fellow who works with kids in detention and does private security on the side. "Hey, Rob, you taking care of yourself? You know, man, you're my role model for when I get older."

I look up at him, feigning hurt. "Hey, man, are you saying I'm an old guy? I just got my first senior's bus pass today. You gotta show me some respect." We both laugh.

Then I go upstairs. Making a beeline for the elliptical machines, I find an open one. Carlos, the head trainer at our club, catches my eye. He's working with a gorgeous young suburban mom who, like most of the women at our gym, does not look like she needs a trainer.

"Hey, Rob, why aren't you back at your office taking care of all those patients who need you?" He says it loud enough so everyone around me can hear. I quip back, also so everyone can hear, "I've got all the business I can handle right here with you, Carlos." Snickers from everyone on the machines.

These men are part of my squad, my gym homies. Our conversation is light, regular, and at times, humorously aggressive. We never get into anything too deep. But within this frame, we notice each other, we're checking in on each other. I need this contact. It makes me feel alive and connected.

I think it's overkill to suggest that men need to trade in their guy shorthand and the easy habits of connection it allows for "something better." Rather, I like to think of it as one level of communication that helps men connect with each other, one that has its own unique value. It's just not the *only* one. Expanding our communication skills set prevents us from getting stuck and allows us to have deeper, more openhearted and satisfying conversations with our guy friends when we need them.

EMOTIONAL INTIMACY: A SHORT COURSE

In our Friendship Labs, Jake and I discover that a lot of guys already have the communication skills they need for close friendship, but they keep them under wraps because they've decided it's not "manly" to talk with other guys that way. Other men in the groups simply haven't developed the necessary skills, or have them only in short supply. All of these guys need encouragement to lean in and commit to make their friendships thrive.

If you believe you have the ability to go deeper in your conversations with your male friends, my advice is: Don't hesitate. Our own and other research clearly indicate that men want more emotional substance in their friendships. If you're not secure about these skills, don't worry; they're learnable. Most men, I've found, just need to develop the abilities that nature has given us, and then put them into play.

There are four important communication skills that will help you have more fulfilling conversations with your buddies. These include creating safety, self-disclosure, emotional expressiveness, and active listening and empathy. Below, I present examples, both personal and professional, of how these behaviors can deepen and enrich your guy friendships. I also share guidelines and exercises from our Friendship Labs that can help you develop the skills to enhance openhearted communication with your male friends.

Safety First

No matter how comfortable guys may seem with words, no matter how plainspoken or direct, no man wants to share private information or feelings without some assurance that he can trust his buddy.

Most close friendships start out with guys working on an intuition that this is a person they might come to trust. As time goes on, this sense is confirmed (or not) through a process of give-and-take, through risking the mutual sharing of personal information and feelings that rewards friends with a reliable bond indicating "we're in this together."

Two qualities are critical for establishing friendship safety. The first is *healthy boundaries*, meaning that friends must share enough with each other to feel emotionally connected, while also providing each other with enough space and privacy so that neither person feels invaded. Simply put, it's about knowing when and how to bring up stuff with your friend.

An example comes to mind. Don, a man I know, described a weekend camping trip with Gary, a close friend of his. Gary was scheduled to go in for heart surgery the following week. When Don had raised the subject prior to the trip, it was clear Gary didn't want to talk about the surgery. Inquiries about whether he was "up for the journey" were immediately rerouted to discussions about camping gear and using traditional maps versus GPS apps. On the trip, Gary had seemed distracted, but when Don gently inquired how he was doing, Gary answered only in monosyllables. My friend read and respected his buddy's signals. The two went on to enjoy the weekend in the physical ways they routinely did when they hiked in the wilderness.

Two weeks later, while recovering from surgery, Gary called Don. "I know I was really down during our hike," he said. "But I really needed *not* to think or talk about everything that could have gone wrong with my operation. You let me do that. You didn't push me and I really appreciated that. And, by the way, I can say it now: I'm glad I survived the goddam operation!"

Keeping healthy emotional boundaries also means maintaining confidentiality. In our Friendship Labs, we ask our men to agree not to talk outside of the group about whatever is discussed by another man, or to gossip with each other outside the group about someone else.

Most people have an alarm system for folks who drop personal information about others. You've probably met this kind of person and thought, "Uh-oh, this fellow is not friend material." Needless to say, if you yourself tend to be loose-lipped, you may need to start practicing keeping a lid on it in order to strengthen your own qualifications for close friendship.

The second requirement for establishing safety in friendship is *communicating respect*. For most guys, feeling respected and admired by other men is important. Guys can be particularly sensitive to signals of disapproval, messages from other men that they're not "living up to expectations." This anxiety is deeply embedded in the male psyche, a consequence of an outdated ideology that prescribes shaming and humiliation as essential to the development of a strong male character.

In *I Don't Want to Talk About It*, author Terrence Real writes,

> Believing it a part of his paternal responsibility, my father was no stranger to the manly value of whipping his boys into line. . . . As was true of many men of his generation, pain was a form of pedagogy. . . . There were no broken bones, no scars—some bruises. . . . Physical abuse? If you had said those words to my father, if you had said them to me, we would have laughed in your face. This wasn't abuse. This wasn't even a beating. My father knew what a real beating felt like. . . . What he dished out to his son was nothing compared to what he himself had received. . . . My father was doing more than meting out punishment for

imagined infractions. He was teaching me, just as he had been taught, what it means to be a man.

Despite a large body of research demonstrating that repeated shaming, both verbal and physical, traumatizes people, limits their chances for happiness, puts them at risk for further victimization, and increases their chances of becoming abusers themselves, men are still ambivalent about the role aggression plays in male relationships.

No doubt, the occasional kick in the pants or heartfelt challenge communicates a genuine caring, a willingness to be candid in order to strengthen your friendship. But the habit of routinely trading insults or *solely* making "innocent" jokes at the other guy's expense with no added warmth or substance can get old and, frankly, annoying over time. I see this at my club as well. There are a few jokers—just a few—in the locker room who, when they run out of stupid stuff to talk about, can be seen walking around dazed, looking for someone to talk to: They've run out of conversational currency, often clueless—and they get no takers.

We have found in our Friendship Labs that men are often willing to trade zingers and even enjoy mutual sparring, but only in limited doses. And while most will *put up* with it, they definitely will not *open up* when it's coming at them.

Disrespect can also be communicated, often unwittingly, in the guise of advice or counsel. Matt, a management consultant in one of our groups, was instructing another guy, Evan, about finding new employment after he'd recently lost a job. While the advice was valuable and well intended, it hadn't been solicited.

In one session, Matt was earnestly instructing Evan, "If you *let* your interviewer talk, make him *think* he's leading the conversation, you'll *definitely* gain his confidence."

I remember thinking, as I watched Evan slouching farther back in his chair, that it would be good if Matt followed his own advice.

Evan finally sat up abruptly, shaking his head, and cut Matt off. "Hey, you know, Matt, I really appreciate the advice. But I've been listening to management experts all afternoon. What I really need now is a break, a little comfort here."

It was an awkward moment, but ultimately educational for both men. Matt apologized, aware that he was coming on too heavy. And Evan realized he needed to speak up better for the kind of support he needed. Both guys got closer, and a little smarter about themselves, as a result.

No matter how savvy you think you are, it's always good to check in first and feel out whether your friend is open to your suggestions. Advice is always more appreciated—and feels less shaming—when it's invited.

Finally, if there is something you genuinely admire about a guy, let him know. No matter how secure you think he is, it never hurts to let a man know what you think is great about him. A few years ago, I listened to Ben, a former colleague, present his work at a national conference. The auditorium was packed, and after the presentation, he received a standing ovation. I remember thinking, "My God, this guy has really arrived!"

When Ben and I went for coffee later that day, I said, "Good job." After we'd schmoozed for a while, he stopped and asked, somewhat awkwardly, "What did you think of the presentation? I mean, *really* think?"

I jammed for a moment, registering that he wasn't just fishing for a compliment. "I was wowed!" I responded. "Your work has progressed so much. Your research is really important stuff. The case presentations were great, and your slides were crisp. You really nailed the presentation." I stopped, caught up in my own emotion. "I'm really *proud* of what you're doing." I wasn't exaggerating. I meant it.

Ben took a deep breath and relaxed. "Thanks," he said. It dawned on me then that my opinion meant more to him than I ever would have imagined. It made me glad that I'd shared this reaction with him.

Opening Up

A second vital aspect of communication in close friendships is *self-disclosure*. This is the willingness to share personal information with other guys about the important things that are going on in your life—in your health, your relationships, and your work. In our survey, men ranked self-disclosure as one of the most important features in their close friendships.

When guys share personal information on a regular basis, it makes it easier, eventually, for them to get down to deeper emotional stuff—the stuff that's incredibly meaningful but hard to talk about. Such as frustration with your partner or worries about your kids. Sometimes it's about good things, like a promotion that you fear might evoke envy in other guys.

It's important to understand that when you disclose something about yourself to a friend, it can be beneficial for *him* as well as for you. Very likely, he will feel good, even honored, that you are willing to share personal information with him. He will feel trusted by you because he knows how difficult it can be to open up about these things. When you let him in, he will be more able, in turn, to share personal information with you. Your willingness to share helps the friendship grow.

For men, sharing personal information can be a loaded issue. Control and dominance play a large role here, the deeply held belief that "real" masculinity involves holding back information, playing it "close to the vest" for the sake of retaining power. A successful real estate broker whom I saw in therapy summed it up this way: "In a negotiation, the person who speaks first loses."

In other cases, men don't share personal information because they fear it will reflect negatively on them, even when sharing this information could help them feel better or solve a problem. How often have you seen a guy, when the topic of job stress, a medical problem, or a disturbed child comes up in conversation, go inexplicably blank or suddenly walk into the kitchen to check if there's beer in the fridge? At this moment, his Machismo Dementor is kicking into high gear, blocking him from saying anything that might "incriminate" him.

In our Friendship Labs, we emphasize two other important emotional skills: *vulnerability* and *reciprocity*. These traits were highly rated by the men in our survey as contributing to their close male friendships. When present, these allow self-disclosure to confidently progress.

Vulnerability refers to our capacity to allow ourselves to be exposed in situations that give us an opportunity to receive help, grow, or heal. In her book *Daring Greatly*, author Brené Brown suggests that we view vulnerability as a strength, and that positive emotions such as joy, as well as difficult ones like fear, all can make us feel vulnerable. In either case, we can grow from this exposure by allowing others to witness and support us in these feelings.

In our Friendship Labs, we suggest that vulnerability is part of our nature, a trait we can actively bring to our relationships to enrich them. When we make ourselves vulnerable to a friend, we disclose information that lets him know us as a real human being— the person we really are—rather than a buffed-up, blow-dried image.

The quality of reciprocity works in tandem here. It means that when a friend shares something personal with you, you give him back something meaningful about yourself that's related to what he has shared. Through this process, guys nurture a continuous, ongoing loop of sharing that deepens a friendship and keeps it alive.

When the men in our groups reveal something sensitive or heretofore undisclosed about themselves, we always thank them. We make it clear that their individual contribution deepens the intimacy of the group. Our analogy is that the more each guy puts his oar in the water, the swifter the boat travels. When a man self-discloses, it invites the other guys to share their own related experiences, something in themselves that resonates with his story.

Exorcising a Demon

I know this from my own experience. In the spring of 1977, I flunked my postgraduate board examination in psychiatry and neurology. I was three years into an academic position in the Department of Psychiatry at Hahnemann Medical College. The overall examination included a written test, along with two live interviews, one with a psychiatric patient and the other, a neurology patient. You had to pass all three parts.

The moment I knew I'd failed this exam occurred seven minutes into the interview with the neurology patient at a VA hospital in Washington, DC. I was standing over a wheelchair-bound man who was looking up at me sympathetically, aware that I had no clue about his diagnosis. Two enormously tall British neurologists towered over me, listening to me hopelessly stumble over their questions. The look in their eyes said, "Rejection bin."

No matter that this was the last year that a live neurology exam would be given to psychiatrists, or that I'd passed the written test and the live psychiatry exam with flying colors. They'd given me a patient here with facioscapulohumeral muscular dystrophy, a disease I would never see again in my entire career as a psychiatrist, rather than a patient with dementia, drug addiction, or cirrhosis of the liver—the kind psychiatrists actually treat, the kind I had studied and hoped to interview at this VA hospital.

Returning to Philadelphia, I skulked around the halls of my department for a few weeks, avoiding conversation. My chairman already knew the results of my exam. He seemed unconcerned. His only comment was "Don't worry. You'll take them again next fall, and you'll pass."

That helped a little, but not much. I felt as if I were walking around with a bright red scarlet *I* (for *Idiot*) on my forehead. What had made me think I belonged in an academic department as a teacher? Mostly, I was embarrassed and didn't want to be within a hundred yards of anyone who might ask me about the examination.

Finally, I agreed to meet my friend Carlos, a psychologist on our clinical faculty, for coffee. He must have recognized that something was wrong when I showed up in a trench coat and dark glasses.

"What's with you?" he asked.

"Oh, f—," I blurted. "I flunked the boards in psychiatry and neurology."

Carlos couldn't contain his astonishment—or his laughter—as I described my patient and the twin towers of punishment who'd interviewed me.

"I can't believe they gave you that case," he said. Putting his hand on my shoulder, he added, "You got totally blindsided. I feel bad for you, man."

A bit comforted, I found myself releasing my deepest, truest upset about the experience. In a near-whisper, I said, "This is the first time I flunked an important test in my life."

He looked at me, incredulous again. "You're shitting me, right? This is the first time? *No!*"

"Yeah," I muttered. I wanted to crawl into a hole.

Carlos sat back and looked at me, squaring me in his gaze, as though recalibrating his whole picture of who I was. "Well, man, think of it this way," he said finally. "This might be the last time you have a chance to flunk a test. You might want to do something with this." I cracked up.

But Carlos wasn't finished. "Do you know how many exams I flunked in college? I was on academic probation every year."

This caught my attention, because Carlos was one of our best teachers, and highly respected in our field. "C'mon, man, you're just saying this!" I protested.

"No," he said. "They finally figured out I had a learning disability. Everyone knew I was smart. They just couldn't figure out why I did so badly on tests and writing. I finally got some educational counseling, and some meds, and it really turned things around for me. But before that, man, it was hell."

We just looked at each other and nodded. I was sad about his story. At the same time, I felt incredibly relieved and unburdened. I think Carlos did, too. I do know that after that conversation, we shared personal information with much more ease and frequency.

I did, by the way, pass the board exams that next fall. But thanks to my friendship with Carlos, I didn't need to wait that long to exorcise my intense shame. The talk did that. I won't lie and say I felt fine about failing the exam, but I did get that it wasn't such a huge deal. It was, well, human.

Expressing Emotions

A third important aspect of communication in close friendship is the ability to express feelings openly and honestly. Most men would agree that this is important, but that doesn't make it easy. Guys are often at a loss about what feelings to share in a close friendship. Will expressing emotion help or hurt? Some of us may not be sure what we're feeling in the first place. Aided and abetted by our Machismo and Dumbo dementors, we often decide to blow off important feelings altogether, hoping they'll just float away without consequence.

There is still controversy over whether men are hardwired to readily process and communicate emotions. Some brain researchers, like Simon Baron-Cohen (yes, Sasha's cousin), claim that men's brains are not constructed to easily manage complex emotional communication. Others, like Daphna Joel, professor of psychology at Tel Aviv University, assert that while biological differences exist, they don't explain the wide variation in emotional capabilities demonstrated by both men and women. What we do know is that the human brain exhibits "plasticity," or the ability to evolve both in structure and in function over a person's lifetime.

Our own observation and research, as well as that of others, confirms that most guys are highly capable of engaging in deep, openhearted emotional exchange with each other. What's more, they enjoy doing this. The men in our survey reported high levels of emotional expressiveness in their close male friendships. In Beverley Fehr's analysis of men's friendships, she found that historically, guys' habitual stiff upper lip has had more to do with a lack of motivation and practice in developing intimacy skills than a lack of innate ability.

But emotional restraint is no longer the badge of successful manhood that it once was. Researchers Barbara Bank and Suzanne Hansford found that emotional restraint is one of the biggest obstacles guys encounter in their attempts to form intimate friendships.

Most guys can read the tea leaves. They understand that the old images of manhood are changing, and they're ready to shuck off the cool, stiff reserve formerly required to keep up the image. At the same time, they're treading unfamiliar waters. Opening up is all well and good as a concept, but how to you actually *do* it?

Not all of the men arrive in our Friendship Labs equally adept at sharing their feelings. Some are quite aware of their emotions and ready to open up to others. Others have been injured previously in this effort and need to rebuild trust in order to risk connection. Still others have trouble figuring out *what* they're feeling at any given moment.

We reassure our guys that no matter where they start, everyone will have an opportunity to learn to connect with others in a more honest and openhearted way. We encourage a team approach:

The more each person brings his feelings to the group, the more the group thrives, and vice versa. Regarding expressing emotions, we focus on three particular skills: accessing emotions, naming feelings, and effectively communicating them.

Accessing Your Feelings

Emotions are complex and involve physical sensations, thoughts, and behaviors. They are affected by biological processes, such as hormones and neurotransmitters, as well as by activity in and between various structures in our brain. Our emotions permeate our experience and bring powerful intensity and meaning to our lives.

In our experience, the language of feeling carries more impact than other elements of conversation. When men discuss their feelings with other guys, it connects them with each other at a deeper, more satisfying level. Also, we've found that encouraging emotional expression in our groups validates this kind of communication for guys, who may have been suspicious of talking with men about emotions in other venues. Women benefit, too: As men become more comfortable opening up, it reduces the pressure on their female partners to always take the emotional lead.

Learning to become aware of your emotions is a first important step. Many of us have learned to ignore any evidence that we're feeling at all. Our Machismo, Homophobo, and Dumbo dementors often converge, urging men to turn off or ignore their feelings, especially in the presence of other guys, to hide any vulnerability that might be construed as unmanly.

My son, Isaac, a therapist who trained at Thich Nhat Hanh's monastery in Escondido, has developed an approach to help men better access their emotions by incorporating mindfulness meditation techniques in his therapy with them. At first, I thought guys might reject this approach as "too passive." I was wrong.

I've seen that meditation can help guys connect with their deeper emotions, through awareness of body sensations and thoughts that come up along the way. They are then able to apply what they've experienced in their daily lives.

To give you a sense of how this works, let me share an example. When our guys reconvened from a silent meditation that we'd sent them on while hiking in Philadelphia's Fairmount Park, a man named Jeff reported that he'd experienced a huge sense of relief—as well as some excitement—while sitting on the side of a steep hill. Listening to the rushing sounds of the creek below and feeling a cool breeze on his face, he'd been focusing on a bunch of tiny yellow flowers that were growing directly out of the rock face of a boulder in front of him.

He'd realized, tearing up as he spoke to the other guys, "If these beautiful little flowers can grow out of a rock, maybe there's a way I can find some happiness, to grow out of these hard times I'm experiencing now." The other men nodded appreciatively, impressed with how Jeff's meditation had taken him to a refreshing place of emotional healing.

If you're with a friend, walking or just sitting together, risk being quiet for a few moments and see how this helps you better connect with your feelings while together.

Naming Your Feelings

Most men come to our groups with some ability to identify their emotions. We encourage them to name these feelings out loud (e.g., "I feel happy, sad, discouraged, surprised . . ."). Even men who possess a strong emotional vocabulary often need this kind of push to counteract the group allergy to emotional language that sets in when guys get together. The default position of men is often to dumb down the emotional potential of their friendships by deleting feeling words. (Expletives don't count here.)

In a session, one of the guys, Darryl, was joking with another, Henry, who'd just won a prestigious award in his professional organization. Though highly successful in his work, Henry worried excessively about other people's opinion of him. Darryl routinely broke the ice for him in the group by joking sarcastically with him: "Now, you know getting the big client was just another day's work, no big deal, right, Henry?" While it was clear from these exchanges and the mutual laughter that these guys liked each other, they never really expressed any of these feelings directly to each other.

I thought I might help deepen their connection by challenging their habit. I interrupted Darryl's jibes with a question. "So how do you feel about Henry's winning the award?"

Darryl shrugged. "I think he wastes a lot of time worrying about these things. We all knew he was going to win." He looked confused. "Why? Do you think I'm jealous of Henry?"

I didn't. "Not necessarily," I pressed on. "But I want to hear how you *feel* about his winning."

Darryl was quiet for a moment. Then he smiled disarmingly at Henry. "Proud of you."

"So *proud* is the word," I repeated. I wanted to give his underlying feeling some exposure, space to breathe in the room.

Henry smiled back at Darryl, looked him in the eyes for a moment, then walked over to him and hugged him.

In our group meetings, we often introduce the Feelings Wheel, a tool used by many therapists to help people identify emotions.

It was developed by psychologist Gloria Willcox and is designed like a pinwheel, featuring dozens of emotions under six broad categories: mad, sad, scared, joyful, powerful, and peaceful. We've found it very useful in helping guys identify and find the words that describe their feelings, which they often find difficult to articulate.

Our guys' first reaction is usually to snicker and then become fascinated as they begin to locate their feelings in one or more sections on the wheel. The wheel, they discover, is a literal representation of the incredibly rich palette of emotions that exists within them and others—emotions they often don't fully notice.

One of our men, Werner, a veteran of self-help workshops, routinely used glib psychological jargon that left other guys in the group confused as to what he really felt. Statements like "I'm not in my truth" or "I hear that you're coming from judgment" flowed freely from him.

When asked to clarify his actual feelings, Werner looked blank; it became clear that he had no idea how to answer. From his stories, it sounded as though he didn't have much connection with his wife and kids, either.

In one session, he'd described how his two college-age sons, home for vacation, showed no interest in spending time with him, despite his invitations. He looked frustrated and crestfallen.

When I asked him how he felt about this, he looked at the floor. "Like I don't count," he finally said.

I pulled out the Feelings Wheel and asked Werner to identify his three major feelings. He first got entangled in all the possibilities but eventually narrowed them down to embarrassed, stupid, and angry.

When he voiced these, other guys in the group perked up and

asked him to elaborate. Before long, everyone was engaged with Werner's issues, offering encouragement and suggestions. Truth be told, he seemed happier than I'd ever seen him in the group. At the end of the session, he threw up his hands jubilantly and said, "Wow, what do I do with all of this great input?"

Jackson replied, "Go home and talk to your kids about all of this." Then he walked over to my desk, grabbed a printed copy of the Feelings Wheel, and put it in Werner's hands. He added, "When you talk with them, make sure you bring this along with you."

Delivering Your Feelings

If you're aware of and can identify your emotions, you're in position to get them across to your friend in a meaningful way. Working on your "delivery" of your feelings may sound a bit mechanical, but given the powerful nature of emotions, it makes sense to do some preparation.

It's important that you communicate your feelings as you intend to. You don't want to send a precious gem in an old paper bag with holes in it. When your friend sees that you've put thought and care into how you communicate with him, I guarantee he'll appreciate it. Guys well know how hard it is to bring up sensitive emotions with another man.

From several decades of teaching communication skills, I've put together a few simple rules for how men can best deliver important feelings to their guy friends. For starters, you should plan to converse in a quiet, private setting, where you won't be rushed. Give yourselves at least thirty minutes, more if necessary, for a conversation.

Your delivery should include:

1   An "I" statement that names the feelings you want to share with him ("I feel . . .")

2   The situation that stimulated these feelings ("This came up when we . . .")

3   The resulting feelings, thoughts, and behaviors you've been experiencing ("Since then, I've felt, thought, done . . .")

4   After giving your friend time to digest your feelings and/or respond, you can make a request for a response on his part. ("What I'd like to know . . ." or "What would be helpful to me is . . .")

I used this process recently with a client named Frankie. He was a private security consultant who had worked for the Philadelphia Fire Department for twenty-five years. Frankie had a group of friends with whom he'd stayed close after he left the department. They met regularly on Wednesdays for lunch.

Over the past few months, Frankie had been missing these lunches because he was recovering from surgery for prostate cancer. While the surgery had gone well, the recovery was tough, and Frankie had begun having panic attacks during the day. Mostly, he made it into his office, but he'd become paralyzed and confused by his panic attacks. He continued to skip the lunches with his friends, even though he was now physically able to attend. "They're not used to seeing me like this," he told me. "They wouldn't know what to say to me." In truth, he really didn't know what *he'd* say if they asked about him.

Frankie was a square-jawed, quiet kind of guy. People who knew him liked and respected him—he was plainspoken, and tenacious in uncovering and preventing crime in organizations. He was fair and kind to people he knew. And tough on himself. The surgery and his cancer had unsettled him. He was unsure if he was completely cured of his cancer and whether his wife, Ellen, and his clients would be able to count on him anymore.

Other than Ellen, I was the only person Frankie had spoken to about these fears. The panic attacks had hit him hard. Between our talks and the medication I prescribed, he calmed down some, but he still kept his worries to himself.

The guys at the department had been calling him, and he'd insisted that Ellen make excuses that he was overloaded and still recovering. "Tell them I'll get back to them," he directed her. But as far as I could see, he had no intention of sharing how terrified and paralyzed he felt most days.

One afternoon, Frankie came into my office, clearly disgruntled. Ellen had told him that three of his buddies from the department had announced they were coming to the house that evening. They wanted to talk with him and wouldn't take no for an answer.

"What are you going to do?" I asked.

"I don't know," he muttered. "But knowing these guys, I'm going to have to say something."

I suggested that we rehearse telling his buddies what was really going on with him. Using the "Delivering Your Feelings" guidelines, I coached him through the steps—identifying his feelings (shame), the situation that brought them up (his panic attacks), and his resulting thoughts and emotions (he had to hide from the guys to avoid being humiliated). When we got to the last guideline—"Let your friends know what you'd like from them"— he was stumped. When the session ended, Frankie took a deep, relieved breath. "This was like the interrogations I do."

"Worse, I'll bet," I replied. "Think you can talk to your friends?"

"I'll try." He added wryly, "My guys are relentless. They take no prisoners." We both laughed.

He called me the next morning to report that he'd told his friends what was going on, in detail. A few of the guys cried for what he was going through. Frankie cried, too. One of his friends was angry with him for not telling them before. "I thought it was something really awful. Like you had a month to live, or something like that!" the guy said. His friend was clearly relieved to hear this wasn't the case. "He told me I was a jerk," Frankie said.

He added, "I figured out what my request was: 'Don't let me get away with hiding anymore, OK?'"

The guys promised.

Active Listening and Empathy

Men are always quick to notice whether another guy is a good listener. They value this trait when they recognize it in another, but they don't necessarily think of it as a "skill," a behavior that can be nurtured and developed.

Charles, a quiet lawyer in his mid-fifties, routinely impressed the men in the group with his thoughtful responses to others. In one session, a guy named Loudon was describing an argument he'd had with his wife, Adrian. In detail, he reported the vicious insults he'd shouted at her until she'd run out of the house in tears. The men were, understandably, alarmed. "Wow, you lost it, man!" "Did she call the police?" "Are you taking any medications for these outbursts?" were some of their reactions. One guy advised him to think about moving out.

Charles, who'd been listening quietly to Loudon for a while, finally said, "Loudon, you just told us that you had an argument with Adrian, in which, because of something she said that you can't *remember*, you unloaded on her. You called her a slut, an imbecile, and a disgrace to the family." He paused. "You also told us that you really don't believe any of those things are true about her, and you don't know why you say these things. You say that in these situations, you just go 'off the deep end,' and wish you could take the words back. Right?"

Honestly, I was in awe of Charles's response, what'd he'd been able to take in and feed back in such a measured and kind way.

Loudon nodded, eyes downcast.

"I can only imagine how painful it must be for Adrian to hear these things," Charles went on. "But listening to you, I was thinking, 'This guy must be in a lot of pain, too.' You must be hurting pretty badly to say these kinds of things to someone you love.

"Your story reminded me of times when I get angry with my wife," Charles continued softly. "Stuff she says or does triggers things in me, and I really don't like the person I am at those times. And I wish I had a way to fix it between us. Does that make sense? Do you ever talk with Adrian about that?"

Listening to him, the guys were all quiet. Loudon's eyes welled up. He started to breathe deeply, as though someone had just opened a window and let in some fresh air. "No, I've never talked with her about it," he said. "But, God, I'd really like to. I would. I can't stand how I am when I'm fighting with her." He looked very sad. Around him, other men were nodding.

After the meeting, a few of the guys stayed in touch with Loudon outside the group. In the next meeting, he thanked Charles and the others for sticking with him. He'd been able to go home, apologize to Adrian, and, he said, "have our first real talk about these arguments." Thinking about what Charles had said, he'd decided to seek help via anger management counseling.

Don't we all wish we could bring Charles's quality of listening and responding to our friendships? When we look closely at what Charles did that was so helpful to Loudon, however, much of it translates into simple actions that most of us can incorporate into our own repertoire of listening skills. In this section, we'll look at three important ones: *receptivity*, *reflection*, and *empathy*.

Receptivity

A good listener, for starters, knows how to quiet his own mind when his friend is talking. Charles was able to listen and respond so effectively with Loudon because he took the time to gather himself, focus, and really take in what the other man was saying.

Think of being quiet as an active process, one that allows you to focus on what's going on *outside* (what your friend is trying to communicate) as well as what's coming up for you *inside* (your thoughts and emotions) as you listen. When your friend is speaking to you, especially about emotionally important subjects, focus on him and what he's saying—not on what you're going to say next. Notice what's coming up inside you, but instead of sharing it then and there, save it for later.

Guys have a reputation—often deserved—for being poor listeners. My suspicion is that men might have a higher regard for listening skills if we didn't confuse *receptivity* (which is critical for good listening) with *passivity*. This latter state can feel unmanly to men, and therefore repugnant and scary.

Men often feel pressure to be active, to say things, to move a conversation along, in order to resolve an outstanding issue. When men listen, they are often gathering information in a somewhat narrow way that allows them to solve a problem, and they may feel impatient if the speaker seems to wander off topic. Their Machismo Dementor nudges them to "get this job *done*," sometimes before they have ample time to really take in what the other guy is saying.

In their book *Listen Up*, authors Larry Barker and Kittie Watson observe that women listen more broadly than men, are receptive to a wider range of information that includes emotional process as well as content—and tend to encourage conversation with small nods and remarks ("yes," "mm-hmm"). Men, who are quietly trying to "make sense" of the speaker, are often misjudged as not interested or not paying attention.

Partly, it's a brain processing issue. Brain imaging scans done by neuroradiologist Michael Phillips at Indiana University show that men listen primarily with their left hemisphere (which emphasizes language and logical processes), whereas women listen with both left *and* right hemispheres (the latter adding an emotional-processing component). Despite these differences, however, Barker and Watson concluded that neither sex had a fundamental advantage over the other in their inherent *ability* to listen.

In our Friendship Labs, we recommend specific mindfulness exercises such as focused breathing and visualization to help men enhance their receptive capacities. For those who find it particularly difficult to dispel the noise in their heads while listening, we suggest extra exposure to mindfulness meditation through group or individual trainings.

The bottom line: Most men can upgrade their capacity for focusing attention and absorbing important emotional information while listening to their friends. When they do, they usually experience a deeper, more enriching connection.

Reflection ○

Aristotle described a good friend as a "second self." He was referring here to a friend's ability to reflect back to us important
things we've been saying. In short, a good friend presents you to
you. The neurobiologist Vilayanur Ramachandran theorized from
his research in 1992 that all humans come equipped with "mirror
neurons," cells in the brain that specifically allow us to experience
what another person feels and thinks and then feed back our experience to him.

This listening skill is called mirroring, and it's been described
in just about every couples therapy textbook written in the past
twenty years. *Mirroring* means feeding back the words and feelings
that your friend has expressed, and then checking back with him
to make sure you've heard him correctly. While this may sound
simple, doing it in real-time conversations can be challenging, because it requires keeping your friend's words and feelings in focus.

Mirroring helps to deepen guys' conversations, first because it
shows you've taken the trouble to listen and remember what your
friend has said. Second, when the other guy is immersed in sharing,
his words may feel complex and even slightly confusing to himself.
So when his words are reflected back to him by a friend in a caring
way, as Charles did with Loudon ("You told us you had a fight with
Adrian . . . you unloaded on her . . . you wish you could take your
words back"), it helps the person make sense of his own feelings.
That understanding can, in turn, help him transform the way he
handles those feelings.

Empathy   ○

The third skill of the listening triad is empathy. Roughly speaking,
empathy is your ability to imagine what your friend must feel and

to communicate this to him. What makes empathy feel so good is that, when it's *accurate*, it connects with the person's own experience of themselves. You allow your friend to feel genuinely understood.

The next time a guy tells you something that's meaningful to him, hold off on the advice giving or problem solving. Instead, try responding with what comes up for you when you hear his story. What does his situation remind you of in your own life? Have you ever struggled similarly? Have you found ways to deal with these situations or feelings in your own life? Share these. See what happens.

We've covered a lot of material in this chapter. So let's take a moment to review. Below is a brief recap of intimacy-promoting skills that can help you to carry on conversations from the heart. If you've incorporated most of these already, you're well on your way to having honest, open guy friendships. If not, pick one or more to work on or develop further. Each one will deepen your connections with your male friends.

CREATING SAFETY

Ask yourself:

Am I giving my guy friend the opportunity to open up with me? Am I being inviting without crowding him?

Am I keeping personal matters between the two of us?

Am I being respectful of him? Am I taking care not to blow off his deeper feelings?

Am I telling him directly how much I admire and care about him?

If you feel you're hitting the mark on all these questions, give yourself kudos. If not, pick an area and work on it.

RISKING SELF-DISCLOSURE

Have you been willing to share personal details of your life with your friend? When he shares with you, do you reciprocate? Remember, self-disclosure benefits both of you.

If you want to strengthen this skill, consider sharing an important personal issue with your friend that you've never before discussed with him. Conversely, if you sense that your friend is holding back on something important, invite him to go deeper with you.

EXPRESSING YOUR FEELINGS

To express your emotions to your friend in a way that he can appreciate and that allows the two of you to feel closer, take these steps:

Allow yourself to breathe, taking the time to notice the sensations and thoughts that arise when you're clarifying your feelings. Take your time with this.

When you share what's going on with you, include words that describe your feelings, not just your thoughts. Naming your emotions shows your willingness to bring more of yourself to the relationship and will foster a deeper connection with your friend. Download and use the Feelings Wheel to help describe the emotions you want to convey. http://msaprilshowers.com/emotions/the-feelings-wheel -developed-by-dr-gloria-willcox/

Use the guidelines for "Delivering Your Feelings" starting on page 140 to rehearse and initiate a conversation about an important emotional issue with your guy friend.

LISTENING AND RESPONDING

Remember that listening and responding are not passive activities, but rather dynamic, essential skills in close friendships. In your next conversation with a friend:

Try staying silent, perhaps for longer than usual, as you listen to him. Pay close attention to his words, facial expressions, and body language. Notice the reactions, emotions, and thoughts that come up for you, but keep these to yourself for now. (You can bring them up later if you choose.)

If your friend says something that you sense is emotionally important to him, wait until there is a pause in his communication. Then, take the opportunity to highlight this by mirroring (repeating back) what you heard your friend say. Check with him about whether you heard it right.

Finally, share with him how you connect emotionally with what he's said. If his communication brings up similar feelings from your own life experience, share these. If not, let him know how you *imagine* you'd feel in his circumstance. The purpose here is not to give corrective advice but to support your friend emotionally in whatever he is experiencing. "I get it" are three of the most powerful words in our language.

CHAPTER 7

Staying the Course

Keeping Your Friendships in Good Repair

> Friendship should be surrounded with ceremonies and respects, and not crushed into corners. Friendship requires more time than poor busy men can usually command.
>
> —RALPH WALDO EMERSON

Developing close, satisfying male friendships is one thing. Keeping them in good working order is something else entirely. After a busy day seeing several psychotherapy clients, hitting the gym for a quick workout, spending what I hope is quality time with my wife, and touching base with my adult kids, it's practically bedtime. When am I supposed to hang out with the guys I care about and enjoy?

Close guy friendships increase in value over time and continue to reward you with pleasure—if you take good care of them. Think of what it feels like to talk to a good friend with whom you haven't been in contact for a long time. You're suddenly telling each other about things that have been weighing on you, things you haven't shared with anyone else, recognizing how good this feels. "This is really sweet," you think. "I want to do this more often."

Well, you can.

In this chapter, I describe some reliable ways I've found to keep male friendships running in first-rate condition. Over the years, I've condensed and refined these methods into a set of tips that I call the Friendship Maintenance Checklist. For each prescription, I give a real-world example and share exercises that we use in our Friendship Labs to maintain strong guy ties. Here's the checklist:

1.   STAY IN REGULAR CONTACT

The more time you spend with close friends, the more satisfying these friendships are apt to be. Face-to-face encounters—what I call dirt time—with your friend is particularly satisfying, because your senses and sensibilities are fully engaged.

For example, my best friend, Jake, and I live within a few miles of each other, so we usually get together twice weekly. Typically, he picks me up at my office and we drive down to the fitness club by the Schuylkill River. There, we work out for an hour, catch some downtime in the hot tub, and then grab lunch. We've been doing this routine for years.

Any lunch or hot-tub discussion might cover a range of material, from what kind of gas mileage our cars get or what service provider has the best cell coverage to why I'm not sleeping well, worries about our kids, or, more philosophically, how to keep beautiful moments alive in the face of aging and mortality. These discussions with Jake create an ongoing, ever-changing newsreel that provides us both with comfort and enjoyment.

Schedule It!

Scheduling time is a constant challenge in our relationship. Witness a recent conversation Jake and I had at the Lunch Box, a little deli hidden inside a nondescript office building across from my office, where we regularly chow down after our workouts.

Jake: "So what's up?"

Me: "I'm feeling nasty. I thought I had a virus. But it hasn't gone away for two weeks. I'm totally low energy."

Jake: "Have you called Brad [my internist]?"

Me: "No. I haven't had time. I should."

Jake, shoving my cell phone across the table to me: "Call him."

I dial Brad's number. Audrey, Brad's administrator, picks up, and tells me the earliest possible time Brad can see me. I'm in luck, but not without complications.

"Shit," I say after I hang up. "He can see me Thursday. But it conflicts with our time together."

We both hesitate, metabolizing this disruption.

"Uh," I say, "what about Friday? I'm good pretty much all afternoon."

"Great!" he says. Then he reverses himself, remembering something. "I can't. Rachel [his daughter] is coming into town, and we're meeting to talk about her moving to Philadelphia from Baltimore."

"What?" I protest, in mock pain. "Your daughter's future is more important than our working out together?"

He smiles. "Yeah, 'fraid so. At least this week."

We look at each other, shaking our heads, with that buck-up-that's-how-it's-going-down look, knowing we're probably not going to meet again until next Tuesday.

"OK," I say, disappointed. "So maybe we'll check in over the weekend." Which may or may not happen. But it's a comforting thought to tide us over until we connect again. He nods his head in agreement.

I'm not complaining here. Jake and I are lucky to have the amount of time we spend together. I'm just describing the administrative details that go into managing our relationship.

Weekly or biweekly get-togethers may not be possible with close guy friends for a variety of reasons—distance, work, family responsibilities. Two of my good friends, Michael and Larry, live in Alexandria, Virginia, and Washington, DC, respectively. When we see each other, we have to plan in advance. Some of these visits are social and include our wives. Others involve getting together at professional conferences.

In these situations, I've found it's important to schedule some one-on-one time with a friend. Couples' chat can be intense and consuming, while professional conferences can be busy. So I try to clear some private guy time—retire to the porch or den, or take a walk outside the hotel—to get a chance to really connect.

Sometimes, you have to simply seize the moment when it arises. During a recent visit to Washington, DC, my wife and I had some scary car trouble along the way. The following morning, my friend Larry and I spent a terrific few hours hanging out in the service lounge of a car dealership, with a supply of coffee, bagels, and cream cheese, as we waited for the car to be fixed.

While my coils were being replaced, we caught up on everything from what our neighborhoods were like in the cities where we grew up (Great Neck, New York, for him, Chicago for me) to how you talk about politics with neighbors you like as people but wildly disagree with (we settled on "sparingly or not at all"). This emergency repair trip, albeit short, gave me some precious time together with Larry.

Flexibility and Persistence

I've found also that it's important to be flexible in how you keep up your contacts with guy friends. Phone calls, letters, e-mails, and texts can all help to keep these connections going, even though they may feel less personal than meeting face-to-face. While there's no evidence that any *particular* frequency or mode of contact between guy friends is required for a satisfying friendship, most men value continuity.

"High-tech, low-touch" modes of contact certainly don't provide the personal juice that, say, hiking together in the White Mountains might. Recent research on Facebook, for example, shows that no matter how often a person uses this tool or how many FB friends they accumulate, it has no bearing on how satisfied they feel with their friendships.

What *is* important, however, is that these tools help us to better manage our friendships. These mini contacts often provide us with opportunities to arrange real-time get-togethers.

An e-mail exchange with an old friend last year revealed that we were going to be on vacation in the Caribbean at the same time. We were able to arrange our schedules, resulting in a few lovely days together that contributed to my revitalizing this old friendship. We got to snorkel together, down some rum drinks, and update each other on our lives and our kids during this time.

Finally, guys often let their friendships wither on the vine because they succumb to guilt, which in turn dampens the energy required to keep up the friendship. In our Friendship Labs, we recommend that our guys put their guilt on hold and focus on the "pleasure of his company"—the enjoyment that their friendships provide. When you think about your friend, your brain is telling you something. If it's saying, "It's been too long," remind yourself that your friend probably misses you, too. Your calling him is not just about assuaging your guilt (although that may be a part of it)—it's about recapturing some lost pleasure that's slipped away for both of you. Most guys in our groups admit that they like being called, especially if the other guy says, "I've been thinking about you. I just wanted to check in (or share something) with you." Trust your brain—and pick up the phone.

2   MAKE YOUR CONVERSATIONS COUNT

While I get as much pleasure as the next guy from nattering about whether it's worth my while to watch the Philadelphia Eagles play football on Sundays, or trying to predict whether Apple products will ever be cool again, you can't depend on these kinds of exchanges to keep your male friendships vital over time. As we discussed in Chapter 6, it's important to bring your EI skills online when you're communicating with your guy friends.

When you're anticipating calling or getting together with your friend, first do a gut check, drawing from your intimacy skills playbook. What's going on in your life that's important to you? How are you feeling about things? What haven't you said or want to know about *his* situation? Make sure you bring up these issues when you're conversing, so they actually get communicated. This kind of commitment lets your friend know you care, and it nurtures your friendship.

My old high school friend Barry called me recently, a few months after our fiftieth high school reunion. His call took me by surprise. It was a snowy day in Philly—no one had gone to work, no patients had shown up in my office. When I heard Barry's voice calling from Sarasota, a warm breeze seemed to blow through the telephone.

"I was just thinking about you," he said. "I don't mean to pry. But I talked to Jeff (another old high school friend) and we both wondered if you were OK after your encounter with Liz at the reunion. I'm just checking in."

I was very touched by his question—and told him so. Liz was an old girlfriend. I'd had a thing for her in high school. The relationship had died, slowly and painfully, in college. "You know," I said, "I had no idea how that would go. It really turned out to be a nonevent, not much energy there." I thought a little more and noticed that I was still feeling some disappointment. I thought I had put this encounter out of my head, but not quite. "Maybe," I reflected, "the encounter with her was a way to help close an old chapter." I felt relieved just talking about it. Barry was quiet, listening. "That's good, Rob," he said finally. "Just wanted to make sure you were OK."

The real event, I grasped later, was Barry's call and the discovery that my guy friends were paying attention.

3   ADD FRESH RITUALS TO YOUR ROUTINE

While consistency is important in maintaining your guy friendships, so, too, is novelty. No matter how terrific your connection is with your friend, repeating the same old routines together can get a little stale. Luckily, the prescription here is simple: Do something different!

This can be as easy as changing a habitual activity or eating place. Sometimes, when we're late for the Lunch Box, Jake and I just hit the sushi counter at the Acme and eat in the car. Other days, when it's gorgeous outside, sunny and breezy, we'll spontaneously decide to forgo the air-conditioning and fluorescent glare of the gym and take a long walk by the Schuylkill River.

You can schedule rituals to celebrate your friendships as well. Several years ago my brother, David, Jake, and I arranged a return hiking trip to the White Mountains in New Hampshire—to celebrate twenty-five years of our yearly weeklong summer hiking trips. This was where we first started the tradition.

Looking down into Zealand Valley, from a high ridge atop Sugarloaf Mountain, a palette of summer greens bisected by a deep blue river line, David and I turned to each other in wonder and amazement. "It never gets old, does it!" I said to him. We were sweating, gulping down water from our old Nalgene bottles. He laughed. "*We* get old." He furrowed his brow in mock desperation. "Where's my elevator? I need my elevator." We both laughed. "But no," he said seriously, "this never gets old."

4   PRACTICE EVERYDAY LOYALTY

Among the most highly prized elements of male friendship is loyalty. The commitment to support your friend, to "cover his back" no matter what the circumstances, elicits some of the strongest positive feelings between men.

Loyalty between men often conjures up images of bonding under duress, as in times of war or other hazardous situations. When it comes to friendship today, however, these kinds of heroics are not what guys expect or are looking for.

In our Friendship Labs, we promote a different kind of loyalty, one that calls upon men to look out for each other not just in times of adversity. Men often provide each other with what I call "instrumental support"—they help each other lift, carry, or build things. They may also give advice on consumer items—which car gets the best gas mileage or which computer is the fastest for surfing the web.

But deeper loyalty involves men giving and getting emotional support to and from each other. In our groups, we strongly encourage guys to maintain contact outside meetings, with regular phone calls and get-togethers. While our men do think about and care for each other, they're often initially reluctant to get in touch outside the group, fearing that the other guy will judge them as intrusive or, if they're asking for emotional support, that they'll be seen as weak or needy, or misunderstood as coming on sexually to the guy.

We educate men about their friendship dementors and how these internalized stereotypes inhibit them from reaching out to each other. We include "reaching out" exercises in our groups, where we ask each man to call or get together with another guy between sessions—to reach out for or offer emotional support. When men learn to do this spontaneously, they enhance the relationship. Some men have great difficulty, however, exposing their dependency needs and letting themselves depend on others.

Visitations

Bob was a fifty-year-old real estate entrepreneur who came into the group with feelings of depression and anger toward his wife, shortly after his elderly mother had moved in with the couple.

While he was caring and empathic, well liked by the men in his group, he revealed that he had a hard time letting people care for him. His relationships were often characterized by his "over-giving" to people around him, almost always followed by resentment and anger on his part. He described himself as a highly responsive but overburdened child. He'd been recruited by his mother to be her confidant during her lonely marriage to Bob's father, an inaccessible alcoholic. Bob's wife, Lois, struggled to understand his moodiness and rejection of her efforts to help him.

When Bob reported that he wouldn't be at the next group meeting because he was scheduled for knee replacement surgery and that he hadn't yet told his wife about this, the other group members were alarmed. They insisted that he inform his wife immediately and pressed him about this odd and destructive behavior. He admitted that he had no good explanation for it. "I just didn't want to put anyone out," he confessed lamely. But he knew this was flimsy, and he was embarrassed. He wife was deeply hurt upon receiving the information.

One of the guys in the group, Charlie, with whom Bob had a close connection, said to him, "OK, my friend, you're in trouble. You're not leaving here tonight until you tell the guys here how we can support you through all of this." Bob looked both sad and strained. "Visit me" was all he could say.

The men (under no direction from me or Jake) organized trips to see Bob in the hospital following his surgery and later when he returned home. They sensed how important this contact was for him. And indeed, his mood and attitude began to change during his recovery.

When Bob returned, he seemed to be turning an emotional corner. "I was really touched by all of your caring," he said sincerely. "But just as much, you've helped me see how much I've been pushing Lois away. She's always been there for me, helping with my mom—and I haven't been able to acknowledge her."

He looked vulnerable, but grateful. "I told her how much she means to me." He hesitated. "Thanks to you guys, I'm learning that it's OK to ask for help."

5   BE HONEST WITH YOUR FRIENDS

It's worth stating here that friendship loyalty is not about robotically agreeing with your friend, regardless of what he says or does. "Support" of this nature is rarely in that individual's best interest.

Instead, as Oscar Wilde said, "A true friend is someone who stabs you in the front." Perhaps that image is a little overwrought, but a good friend is someone who calls it like he sees it, who is willing to tell you the truth, to confront you even when he knows that it will make you uncomfortable—because he really *does* care about you.

Mario, a longtime group member, stunned the guys one evening when he announced that his wife, Adele, had just threatened to leave him. Mario was a highly respected psychologist and educator. He was well liked by the guys in the group and a great listener for the other men. While he'd openly shared his stress over his busy work schedule, he'd never before said a word about marital trouble. He looked defeated.

"She said I'm delusional," Mario said listlessly. He went on to describe his wife's litany of complaints about his emotional unavailability and his chronic failure to follow up on things she'd asked him to do.

The other men in the group rushed in to comfort him, flooding him with questions. What was going on with Adele? Was there an affair? They were shocked.

Randy, a man who wasn't known for mincing words, had been quiet amidst this flurry of support. He was a close friend of Mario. Finally, he spoke up.

"Is she right?" he asked Mario, point-blank.

"About what?" Mario responded.

"About your being delusional, living in a dream world, acting like everything was fine, overlooking her pain and disappointment?" He held his friend firmly in his gaze.

The guys in the group went quiet.

Mario wilted further. "She might be," he admitted, looking discouraged. He confessed that he'd *heard* Adele's words before, *thought* he was being attentive, but—maybe not. He said he couldn't believe that things had deteriorated to this level, but he did know that he loved his wife very much. "I feel sick to think I might lose her," he said.

Randy continued to hold Mario in his gaze and said, "Then you'd better turn up the volume in your hearing aids, my friend, and start listening."

While I could hear the compassion in Randy's voice, it was clear he wasn't letting Mario off the hook because he knew how desperately Mario wanted to save his marriage.

Taking their cue from Randy's steadfast honesty, the rest of the group began to side with this effort, nudging Mario (both within and between group meetings) to keep things moving forward with his wife, to pay more attention. Gradually, these efforts paid off, and Mario and Adele were able to pull their marriage back from the brink.

6   INCLUDE YOUR FRIENDS IN YOUR OTHER KEY RELATIONSHIPS

When men talk privately with their close guy friends, they often share experiences that they share with no one else. Our MFEI Survey found (and other friendship research confirms) that men hold their closest friendships in as high regard as other important connections in their lives, including their relationships with their spouse, their children, and their parents.

Problems can arise, however, when men erect boundaries around their friendships that isolate them from their other important relationships. This quarantine policy can strain your friendship and turn your friend into an "outlier" or a competitor with the family for attention. An errant Misogyno Dementor, harboring negative attitudes toward women, sometimes encourages guys to invite their friends to join them in behaviors that are destructive to their relationships with women.

Several years ago, Lon, a forty-eight-year-old stockbroker in one of our groups, was confronted by two of the other men. Lon was constantly complaining about how his wife, Denise, tried to interfere with his guy friendships. It turned out that Lon had been calling some of the guys in the group, pressuring them to go with him to Delilah's Den, a local strip joint, after the groups were over.

One of the fellows, Gerry, said to him, "Lon, I'm worried about you. These 'after hours' escapades of yours are destructive for you and your marriage. No wonder Denise is all over you about going out with the boys. Sorry, man," he added firmly, "I can't support that." The men in his group continued to press Lon to do a lot more thinking about how he was contributing to his own marital problems.

On the other hand, if you can find positive ways to integrate your close guy friendships into your life, it can greatly enrich these relationships *and* support your family ties.

Arranging social get-togethers that include your partner and your guy friends can help enormously to build bonds. This gives your friends and your partner a chance to get to know each other and, hopefully, come to like each other.

When my friend Larry was going through a difficult divorce, he came to visit us in Philadelphia. The visit not only brought us closer, but it gave my wife, Sandy, a chance to get to know and really like him. I had previously told Sandy about getting together with Larry at a men's conference and how positively I had connected with him. During his visit with us, I returned from a trip to the deli, carrying a bag of bagels and pastries. Sandy and Larry were huddled over our kitchen table, sharing war stories about divorce, kids, and their opinions about Brooklyn as a good place for young people to live. It was a great feeling seeing my wife bonding with my new friend.

Another memory surfaces: Several years ago, when I returned home from the hospital, following hip replacement surgery, I remember seeing, in an analgesic glow, Sandy and my best friend, Jake, hovering over me, helping me to get situated in a room in our house where I could comfortably recover. Exhausted and grateful, I remember thinking, "Wow, I'm surrounded by the people I love!"

As corny as this may sound, it underscores my belief that in our world today, creating "a village" that includes our closest friends helps optimize and expand our experience of love. It's worth inviting your close guy friends to enter that village.

7   TREAT YOUR FRIENDSHIP AS A LONG-TERM INVESTMENT

The value of a close friendship appreciates over time. But relationships are also in constant flux. While we may treasure certain features of our guy ties, we also need to be able to hang in there through the inevitable life changes, including moves, job shifts, marriage, new fatherhood, illness, and loss.

Sometimes it's geographical distance that challenges a close friendship. Whether we admit it or not, having a guy friend within easy striking distance, where you can run out to catch a movie on a whim, plan a spontaneous bike ride on a Sunday morning, or share an experience hot off the presses—like your fourteen-year-old daughter's boyfriend asking you what time she needs to be home from the date—is a huge plus.

When a geographical disruption occurs in a close friendship, you may need to do some serious emotional processing, talking, and planning with your friend to continue nurturing your friendship.

The Playground Chronicles

Tom and Carl met each day in their neighborhood park with their three-year-old daughters, Amy and Carolyn. Both men were at-home dads who were the primary caregivers for their daughters. Their wives were physicians who worked at a busy, high-volume suburban medical practice. Tom was a temporarily unemployed book editor, Carl a software developer who freelanced from home.

For the past two years, the men had braved the streets of Center City with strollers, shopped together in local food marts, and covered for each other when the occasional work gig required them to be away. They'd taken special pleasure in wearing down the resistance of a local group of playground moms, who'd finally accorded them "real parent" status after one reluctantly approached Chris for advice about how to handle her defiant seven-year-old son. The men had high-fived each other on this major breakthrough.

When Carl learned from Tom that he and his wife, Ann, were moving to Los Angeles because Ann had received a "can't refuse" offer to run a large primary care practice, both men went into shock, struggling to absorb the likely effects on their friendship and families. But they spoke little about it to each other.

A few weeks later, Carl's wife, Susan, arranged a dinner to

celebrate Ann's professional coup and the big move. Both Tom and Ann had family on the West Coast. This would give them more chances to see them.

Carl and Tom tried to be upbeat, but sadness lurked behind the toasts and laughter. When the day of departure came, the families drove to the Philly airport together. Ann and Susan chatted in the car, discussing when schedules would permit the families to meet for the holidays. Tom and Carl were uncharacteristically quiet. They both helped unload the carry-on bags, gave each other a hearty man-hug, wished each other good luck, and kissed the women good-bye.

"We'll talk," they said. And that was it.

Over the next two weeks, Carl remained unusually quiet, continuing his daily routine with his daughter, Carolyn, and making no mention of Tom or his family's absence. Susan noticed he was not sleeping well. She didn't probe but was gentle with him, knowing he would talk when he was ready.

Two weeks later, waiting in the checkout line with Carolyn at Trader Joe's, Carl got a text—a photo of Amy sitting atop a brightly colored playground jungle gym, holding up a cardboard sign inquiring: "Where is everyone?"

The text message read, "Call me."

Immediately, Carl punched in his friend's number.

"Hey," said Tom. "How are you?"

Before he could edit himself, Carl responded, "Pissed."

"Me, too," Tom said. "Every place here is pushing vitamin shakes and quinoa salads. There's not a single down-to-earth Philly dive around here. And there are no moms *or* dads on the playgrounds. Only nannies. Who are all reading books on how to raise kids!"

"Ugh," Carl groaned, pleased to hear how bad things were at that end. After a small silence, Carl said, "Carolyn keeps asking for Amy." Another silence. He breathed deeply. "This is depressing, man. What am I supposed to do here without you?"

"Yeah, likewise," said Tom. "I guess we're gonna just have to keep texting and calling." He grinned into his cell. "Until I can find someone here who remembers to bring coupon clippings along with him to the grocery store. But I doubt that's possible. Too weird, right?"

"Not possible in this lifetime, my friend." Carl rocked back on his heels, relaxing. He and his buddy were connecting again.

The guys agreed to keep sending pictures and texts. That's what they could do now. Maybe they'd try to get in a phone call at least once a week.

Susan noticed that Carl slept better that night. He told her about the conversation with Tom. They talked about planning a visit to L.A. in the spring. At breakfast, he piped up, "This moving stuff, losing our friends really sucks, doesn't it? It's a lot harder than I thought it would be." Susan nodded in agreement. She knew exactly what he meant.

The Flexible Friendship

Adjusting to phone calls, texts, and planned visits when you're used to easy day-to-day contact, as Tom and Carl were, can feel like quite a stretch when a friendship changes. The value of this effort to stay connected and adapt to these changes, however, emerges over time. We realize how comforting it is to have a friendly face or voice, *someone who really knows us,* when we are going through new, sometimes daunting life challenges.

Disruptions of other kinds, ones that feel more hurtful, from emotional injuries or neglect, can arise in men's friendships. All too often, these friendships wither or drop off, when in many cases they could be healed or salvaged with the right approach. We examine this phenomenon in the next chapter, "Friendship First Aid."

CHAPTER 8

Friendship First Aid

Managing Conflict

Because we get to choose our friends, we tend to believe that these relationships are immune to conflict. If only. Guys often try to ignore the tensions and hurt feelings between them, but the issues rarely disappear on their own. Unaddressed injuries can fester, deepen, and ultimately put your most important male friendships at risk.

I was chatting with James, a man in his twenties, in the hot tub at our health club. He plays basketball with a group of his guy friends in the afternoons. I was asking him about one of his buddies, Jamal, whom I hadn't seen around lately. "He's not talking to me now," James said somewhat offhandedly.

I couldn't resist: "What's up with that?"

James looked around to make sure no one was listening. "He's mad at me," he said in a low voice, "'cause his mom died and I didn't call him up. I mean, I was at the church, the funeral and all that. But I didn't call him after that. So now he's not talking with me."

He looked glumly into the water.

I realized that I'd wandered into something pretty intense for James. I hesitated, wondering whether this was really any of my business. But I liked James. And I got the feeling that he wanted to talk.

"So how bad is it with you two?"

He shook his head determinedly. "I'm not going to *let* it be bad. Jamal and I go back to grade school. We're close. He knows my mom." He took a deep breath, looking down. "Yeah, I was stupid! I should have called him." Long pause.

"It's gonna be OK, though," he continued. "I'm gonna keep calling him. I think he'll come around. We go back a long way." He looked up. "You can't just give up on your friends, right?"

I nodded. "No, you can't. I think Jamal will come around." Listening to James, I believed this was true.

Research shows that most men want to do what it takes to preserve their close male friendships. In our own survey, men were deeply saddened by losses suffered in their friendships with other guys, whether due to disagreements, relocation, illness, or death. Most guys in the study reported that they'd taken action to lessen the stress in their guy friendships—by speaking directly with their friends, getting advice from another party, using gentle humor, or taking a break to de-escalate tension.

Sometimes, traditional male behaviors such as aggressiveness, competition, and the need to control can generate conflict in men's friendships. Other behaviors, such as emotional restraint, withholding information, and hiding vulnerability can keep guys from addressing and repairing injuries when they arise.

Psychologist Niobe Way observes that as boys move into their late teenage years, they tend to let go of emotionally intimate connections with their close guy friends. These deeply trusting bonds give way to the more wary, isolating habits of traditional masculinity. I believe that when young men constrict themselves in this way, they also shut down their emotional immune systems—their capacity to identify and respond to conflict when it arises in their friendships.

In this chapter, I show how guys can reactivate these restorative powers and heal relationship injuries through a process I call friendship first aid. I introduce you to several of the culprit behaviors associated with the traditional Male Code, along with their accompanying dementors that contribute to common friendship injuries between men. I share some stories—some personal, others from our Friendship Labs—of how men have learned to recognize and address these problems as they arise. Finally, I describe a more extreme response—a kind of "friendship resuscitation"—that I used to save an important relationship in danger of expiring.

THE POWERFUL PAUSE

Close friendships fare better when guys are attuned to emotions—their own as well as their friend's. If a buddy's comment strikes you as harsh ("How stupid can you get?"), take a moment to think about where this might be coming from. Is he responding to something hurtful you've said, perhaps unwittingly? Or is it coming from him, out of the blue? Are you overreacting, nursing a cold, lacking enough sleep, or feeling especially sensitive?

I consider this hesitation a preventive "stutter step," an opportunity to reflect rather than react. Sometimes a friend will pick up on the pause and correct himself: "Sorry, that was obnoxious." Or I will ask, "Do you really think that was a stupid move on my part?" I want to clarify his comment so that I can begin a constructive conversation rather than just sit there silently and feel pissed off.

Attunement goes both ways. If I make a remark and my buddy tenses up or goes pale, I try to check in with him right away: "Whoa, what's going on? What did I say? Did I just freak you out?" Developing this discipline of paying attention and checking in is the most valuable preventive step you can take to protect your close friendships.

THE COSTS OF CLUELESSNESS

Upsets occur in all sizes and shapes in men's friendships. Many of these originate from unintended acts of insensitivity, aggression, or neglect. While we may write these off as "typical guy behaviors," it pays to be cautious here. Men, even the men we think we know well, don't metabolize these experiences in ways we can predict.

Some men like to think of aggressive or insulting behavior as a kind of primordial bonding rite, like soldiers in a Hemingway novel who drink, brawl, behave badly toward each other, and wake up best friends the next morning. But this romantic image covers a bundle of insecurities that real-world guys experience, including hurt, shame, and a painful sense of inadequacy. Left unchecked, chronic aggressive behavior can destroy a friendship.

I witnessed such a collapse on a racquetball court several months ago. One fellow, who'd been playing with his guy partner for nearly a decade, stormed off the court, shouting, "That's it. I'm not putting up with this anymore!" Normally a reasonable person, the fellow had lost it after his partner, a man who routinely belittled him about his game, often throwing tantrums on the court, had smashed his racquet on the floor to make a point.

"One more lucky point for you—if it was really in bounds at all!" his partner brayed. His Machismo Dementor had shifted into high gear.

It was an unsettling scene to witness, but those of us who had experienced how volatile this partner could be were relieved for the fellow when he walked away.

Similarly, chronic neglect—forgetting to return calls, not showing up on time, or ignoring important events in the other guy's life—can undermine your friendship. These behaviors communicate indifference and lack of respect. A Dumbo Dementor may be speaking here: "Oh, well, you know. Guys are busy. I'm busy. Whatever. We'll catch up sometime."

Now and again, we're all guilty of this kind of inattention. But if you neglect your buddy often enough, the friendship may erode—or even evaporate right under your nose.

When men can get their Machismo or Dumbo dementors under control, these injuries can be nipped in the bud. Three steps can help:

1   Identify the offending or neglectful behavior(s) in
    your friendship.

2   Offer a genuine apology to your friend for the harm
suffered.

3   Agree on a plan that makes it unlikely that this
injury will occur again.

Foot-in-Mouth Disease

Griff, a fifty-four-year-old computer engineer, joined one of our Friendship Labs because his wife, Madeline, could no longer stand his knee-jerk sarcastic remarks. He admitted to the group that his penchant for off-the-cuff rudeness made it difficult to keep any friends. He felt he was on the verge of ruining yet another friendship with a guy at work, Dom, who was clearly getting turned off by Griff's chronic insensitivity.

During Griff's first meeting with us, a group member named Rick described a recent upsetting incident with his wife. The two of them had driven past a restaurant that Rick used to frequent with a woman with whom he'd had an affair. Rick and his wife were now in couples therapy trying to repair their marriage. A year later, driving past this scene still triggered painful reactions in both partners.

Griff leaned toward Rick, grinning broadly. "How dumb was *that* to drive past *that* restaurant? I wonder if your wife was thinking, 'Why did I stay with this jerk?'" His tone was chummy, as though he thought this was an amusing, guylike observation.

Rick stared at him, incredulous. Finally, he shook his head and responded: "Griff, I totally understand why your wife wanted you to come here. And why you can't keep friendships with guys. Your remark made me sick. Saying stuff like that is hurtful, man!"

Griff looked discouraged—and remorseful. He held his head in his hands. "Here I go again, putting my foot in my mouth. Just like I do with my friend at work." He looked genuinely sad.

Jake, my co-therapist, asked, "Griff, do you think before you speak?"

Griff replied hastily: "Probably not."

"Seriously?" Jake asked. "Why not? Because you say you want to have good friends. If that's true, wouldn't you want to first carefully check inside about how you feel, and then give your friends the kind of thoughtful response they deserve?"

It was more a statement than a question.

"Yeah," Griff replied, nodding slowly. "But I think I'm kinda primed to go the other way." He went on to describe growing up in a family where everyone, including his parents, let loose with nasty criticisms whenever they felt like it. It got so bad that Griff left home when he was sixteen to live with the parents of a friend, where, he said, "the adults were kind, and sort of put up with my goofy behavior. It was the first time I felt loved in my life." Griff had married a woman who also was kind, but he'd continued to behave as though he were still living by his parents' rules—attack hard and often. He said he felt strongly that he wanted to change this, to respond kindly to the people who loved him and whom he loved.

Griff looked at Rick, and as though he were just waking up, said sincerely, "I'm really sorry. I didn't mean to hurt you."

He asked for support from the guys in the group to help him alter his knee-jerk habits of throwing out hostile, insensitive comments. You could tell he was serious about this request. And the men in the group took this task seriously. When we were soliciting feedback from guys, they all took pains to encourage Griff to slow down, identify first (with the Feelings Wheel) *what* he felt, and then what he wanted to communicate to others. Jake and I worked with him on empathy: He started to practice, responding with phrases like "Wow, that must have felt awkward." Or "I would have felt angry in that situation." Certainly more restrained, a little stilted, but far more effective than, for example, his normal "Boy, that was a dumbass move" responses.

Once he'd committed to this path, Griff was a quick study. As he began to expand his "emotional toolbox," he was better able to intercept his impulsive statements before they left his mouth. In the group, his comments became gradually less caustic, more responsive and positive. A number of guys also noticed that Griff's body language was changing: He appeared calmer and more focused.

Outside the Friendship Lab, Griff was garnering praise from his wife, Madeline, and establishing better rapport with his friends at work. He reported that Dom was beginning to warm up to him, seeking him out to chat during the day. Toward the end of his first year in the group, he reported that Dom and his wife, Beverly, had invited them over for dinner at their house. Everyone applauded.

Winning to Lose

We're told that competition in relationships is healthy, good for a man's character as well as for bonding with others. And in many situations, it does work this way. Certainly, for example, a rousing game of one-on-one basketball, with both opponents scoring and defending well, can foster a positive connection, enjoyment, and mutual admiration. These competitions often initiate the beginnings of close friendships between guys.

But competition is complex. When the pressure to win or maintain control gets out of hand, feelings of shame and humiliation can quickly come to the fore. Guy friends can find themselves shockingly angry or, alternatively, so hurt that if these feelings aren't resolved in a timely fashion, they may head for the exit at warp speed. Virtually all of the men in our survey indicated that they had had to develop specific techniques to address destructive competition in order to get their friendships back on course.

A painful example comes to mind. In my early academic career, I found myself in a confrontation with Andres, a friend and colleague who worked in the training program I directed. He'd asked me to find someone else to work with a trainee he'd been supervising because, he said, "She has too many personal feelings for me." I found myself intensely annoyed with his request—for reasons I couldn't immediately put my finger on.

All I knew was that, at the time, his request felt frivolous to me and, frankly, insensitive to the enormous time and energy I'd been expending to match students with supervisors. He wanted me to make yet another set of phone calls because some female trainee had a crush on him? "Deal with it, man," I thought.

But instead of saying some version of this, or offering to work out some compromise, I just stood there, stony-faced. "Sorry, I can't do this," I said coolly. "It's too late to change the assignments."

We stared at each other for a long time. Finally, in an equally frosty tone, Andres said, "Fine. I'll see her. But if you won't change this, our friendship's over."

I was too shocked to speak. We stared at each other some more. Then, finding no way out of the emotional dead space, I shrugged my shoulders and walked out of the room.

Over the following weeks and months, Andres and I would pass each other in the hall, acknowledging each other politely. But we never discussed or resolved our impasse. Our friendship never recovered the closeness we'd had before, and ultimately fizzled out.

I often think of this episode when men in our Friendship Labs find themselves embroiled in destructive contests with friends. It's clear to me now that while Andres and I liked and admired each other, there was a strong, unacknowledged competitive streak between us. I'm sure I felt jealous of his charisma with my students, and he may have felt put off by my asserting my authority over him as the training director of our program.

Under the spell of our Machismo Dementors, Andres and I did what men in this situation often do—we dug in our heels and tried to stare each other down to see who would blink first. At that time, neither of us had the words—or more important, the emotional skills—to voice our hurt feelings, listen to the other with an open heart, and explore compromises that might have salvaged our friendship.

In our Friendship Labs, we underscore the importance of finding ways to balance competition with an attitude of cooperation. Cooperation means recognizing that "we're in this together," that while we're striving for a goal, we can keep our feelings of jealousy or envy under control and stay open to our vulnerable feelings, and communicate honestly. This allows us to compromise and find positive areas of mutual support in the relationship.

DISCOVERING THE TIES THAT BIND

Behind competitive feelings and verbal jousting, men hide more sensitive and tender feelings that connect them. Sol, a forty-year-old businessman, and Barry, a forty-three-year-old physician, were constantly taunting and one-upping each other, even when sharing their personal stories in the group. Within a short time, the other men in the group began to tire of their antics.

During one testosterone-charged verbal duel, Randy broke in: "You two are like siblings, squabbling for attention in a family." He added, "I want to say, 'Take it outside to the playground—or work out whatever is going on between you.'"

After a brief silence, Sol spoke up. "Funny you should mention this, because Barry does remind me of my older brother." His brother, Alex, had become a physician and worked in their dad's cardiology practice. "We've always fought, and to this day, at family events, we can't agree on anything—even on whether it's raining outside or not." Even as he described his constant arguments with Alex, I heard a note of tenderness in his voice.

Barry gazed at him, incredulous. "*You've* got a brother like that, too?" It turned out that both men had siblings with whom they'd ferociously competed for parental attention and approval. Barry's younger brother, Roger, was an entrepreneur who helped start-up companies develop their business plans and secure funding. Barry's dad, a businessman himself, was always on the phone with Roger, "chatting about business ideas." He didn't call Barry as much, saying, "You're probably too busy with your patients for us to talk . . . right?" Barry had never responded to this, but he felt hurt.

When we identify competitive behaviors between men in our Friendship Labs, we try to help them discover what's behind these feelings. What are they competing for, emotionally? For Sol and Barry, as for many guys, the stakes were approval and attention. When they were able to acknowledge this shared connection, they began to feel more relaxed with each other.

We also try to help our men identify and eliminate behaviors that trigger feelings of shame or jealousy in the other, or that escalate unpleasant exchanges. Sol, for example, never missed an opportunity to point out to Barry how current medical practices and physicians' lack of education about the economy contributed to social problems, such as unequal access to health services in the United States. Not missing a beat, Barry was equally quick to point out how the nation's poor eating habits and the food industry's marketing of unhealthy products created equally serious health problems associated with obesity and diabetes.

Since Sol was somewhat overweight and also had a major client in the food industry, Barry's dig was clearly a personal one. The guys in the group repeatedly pressed Barry and Sol to stop firing these cheap shots at each other. With some embarrassment, each agreed.

We point out, too, that competition between men is often fueled by feelings of deficiency. We perceive that the other guy has something we want but don't have—a particular personality trait, set of skills, relationship, or resources. We suggest to guys that they can convert those feelings of jealousy and shame to expressions of admiration and appreciation.

Behind their jousting, it was clear that Barry and Sol did have positive feelings for each other. They each had previously indicated admiration for the other—but through backhanded comments.

We began to encourage them to share their positive feelings more directly.

This wasn't easy for either of them at first. Barry shared how awesome he thought it was that Sol had single-handedly developed a successful online marketing agency. You could tell by his smile that Sol appreciated this acknowledgment. Similarly, Sol voiced how much confidence he felt in Barry, hearing him speak about his patients and his medical practice. He'd actually referred a family member to Barry's group. Each was clearly happy to hear these positives spoken directly by the other—and the bantering between them began to diminish more rapidly.

Letting up on their macho, competitive behaviors and substituting positive ones allowed Barry and Sol to reposition their relationship from one in which each guy felt diminished by the other to one in which each supported the other's self-worth.

KNOWING WHEN TO FOLD

Sometimes a friendship can't be saved. When the relationship has gone bad and you've tried hard to correct or revive it, the healthiest decision may be simply to let it go.

Some friendships fade out because of loss of motivation due to time constraints, distance, and reprioritizing commitments. If this is the case, it may be good to acknowledge this with the guy. Just as often, you and he can find a way to keep the relationship going in a scaled-down fashion. At least if it ends, you can part with no bad feelings.

Betrayals, such as lying, breaking important confidences, knowingly misleading a friend, especially for personal gain, or cheating with a partner are transgressions most likely to cause irreparable damage.

This breach occurred between Walter and Terry, who were partners in a small, successful matrimonial law practice, along with a third colleague, Ron. The three men had been chums since law school. Now each was married, with young children. They saw each other every day, shared cases, and celebrated holidays together with their families.

One morning, eight years into the practice, Terry stepped into Walter's office and asked him to do him a favor—speak with a representative from the disciplinary board of the state bar association to attest to his character. When Walter asked why, Terry said it was no big deal—a frivolous complaint from a female client. He wasn't at liberty to discuss the details.

Walter said he'd be more than happy to vouch for him.

At the interview the following week, Walter presented a glowing picture of his friend's character, adding that he couldn't imagine how a complaint about Terry could ever get to this level with the board. The representative wriggled uncomfortably, and then responded. "If a female client in a law firm came to you and reported that she had been solicited to have sex with her divorce lawyer, and if it weren't the first such complaint about this lawyer, would you think it worth investigating?"

Taken aback, Walter managed, "Yes, of course." He drove back to his office in a daze.

He told Ron what had happened, and the two men confronted Terry, who denied engaging in any inappropriate behavior. He insisted that an angry female client was manipulating him, and that he had no knowledge of any other such complaints.

Still uncomfortable about the allegations, Walter arranged to meet alone with Terry at a local diner. Sitting across from his friend in a booth, Walter plunged in.

"Look, Terry, if there's anything going on that you haven't told me, please say it. We're best friends. We're all in this together."

Terry met his gaze. "Walter, I know you and Ron are concerned about me," he said. "And I appreciate that. But your support is all I need now. There's nothing to worry about. Thank you."

Three weeks later, Terry announced to his partners that he was taking a leave of absence from the practice. When pressed, he admitted that his license had been suspended pending further investigation by the board, and that he also might be the subject of a malpractice suit. Shortly afterward, a report from the local investigating board appeared in the local newspaper, stating that Terry had been found culpable of soliciting sex from several female clients, and that further actions were pending. Walter and Ron had been told nothing about this.

Walter spent weeks trying to reach Terry on the phone, alternating between feelings of rage at being lied to and guilt that he'd somehow missed something, had let his friend down. Terry didn't return any of his calls. Walter and Ron eventually worked out a separation agreement with Terry, and subsequently disbanded the practice.

As close friends as they'd been, Walter told me, he'd come to feel that this breach of trust—Terry's lying and disregard for his and Ron's well-being—was a betrayal that could no longer be mended. Dissolving the practice was difficult, but letting go of the friendship, he lamented, was the hardest part of the whole experience.

RESUSCITATING A FRIENDSHIP

Fortunately, the fatal breach of trust that Walter suffered in his friendship with Terry is relatively rare. With some effort, most men can find ways to address and resolve problems that occur in their friendships, allowing the relationships to remain vital and stay on course.

George Washington said, "True friendship is a plant of slow growth, and must undergo and withstand the shocks of adversity, before it is entitled to the appellation." Oftentimes, disruptions even in long-standing friendships occur due to emotional cutoffs, real-world losses, such as a friend's geographic move or serious illness, or changes in family structure, such as divorce or remarriage. During these times, guys may sideline or lose track of their friendship. In some cases, one friend may feel abandoned by another.

These life changes can test the resilience of the relationship, challenging guys to take a hard look at the importance of the friendship to them and what's called for to resuscitate it. A story involving one of my own close friendships comes to mind here.

I met Michael during the first year of my psychiatry residency in Madison, Wisconsin, in 1971. He stayed for just one year before transferring to the U.S. Public Health Service in Washington, DC, but we stayed in close touch.

Michael and I had connected immediately. Both of us were recently married Jewish guys from big cities (he, New York, and I, Chicago). Michael was smart and had an edgy sense of humor, which I enjoyed. We ribbed each other about politics, debating liberal (mine) versus conservative (his) positions on just about everything. Underneath, I sensed a gentleness in him that allowed me to feel, from the beginning, that I could trust him as a friend.

After residency, I moved to Philadelphia and settled there. Around the same time, Michael moved to Alexandria, Virginia. Those first years were tumultuous for both of us, fraught with unexpected divorces, professional uncertainties, and family up-heaval. Later, when each of us remarried and had children, we faced the new challenges of parenting. While Michael and I saw each other infrequently—two or three times a year at most—we stayed in close contact and managed to continue to share our deeper feelings and support each other in the personal changes we were encountering.

It was with great surprise, then, that I received a very up-setting letter from Michael.

Uncharacteristically direct, he described how hurt he'd felt by me. He recounted the many times he'd called me over the past several months, and I'd failed to get back to him. He reminded me that he'd told me this was a particularly stressful time in his life because of family issues, and that he felt I was missing in action for him. He went on to say that he needed me to think about just how important our friendship was to me, because he didn't want to go on feeling this way—ignored and disrespected.

A whole litany of excuses flooded my mind. I'd been away on vacation. I had so many work deadlines. I don't usually check our home answering machine. Anyway, I couldn't really have *ignored* all of those calls, could I?

An unwelcome, sober voice in the back of my head, however, replied, "Yes, you could. You did." I'd been in what I imagined to be a go-with-the-flow mode, letting a lot of Michael's calls go by and thinking, "It's all cool. I'll get back to him later."

In retrospect, my Dumbo Dementor had probably been snoozing along in High Siesta mode.

I felt sick in the pit of my stomach and, frankly, scared. Here was my good friend telling me that I'd dropped the ball on our friendship, causing him pain and jeopardizing our relationship. Plus, I knew it had taken a lot for Michael to write this letter. He was not an "in your face" kind of guy. Conflict was not his thing.

There was no way I wanted to lose Michael. My first instinct was to pick up the phone and try to patch things up, telling him all the good reasons I hadn't called him. But something made me hesitate. I realized that I needed to think this through first, not just let loose with a bunch of dumbass excuses for my behavior.

Upon reflection, I realized that I'd been relying on Michael *for years*—not just recently—to pick up the slack when we hadn't been in touch for a while, or when I neglected to return his calls promptly. He was usually the one to make the second phone call, and often the third. He just hadn't said anything about it—until now.

When I mentioned the situation to my wife, Sandy, she looked up from her newspaper and nodded. "So you've been taking your friendship with Michael for granted," she said. "Fix it."

I called Michael, apologized, and told him how important he was to me. I promised I would be more prompt in returning his calls and not let things go so long between our contacts. He was glad to hear this from me, and quick to forgive. Since then, I've definitely upped my return-call rate, and just as frequently, I'm the one to initiate our contacts. We've had a lot of good talks in the last year about how our lives are going professionally, healthwise, and with our kids getting married. It's a good feeling.

This experience was a wake-up call, but not only about my behavior with Michael: It made me realize that I'd been neglecting my other friendships as well. Somehow, I'd needed to feel "special," to be the one *others* tracked down, at the cost of not holding up my end of the bargain. Michael's courageous letter gave me an important opportunity to better care for all of my friendships. Now I make a conscious effort to promptly get back to everyone, and to pick up the phone (or text) when the feeling of missing someone arises.

For this and more, I am grateful to Michael.

PART 3

SPREADING THE WEALTH

CHAPTER 9

The Men Behind Your Marriage

Maintaining a strong marriage may not take a village, but it can usually benefit from a little help from our friends. Women seem to know how to do this more easily. Men indicate they'd like to share more about their marriage or committed partnership with their friends, but often find it hard to do so. Our study shows that men who have more emotional intimacy in their friendships talk more and get more support from their friends about their intimate partnerships.

Marriage is changing today. Men are struggling to redefine themselves as partners. They've enjoyed a long, comfortable run in traditional marriage. During the last half of the twentieth century, men reported very high satisfaction levels with their marriages, significantly higher than those of women. Today, marriage feels more fragile than ever before, more uncertain for men.

The guidelines of Male Code in place thirty years ago—the ones that encouraged men to be strong, silent providers, exempted from talking, child care, and housework—no longer work. These rules may in fact contribute to problems within marriages. More women than ever before are leaving their marriages because their guy won't talk or engage with his family.

The emotional skills that we've identified as so important to men's close friendships are also the traits that partners are seeking in their intimate relationships. The philosopher Nietzsche stated years ago that it is not a lack of love but a lack of friendship that makes unhappy marriages. Close male friendship can help men support loving communications and reduce tensions in their marriage. By being trustworthy sounding boards for questions and emotions, guys can help each other engage more constructively with their intimate partners.

WHY MEN DON'T TALK ABOUT THEIR MARRIAGES

Given the success women have had in supporting their intimate partnerships and families through friendships, it might seem odd that men haven't done this more for themselves. Admittedly, things may be changing here. Our study revealed that 40 percent of our men said they'd received some help with their romantic relationships when they spoke with close guy friends.

Still, there's quite a bit of resistance to this topic. Let's examine why.

Men are generally very loyal to their spouses. Even when

they're feeling angry, hurt, and alone, they carry deep protective instincts about their partner and the relationship. They are loath to reveal private details about these relationships, even when it might really help them.

Male Code continues to play a strong role here. When things are going badly between a man and his partner, he often won't say anything about it to his guy friends, to avoid feelings of shame and discomfort. Admitting his pain and suffering can feel as if he's exposing to the world that *he's* failed as a spouse.

Not admitting there's a problem, however, often blocks a man from receiving support he needs from a close friend.

Between Stocks and Bonds

Roger, a forty-two-year-old graphic artist, called his friend Harry on a Sunday evening for an "emergency consult." Roger's wife, Tina, was in the hospital recovering from surgery, on heavy-duty pain medications, and had called Roger to ask him to pay some bills that needed urgent attention while she was recovering. Harry could hear the tension in Roger's voice. "I don't normally do the finances. Would you be so kind as to come over and give me a crash course on the software program that Tina uses?" It wasn't just tension; it was also anger, Harry thought.

Harry, an IT software developer, had been a friend and neighbor of Roger and Tina for many years. The men liked each other a lot and took long bike rides together on the weekends, but they hadn't shared many of the details of their personal lives.

What Harry was hearing in Roger's voice, though he couldn't know it at the time, was the unresolved frustration in Roger and

Tina's relationship about how they managed their finances together. Tina, a bank executive, had been handling these matters on her own for years. She'd found it difficult to get Roger to sit down with her and go over them. He'd complained that she was too "controlling" and couldn't explain things well to him. "I always end up feeling humiliated," he told her and the therapists they'd seen.

Roger had grown up in a family where his father quietly handled the bills and never discussed money with his kids. As a graphic artist, Roger hadn't needed to learn much about money—they'd inherited some from his family, and Tina earned a lot. His mother had delighted in his creativity and seemed to dismiss his father's more "mundane" interests.

It was more important, Roger told people, to be open about feelings and connect through your creativity than to focus on material concerns. He liked to boast that he didn't "know the difference between a stock and a bond."

When Harry came to the house, Roger gave him a file folder of information about how to open up the financial software, apologizing from the start how complicated and difficult all this must be and complaining about how controlling Tina was when she insisted he learn it. Harry listened quietly while surveying the program that Tina had set up. After a couple of minutes, he shushed Roger and motioned him close to the screen.

"Look at this," Harry said. "This is beautiful. Tina set this up herself? It's a lot of complex information that you can access very easily and do your transactions as well. Here you see all of your accounts . . ." Through Harry's eyes, Roger began to marvel at how efficiently Tina had set up their financial system. In a short time, less than ten minutes, he was able to pay the outstanding bills and to understand more about how their finances worked.

Harry looked up from the screen, gazed at Roger directly, and said, "My friend, since I walked in the door, you've been criticizing your wife about how controlling she is, and how complicated your finances are. The truth is, Tina's done an amazing job of organizing this information. She's been managing it herself, and she's made it easy for you. You just saw for yourself."

Roger was quiet. He felt a great weight lifted off his back. He realized how utterly he'd been taking his wife for granted, and was ashamed. But he also felt relief.

To Harry's surprise, Roger leaned over and gave him a big hug. "You've helped me more than you realize," he said, smiling.

Tina was delighted to get Roger's call telling her "mission accomplished" on the bills getting paid. But she was utterly flabbergasted to hear him praise her and apologize for dismissing the amazing work she'd done on their financial system. Thanks to his friend's expression of authentic regard, Roger was able to step up to his financial responsibilities and start to let go of his old battles with Tina.

INSIDE THE FRIENDSHIP LAB

When men feel it's safe to speak with each other, they talk about their intimate partnerships a lot. Their conversations cover a broad range of topics, from intimacy to work-family balance, from divorce to remarriage. In later life, they discuss the impact of health issues and retirement. With some, violence, infidelity, and addiction have affected their partnerships, requiring a good deal of healing and repair.

In our Friendship Labs, we introduce exercises, mini retreats, and group process to specifically help men address issues with their marriages and partnerships. These can help guys clarify their own values and feelings as well as figure out how to effectively communicate with their partners. We emphasize that this work is a part of their friendship training: High levels of sharing about marital issues correlated with higher emotional intimacy in the friendships of the men in our study.

Being a Good Partner: Reviewing and Revising Our Models

In one exercise, we start by asking men to recall what they learned from their fathers, via observation and advice, about being a strong, committed partner. (We recognize that many men grow up without their fathers around much—or at all. For those men, we inquire about who influenced their ideas and behavior about being a male partner.) In these go-arounds, men discuss their histories with each other and get feedback and support about their current marriage and their role as partners.

We've extended this exercise into a daylong mini retreat on marriage. Each man chooses from the questions below and speaks on the topic, while receiving feedback from the other men.

Take a minute or two to think about each one. Consider reviewing these with a good friend when you have some private time together.

1   How did my father (or other male role model) behave as a husband? What did I observe about how he

negotiated his role and relationship with his wife (my mother) while I was growing up?

2   How did he influence my expectations of myself as an intimate partner? What qualities or traits have I wanted to emulate? What have I wanted to let go of or avoid?

3   Who else has been an important influence on my expectations of myself as a partner? In what ways have these people influenced me?

4   Have the changing roles of men and women affected my ideas about what it means to be a "good husband" today? How?

5   Finally, how successful have I been in living up to my own expectations of being a good partner? What would I like to change or improve upon?

You might be surprised how discussing these questions can lead to more openhearted discussions with your partner, even to resolving some difficult problems between you. We strongly encourage guys to bring their "best selves" to their marriages. Even if a man (or we, as therapists) senses that his partner is not making her/his best effort or seems poorly motivated, we push the man to "up his game" anyway. Our belief is that setting the bar high encourages *both* partners to try harder.

How to Talk About Marriage with Your Buddy

If your friend is struggling with conflict in his marriage, consider the following guidelines in your discussions with him. It may help you to review Chapter 6, "Conversations from the Heart," in preparing for this talk. I find that it's good to have a thoughtful game plan when introducing a sensitive subject.

1 Notice, Ask Questions, and Listen.

Don't be afraid to notice your friend's stress and bring it to his attention. You can ask him how he's doing when you are with him, one-on-one. For most guys, this kind of concern and inquiry is appreciated; opinions and judgments, usually not.

It's best to start with what you've observed: "*You've seemed down* around Janice lately. Is anything going on with you two?" Or "*You've been a bear* with Janice lately. *You seem angry.* Are you?"

Wait for an answer. If your friend is downplaying the problem, you can say something about how you feel (or felt) observing this: "It's *troubling* to see how different you are when you two are together!" Or "Hey, man, that was *upsetting*. You nearly took her head off. What are you so angry about?" Your feeling responses will let him know that you care and are reacting to what's going on.

When he's describing emotional events, it can be helpful to ask your friend about the *details* of what happened:

"So you innocently asked why she got in bed so late last night, and she jumped all over you? Then what did you say?" (Answer.) "OK, and then what did she say?" (Answer.) "OK, and then what happened?" And so on.

The old adage "The devil is in the details" applies here. This kind of inquiry can help your friend begin to hear the issues he hasn't been able to hear in the midst of highly emotional exchanges, to get some perspective and start to figure out how he might communicate more effectively in the relationship.

2   Respect His Relationship.

No matter how angry or hurt your friend is—even if he's talking about divorce—remember that marital loyalties run deep and attachments are powerful. Whether you think his marriage might be on the rocks, or whether you know his wife and have an opinion about her or about their relationship, the most important thing is to support your friend in figuring this out for himself. Hold off on weighing in or predicting an outcome.

3   Resist the Temptation to Attack His Partner or to Pile on
      with Complaints About Your Own Relationship.

Your friend needs the opportunity to vent—and then decide how he's going to handle these feelings in a constructive way. He needs you to be a calm, steady listener. Guys are very attuned to these negative reactions, and they may have the opposite of the desired effect, causing your friend to withdraw or become defensive of his spouse. Not helpful.

4   If Your Friend Asks for Your Opinion or Suggestions,
      Share Your Own Experience and/or Offer Empathy-Based
      Suggestions.

If you've been through a similar experience in your own marriage, let him know how you and your partner handled it. Your situation may not be entirely applicable to his, but at least he will know he's not alone with this problem.

Empathy-based suggestions sound like "If I felt that way, I'd want to . . ." or "Have you considered . . . ?" You can express empathy for your friend, his partner, or both.

An example: Say your friend tells you that his wife has seemed remote lately. She's not responding to his efforts to be super-nice or to his requests for sex. He tells you he's feeling hurt and starting to get angry. You could say, "Wow, that sounds painful and confusing. If I were in your situation, I might feel frustrated and a little scared."

5   Be Patient and Trust Your Efforts.

When you speak with your friend about his relationship, he may not be ready to open up and reveal his deeper feelings to you. Be patient with him—and his relationship. Even if he does open up, he may not be ready yet to act on his feelings.

Remember that listening to him *itself* is a helpful intervention. He'll carry your support and may return to some of your ideas later, when he can use them.

Dan and Ethan were walking buddies who'd first met through work at their pharmaceutical research company. Both were in their mid-forties and lived in the Washington Square area in downtown Philadelphia. Dan lived with Wallace, his committed partner of seven years. Dan and Ethan had been friends for many years, having dated briefly earlier but discovered that they worked better together as friends. Ethan knew Wallace, and liked him.

On one of their morning walks, Dan casually mentioned that he'd had another "spat" with Wallace over the weekend. But no biggie, he added, his voice slowing to dismiss any concern, just another routine fight.

He was ready to move on to another topic of conversation, but Ethan wasn't. Something was bugging him about this: Dan had been reporting his fights with Wallace with increasing frequency—and communicating no sense of urgency that anything needed to be done about them. Ethan wasn't convinced. During their last fight, Dan said he'd knocked over a table.

"Tell me what happened," Ethan urged.

Dan smiled tightly and shook his head, a little embarrassed. "Really, I can't remember it. They're all so stupid. I don't think they're worth remembering."

"Try," Ethan pressed. He sensed that there was something important here.

Dan seemed somewhat annoyed—as if he wanted to escape Ethan's questions. Then, slowly, he began to reconstruct a scenario that, as it developed, had Ethan opening his eyes wide.

"I'd asked him about getting some insurance papers taken care of while I was away," said Dan. "He told me he didn't have time to do it."

He shrugged his shoulders as if to say, "That's it."

"Then what happened?" Ethan persisted.

"He started shouting at me that I'd told him I wasn't going to be traveling so much this month."

"Shouting?" Ethan asked. "Really? How loud?"

"Pretty loud, I guess." Dan was getting more uncomfortable.

The men stopped as they were passing a bench. Ethan said, "Let's sit down for a minute and continue this." They sat.

"Then what did you do?" Ethan asked.

"I started shouting back at him, like 'Are you deaf?'" Dan said. "I'd told him I'd be away a lot this month." His face was turning red and he was clenching his fists.

Ethan had never heard Dan shout or even raise his voice. "Then what happened?" he asked. Listening to his friend's story, he was starting to feel strangely sad.

"Well, Mack, our Sheltie, started barking like crazy, running all over the room, upset."

"And?"

"That sort of helped. . . . It helps. Mack does that when we fight. We stopped. But we didn't get the thing resolved."

"How often are you and Wallace having these 'spats' now?"

"Pretty much weekly," Dan replied. He looked downcast.

He glanced up at Ethan and saw the look of concern on his friend's face.

Ethan said tenderly, "I'm worried about you—both of you. If I were in your situation, frankly, I'd be scared. Are you . . . doing anything about this? Talking to a therapist?"

Dan shook his head no. Reflecting for a moment, he then said, "Wallace and I love each other—but we're not handling this well. *I'm* not handling it well." He paused, then continued, "I don't like to think about it, and I suppose we've both been hoping that it all goes away." He hesitated. "But I guess it's not."

He then signaled Ethan a look of exhaustion that communicated he'd said as much as he could, for now. Ethan put his arm around his friend's shoulder and hugged him.

Over the next two weeks at work, no mention was made of the conversation. But Ethan noticed a definite look of relaxation in Dan's face as the days progressed. At the end of the following week, Dan called him to make a weekend date to go bike riding. Just before getting off the phone, he said, "By the way, thanks for that talk. Wallace and I talked a lot the last couple of weeks. We've decided to talk to a counselor. I think that really might help us now."

"Great," Ethan replied. He noticed a sigh of relief within himself, thinking that it sounded like Dan and Wallace might be starting to get their relationship back on the rails.

"See you, then, this Saturday?" he said.

ENLISTING MARITAL SUPPORT
FROM YOUR FRIENDS

There are times when you may want to solicit support or advice about your marriage from your male friends. You can prepare yourself by understanding how *triangles*, or relationships involving three people in a system, can support couples (or *dyads*) to moderate tensions between themselves and to empower each other to better deal with their relationships.

We know that triangles, badly managed, can bollix up relationships (bad-mouthing a friend behind his back, for example). So how to nip these problems in the bud, to prevent unhealthy triangles from forming in your relationships? The following guidelines can help you to optimize your sharing with a good friend.

Confidentiality and Respect

I've discussed the importance of confidentiality in sharing personal information with your friend. This is even more important when you're talking with him about your partner and your relationship. If you want it absolutely clear that what you share is "for his ears only" (and not for, say, his wife's or partner's or another close friend's), then you must ask him if he can honor that request.

This can save you a lot of grief. Recently, I heard about a major blowup between two guy friends over a careless slip. The man's wife walked into her book club meeting and was met with a rush of heartfelt condolences over a recent miscarriage, her third. She hadn't shared this with anyone except her husband. Her husband's friend had told his spouse, a notorious gossip, who'd passed this sensitive information on to all of the women in their group. The wife was livid, her husband had hell to pay, and the friendship took a serious hit.

When you're sharing personal feelings about your marriage, it's important to be respectful of your wife *and* your friend. Ongoing negative carping about your wife can weigh heavily on your friend. It can predispose him negatively toward your marriage in ways that aren't helpful, and that you don't intend. Express yourself openly, but be explicit so your friend hears exactly what you want him to hear.

This also applies to conversations with your partner about your talks with your friend. While these are private, if you're talking with your friend in good faith, you should be able to tell your partner that these talks are mostly about *you* and how you can better handle things when you get bent out of shape. If she's seen you after you come back from walks with your friend in a better mood, better able to communicate with her, she'll know this is true.

The Benefits of Privacy and the Complexity of Secrets

Close male friendships are private. What gets discussed is between you and your friend only. This privacy provides a wonderful opportunity for your intimate relationship. Because your friend has your best interests at heart, he can safely hold thoughts and feelings that you struggle with in your marriage, and help you sort these out. Privacy offers a space where thoughts and feelings can incubate without judgment or pressure and have a chance to mature into thoughtful communications and strong, compassionate action.

Secrets differ from privacy. Secrets are complex: Their purpose is to shield information from others. Keeping secrets in your marriage can be fine if they're short-term, like a surprise birthday party, or involve issues that are not directly relevant to you and your spouse. For example, a friend's confidences that have no bearing on you and your relationship are not secrets you need to reveal.

Secrets become a problem in a marriage when they involve actions that can have damaging consequences for a man, his partner, and the relationship. The secret can both perpetuate the offending actions and protect a man from having to address the relational consequences with his spouse. Common examples include affairs, addictive behaviors such as drinking, drugs, and gambling, and work-related problems involving a potential job change or loss.

Men often don't share these secrets, even with close friends. Feelings of embarrassment, shame, and guilt may contribute to this withholding. A guy may also fear the consequences, including the possibility that his marriage could dissolve if the secret is revealed. In other cases, men don't want to share the secret because they don't want to have to address the issue or stop the offending behavior.

In such situations, a man's isolation often clouds his judgment. This blurring, in turn, interferes with his taking action to resolve the problems and stop the damage from increasing.

Secrets can go on for years in some marriages. But they have an erosive effect over time, blocking the couple from developing deeper trust. They also foster chronic instability in the relationship, setting the stage for marital ruin when external circumstances change. At this point, the long-buried, incriminating information erupts, and the man suddenly finds himself in a shit storm with his wife, kids, and whoever is involved in the secret.

Last year, I saw a man in crisis, a father of teenage children who had recently been thrown out of the house by his wife. She'd been suspicious of his affairs for the past two decades. When she went back to school to finish her college degree, she became computer literate and figured out how to track his deleted e-mails to other women going back several years. He found himself faced with a long trail of emotional debris resulting from this clandestine escapade—which he hadn't begun to address.

Many people, both men and women, hold the belief that secrets allow a couple's relationship to remain stable over time. But from my observation, the opposite—an increased vulnerability to disruption—is far more common.

Sharing a painful or perilous marital secret with a good friend can be enormously helpful, with some provisos. First, don't ask your friend to listen in order to simply rubber-stamp your secret. This invites him to become an accomplice in your troubled relationship and could well feel disrespectful or be a turnoff to him. On the other hand, Misogyno Dementors (yours and his) may flock to this situation to further exacerbate your already troubled relationship.

Ask him, instead, to help you think through the consequences of this secret, the feelings it's hiding, the costs of keeping up the facade, as well as what would be required to change the circumstances that keep it in place. Your friend is probably not a therapist, but he ought to be able to listen well.

In this way, wise and compassionate action starts to become possible. The steps involved may be painful in themselves, sharing details, seeking forgiveness, and making restitution for infractions, possibly couples counseling.

Recovering from an Affair: Stepping Up

Several years ago, I saw Liam and Maryann. Both were in their early thirties and, though unmarried, had been together for fifteen years. Liam had been having an affair for a year. He'd revealed the affair to his friend Randy, who'd urged him to get couples therapy with Maryann.

A month or so into counseling, Maryann discovered several months of unexplained credit card charges from Liam's trips, and he admitted to the relationship. When he couldn't explain to her why he had the affair, Maryann moved out of the house to stay with her parents. She said she didn't want to stay with a man who didn't talk and had no clue about why he'd betrayed her. I could see that Liam was devastated.

At this point, I suggested that Liam bring in his friend Randy for a session. Randy had known Liam since childhood. They'd grown up together.

With Liam there, I asked Randy to tell me what he thought "made Liam tick." Without hesitation, Randy shared how Liam's parents had divorced when he was eleven, and how Liam had stopped talking and adopted this John Wayne strong-guy manner, which he'd maintained to this day.

I asked Liam if this were true. He affirmed it and told me that his parents never explained why they divorced. After they separated, he and his brother lived with their mother. He visited his father every other week.

"The man didn't talk much," Liam said. "He was mean and indifferent. I never wanted to be anything like him. Except now, I guess I am."

He said he loved Maryann. They had been high school sweethearts. Even so, he hadn't felt confident when she urged that they move in together, nor more recently, when she'd been pressing him to have a child. He hadn't said anything but passively agreed to move in with her.

The girl he'd had an affair with was younger, twenty-two, a bartender who made him feel "like a big man. I don't know what I was thinking."

I asked Liam if he could talk about these things with Maryann present. He looked over at Randy, and I saw panic on his face. Randy looked back at him squarely and said, "You damn well better, man. She's not coming back unless you start talking."

Liam nodded. There was a flicker of recognition, as though he knew it was now time for him to step up and let go of his hurt past.

With more therapy and time, the couple was able to heal from this breach of trust. Liam's willingness to talk with Maryann about his lack of confidence and his parents' divorce was a major breakthrough for the couple. Goodwill, commitment, and family support all contributed to a gradual restoring of trust between them.

Plus, as Liam acknowledged, a little help from his friend.

Avoiding Sexual Betrayal

Of all the unhealthy triangles that can occur among friends, the most damaging is the one that involves an affair with a friend's partner. There's not a whole lot to say about this—except to avoid it at all costs. Only bad things happen here. If you are in a committed partnership, if you have children, if the other couple has children, and/or if you value your friendship, this common form of thrill seeking is guaranteed to create long-term bad outcomes for you and everyone else involved.

Sometimes the feeling of falling in love comes up at strange times in strange places. Your relationship with your friend's wife, or his with yours, plays off of intimacies that are complicated, fraught with more emotional dynamics than the average man or woman can even imagine. Your or his marriage may be in a vulnerable place, there may be unacknowledged competition between you, or a partner may act out conflicts by flirting.

If you experience a sexual vibe between you and your friend's partner, just notice it. You don't have to comment on it or encourage it in any way. Don't go overboard interpreting a single episode. If the extra-long hug was the wine talking, you need to let that go. And face it—you participated in that hug. If there's an exchange of guilty looks the next time you're together, take an attitude of graciousness and humor. As in "It's fine. We're friends." That also sends a message, a positive one.

On the other hand, if you start getting texts and discreet lunch invitations from your friend's partner, politely demur. If these continue, you may need to talk with her/him directly about these invitations while sending a clear signal that you are not open to secret get-togethers. If your message isn't getting through, you may want talk to your friend about his marriage.

On the other side of the aisle, if you see something that makes you uncomfortable, such as overfamiliar or sexually suggestive behavior between your partner and your friend, call it to their attention separately and in private. Be firm and unapologetic: You didn't like what you saw, were hurt or uncomfortable. Please stop. Say this to your friend as well as to your partner.

Taking these actions should be more than enough. If your concerns go ignored and the behavior continues, there may a problem with your marriage and/or your friendship that you've missed.

Resolving Jealousy and Competition

Another less drastic but still troubling triangle occurs when jealousy and competition arise between your partner and your best friend. A man may hear his spouse complaining about why he spends so much time with his guy friend, grousing about the friend seeming to be more important than she is. Conversely, the man's guy friend may make subtle disparaging remarks about, and occasionally even directly to, his partner. There are no long-term benefits in letting this kind of dynamic persist. It's wearing and debilitating for the relationships.

So it's important to ask yourself why this is going on and what can be done about it. Why are two people you deeply care about at war with each other, rather than being at least cordial and friendly on your behalf? Have you been clear that you *want* them to be friends, or at least positively disposed toward each other? Have you done all you can to encourage a positive alliance between them? After all, the main thing they have in common is you.

Unless you enjoy watching gladiator sports, managing two close people in battle with each other is downright exhausting, and tends to erode each of their relationships with you. Jealousies and competitions between a man's friend and partner can proliferate when the man is unconsciously trying to solve his own problems through their struggle. Psychologist Carl Jung called this the participation mystique. We project ourselves into other people's interactions to experience some missing part of ourselves, some missing parts of our own relationship.

When tensions occur between the friend and spouse, rather than stepping in to quiet or help resolve them, a man in this situation will become a passive observer or even a subtle accomplice who foments the trouble. Even though he hears complaints from both sides, he thinks perhaps that his own problems may be solved within this battle.

What he hopes to achieve here, of course, can never come to fruition in reality.

Some highly narcissistic folks simply can't balance having a partner and a close friend at the same time. Their need to have people fighting over them all the time doesn't allow them to give up being the center of attention, something they need to do to foster a positive relationship between a partner and a friend.

In most cases, however, when a man comes to understand that he has to be responsible for his own personal and relational needs, that the drama of jealousy and competition between his friend and intimate partner can't replace his own authentic emotional commitment, he can then begin to bring these fights to a close. He can step up for himself in each of these relationships and not ask others to solve his problems.

Running Interference

Angela and Tim had been happily married for twenty-two years when their relationship hit a speed bump. Angela's mother, Rose, widowed and living in Florida, had begun to show symptoms of

Alzheimer's disease and needed to be moved to a nursing home. Usually vibrant and upbeat, Angela was devastated about her mother's decline and turned to Tim for emotional support.

But Tim, unaccustomed to providing this kind of comfort, was unable to respond. The couple found themselves at a miserable impasse, sniping at each other and then withdrawing. All of this was going on while they were doing their best to support Angela's mother. Both of them felt awful.

Over the years, they had worked out a caring "opposites attract" kind of marriage, which had worked pretty well until now. Angela was a fifty-year-old interior designer, a New Yorker from a boisterous, animated Italian family. Dinner-table discussions in her home, which she described with affection, sounded like people shouting at each other on subway trains. Tim was a fifty-two-year-old social services administrator. He grew up in Iowa, in a reserved Catholic family in which "Pass the butter" would have been the highlight of the dinner conversation during an otherwise silent family meal.

Typically, Angela was the emotionally expressive one, free to share her opinions and enjoying vigorous give-and-take in conversations. Tim was the quieter spouse, reluctant to readily offer his feelings or opinions. These differences, usually comfortable, now had become exaggerated and felt at odds with the altered needs of their relationship.

Tim shared this struggle with his best friend, Louis, a forty-eight-year-old real estate developer, now divorced. Louis, like Angela, was from an expressive Italian family. He was a highly energetic guy who was also caring and openhearted. But he had a tendency to overshoot emotionally, which often resulted in his stepping on people's toes and then having to backtrack and apologize later. He was a loyal and devoted friend to Tim, and had developed an affectionate, humorous relationship with Angela.

But now, whenever Angela criticized Tim—usually for not tuning in to what she was saying—Louis would jump out of his chair in frustration. "You can't talk to him like that!" he'd protest. The two would then proceed to go at each other, Angela attempting to justify her comments about Tim, and Louis flailing in a somewhat disorganized way to try to protect his friend.

Both Angela and Louis had grown up in households where flash-flood bickering was standard operating procedure. Neither seemed terribly upset by these skirmishes. It was as though they were creating a noisy distraction from the painful communication issues between Tim and Angela.

For his part, Tim sat back and enjoyed the attention as his wife and friend argued about him. He seemed not at all worried about the outcome and was reluctant to intervene in their skirmishes. After a while, everything would settle down, though nothing had really been resolved.

Weeks passed. Louis and Angela's fights had become part of the background of the unresolved tension between Angela and Tim. It was becoming clear to Tim that his friend was not going to be able to resolve his differences with his wife for him. And he certainly didn't have the personality to go toe-to- toe with Angela himself. Around this time, he sought individual therapy from me, and also joined one of our Friendship Lab groups to try to sort it all out.

Two things happened for Tim over the ensuing months: In the group, he was able to talk about his struggles with expressing himself in a loving, supportive way—the very issue that Angela was finding painful at this time. He received support and feedback from the men about this. In our one-on-one therapy work, he acknowledged how important it was to have Louis, and the group members and me, take an interest in his feelings, in contrast to the barren emotional landscape of his childhood.

At home, he started to be able to listen to and support Angela in ways she'd never experienced before. Her anxiety and agitation levels dropped several notches. Her mother was getting settled in the nursing home. Angela and Tim's relationship began to thaw. Warmth and good feeling began to return, with Tim more emotionally present than he'd been before.

Louis, for his part, was relieved for his friend and relieved not to be bickering with Angela. He was also learning something, watching Tim show more interest and skill in listening to his wife.

"Wow, I like the new you," Louis told him one morning when they were tossing a football around in Tim's backyard. "I'm writing down some of your moves with Angela in my playbook—giving her attention, feedback, etcetera. Do you mind?" He was joking—but also not.

Tim tossed him the ball—hard, and smiled. "Not at all, my friend," he responded. "It's my pleasure. You've been running interference for me in my marriage for too long. 'Bout time I stepped up, don't you think?" They high-fived.

CHAPTER 10

The Father's Club

While many men are discovering that being a "present and accounted-for" dad is a rewarding venture, it also requires emotional skills that can feel beyond our pay grade. For most men, fatherhood feels like entering an entirely new world, one that can be incredibly joyful yet at the same time feels daunting and exhausting.

Times have changed, and men are taking their roles as fathers more seriously than ever before: The old notion that parenting young children is something a guy "fills in for" or does as a favor for his wife has all but disappeared. Like women, guys are having to find ways to balance work-family time while mastering a new set of emotional and practical skills to help support their little ones through the rapidly changing years of childhood and adolescence.

While advice literature abounds, men are still wading cautiously into the waters of engaged parenthood. Learning from our wives can be a wonderful advantage, but ultimately, men want to forge their own particular style of "dadship." Male friendships can be important crucibles for helping guys develop comfortable ways of connecting with their children.

Men often underestimate their value to each other as they enter their parenting years. Male friends who share the experience of having been fathered in a different era can uniquely support each other in passing on valuable old-school traditions of fathering, as well as leaving behind others, in parenting their children.

Our own MFEI Survey confirms the value of close male friendship in parenting. There was a significant positive correlation between men who had more emotional intimacy in their friendships and those who received help in parenting their children.

HOW DADS ARE CONNECTING WITH EACH OTHER

Men are looking for new ways to connect with each other about parenting. Jim DiMeo, a local Philadelphia software developer who was a stay-home dad for a time, set up PhilaDads.com, a website on which at-home dads could share questions and observations about parenting. He told me that meet-up groups for fathers (see National At-Home Dad Network, AtHomeDad.org) are springing up all over the country.

He described a recent conversation, a callback from the CEO of a software company, a young guy around his own age whom he'd contacted about a job. "As we started to talk," DiMeo said, "the guy heard some background noise on my end. It was my one-year-old daughter fussing about something. He started asking me all kinds of questions about my situation as a stay-home dad, my website, and so on. He said he had young kids at home, missed spending time with them, and wished he were there with them. We got into comparing notes about our kids. We talked for a long time about this. I almost didn't get to talk to him about the job."

My, how times have changed.

OUR FATHERS, OUR FRIENDSHIPS

It's fitting that when we talk about men raising children, we think about the roles our fathers played in our development. It's through those relationships with our dads (or with other important male figures) that we first learned about emotional intimacy with other men. In *Finding Our Fathers*, author Samuel Osherson emphasizes the hunger for and, at the same time, obstacles that often arise around emotional intimacy between fathers and sons.

In our own recent survey, we found a strong correlation between men having close male friendships as adults and their fathers themselves having enjoyed close male friendships. Interestingly, this correlation was even stronger when, in addition, our subjects had enjoyed positive emotional intimacy with their fathers or other important men during childhood. Sociologists Barbara Bank and Suzanne Hansford discovered a similar correlation between fathers modeling intimate male friendships and their sons having their own close male bonds.

My relationship with my father was complicated, bittersweet—and ultimately loving. I revered him as a boy, and wanted him to feel proud of me. I knew he loved me, in his own fashion. He took pleasure in my accomplishments, and he positively supported my friendships. He also placed great value on his own friendships and had several close guy friends.

He was a difficult person for me to feel close to, however, in my later childhood and early adulthood because of his own childhood and subsequent physical trauma. I learned a lot from my father directly about the importance of close male friendships, and ultimately, I was able to find a way to achieve emotional intimacy with my guy friends that I wasn't able to have in my relationship with my dad.

As you read through this section, consider how your relationship with your own father and/or other important men in your childhood has influenced your close friendships with guys today—in both positive and negative ways.

Healing the Wounds, Bridging the Gaps

Growing up, my dad, Milt, struggled with a tough family life. His dad was a poor Jewish immigrant from Poland and his mom, also Jewish and Canadian born, was mentally ill, in and out of hospitals through most of his adolescence. His parents worried and fought about money, and my dad found himself in the role of a parental child, feeling responsible for and taking care of his two younger brothers in the midst of this turmoil. He was verbally humiliated by both of his parents when he tried to intervene in their fights.

Later, after my dad's youngest brother left home, his mother left his father and moved to California with her parents. Until my mother and her family came along, my dad's only emotional support had come from his brothers and a few guy friends. His father died (some said of a broken heart) shortly after my dad returned from the war, the year I was born.

When I was eight years old, Milt was hit by a second major trauma (the first being his childhood). As a young father just starting a new business, he suffered sudden bilateral retinal detachments, from no obvious cause, that left him almost completely blind.

With heroic determination, he returned to work in a few months. He plowed on in a state of emotional denial as though nothing had changed in his life. To the astonishment of his partners and colleagues, he went on to develop a successful advertising business. So effectively did he hide his visual impairment that many of his clients had no idea they were in the presence of a legally blind man.

Emotional vulnerability was not my father's strong suit. He was a fiercely proud man and never considered using a seeing-eye dog or a cane. The words *blind* and *handicapped* were never uttered in our home.

From the time he returned home from the hospital, my mother orchestrated an atmosphere of upbeat pseudonormalcy that permeated our household. We never discussed anything about my father's altered condition that might upset or anger him.

There was this unspoken sense that he might lose what little vision he retained if he got upset or angry—if *I* made him angry—and that our fragile arrangement would utterly collapse. He had a wife and three young children who depended on him, and he wasn't going to let them down—or even appear to do so.

As a kid, I revered my father: He was my absolute hero. Soon after our lives had returned to "normal," he insisted that we move from Chicago to suburban Evanston. It was the best school system, he told us. With his meager vision, he was able to find his way to our local train station (or, once in a while, spring for a taxicab), traveling downtown to his office in Chicago.

When I was ten, he taught me how to "pick a spot on the backboard," to shoot a basketball off of a backboard he could barely see. That same year, he once got out of bed at five A.M. on a winter morning to help me drag my sled, piled with *Evanston Review*s to be delivered in the middle of a snowstorm. I had come back to the apartment in tears because I couldn't navigate the sled in the snow. Together, we dragged the sled and got the magazines delivered. He had no idea where he was going. He just pulled, and I directed: a blind man and a kid in a snowstorm.

The hard part for me from the time he returned from the hospital was feeling that I'd lost him and the family I'd lived in. I missed him terribly, without ever being able to say it. He could no longer see me the way he had before. It was disconcerting when he looked in my direction, talking to me, and my knowing he wasn't really registering my face.

Worse than all of this, however, was not being able to talk about any of these feelings. To say out loud how we felt about this loss, this disruption of our lives—one that we all needed to grieve—was beyond the emotional capabilities of either of my parents.

My dad's approach to parenting was to model strength and invulnerability. The times that I asked for openness, for him to "see" me emotionally, he drew back, hurt and offended. I think he must have felt disrespected, as though acknowledging this pain was some indictment of a failure on his part to overcome his injury and save his family. He wanted me to be like him—the strong, invulnerable oldest child who would rise above the emotional fray.

As he hid behind his determinedly upbeat demeanor, avoiding anything that would bring up shameful feelings, I gradually came to feel that my only option for a connection with him was to join him in putting on this brave show for the world.

I remember early in his recovery my standing on the corner at Sheridan Road, throwing rocks at cars (not my usual pastime). I must have been pretty desperate, looking for someone to notice how upset I was feeling. A cabdriver slammed on his brakes, got out, and dragged me back to my apartment, making sure my grandmother heard every detail of my dangerous escapade. She decided not to tell my parents because this would upset them.

I think I must have given up the battle somewhere around then. My pain and anger just weren't worth talking about. I'm sure I gave up and decided to enjoy my life as a kid as best I could with my family and friends. And I did just that, while this abscess of pain and denial closed around us all.

An uneasy tension remained between me and my father for many years, I wanting him to listen and talk with me about his and my feelings, and he wanting me to ignore these things and move on. When I went into psychiatry, I could almost feel him cringe: Oh my God, not more emotional discussion, please!

The sad truth, when I think back on our relationship, was that I never really could ask him for what I needed. I felt too guilty. I kept telling myself that what *I* needed must be so insignificant and unworthy in comparison to the suffering *he'd* endured that I wasn't even entitled to ask. I was angry with myself. I drank the Kool-Aid.

Meanwhile, Back at the Friendship Oasis . . .

I was always curious about, and maybe a little jealous of, my dad's friends. He seemed able to relax with them, to be very different from the serious dad I encountered at home. Two of his favorite guy friends were Harry and Nat.

Harry was a shrewd businessman whom my dad admired, and vice versa. Nat was my dad's oldest friend, going all the way back to junior high school, who, like my dad, worked in advertising (yes, during that *Mad Men* era). I liked Nat a lot. There was a kindness in him that came through to me.

After we moved to Evanston, each of these guys would regularly walk or drive over and pick up my dad, and they'd go off together for long walks along Lake Michigan. I was never privy to their conversations, but I could see how upbeat my dad often was when he returned from their outings. While he never went into detail, I could see he was relaxed and energized by their visits.

I spoke with Nat's widow, Phyllis, a former social worker, last year. I asked her what she knew about Nat and my dad's friendship. Had Nat ever talked with her about it?

"I think the important thing," she said, "was that Nat let your dad, Milt, help him. Your dad wanted to feel important to people. Nat, being in the advertising industry, had a lot of questions about his career. He confided in Milt. At the same time, Milt felt comfortable with Nat and trusted him. They'd known each other from when they were kids, with all the problems in your dad's family, and before his . . ."—she hesitated—"eye problems." She didn't say "blindness," either. I felt curiously at home with her here.

She continued. "Your dad didn't have to keep his guard up

so much around Nat. He let Nat drive him around and guide him places."

She suddenly looked at me directly. "You know he was proud of you," making sure I was paying attention. Then, just as quickly, she shifted back to the topic. "But they were good together. They were best of friends; they took care of each other."

She was telling me not to worry. She knew that he and I hadn't had an easy time together, but it was OK. My dad had been OK. He'd had his friends, and he also loved me.

Revising My Own Code

By the end of my young adulthood, I'd made the painful decision to let go of being the person we'd both hoped I would become— that strong, super-responsible son who'd keep the family together while rising above the emotional fray. This role had worn thin. It had already cost me a huge amount of anxiety and depression, struggles in my relationships with both men and women, and, ultimately, a divorce. The cost was too high for me. I was that guy struggling between the two worlds—one of the Male Code and the other that allowed for emotional intimacy.

I began to resign from this failing enterprise sometime in the late 1970s. A therapist I was seeing in Philadelphia met with me and my father. During a long session, he kept asking my father if there was any way he could let me help him. My dad spent much of the hour avoiding answering these questions.

I could tell my dad had been uncomfortable with the personal questions the therapist was asking about his visual limitations and about his relationship with me. The next morning, he came into the kitchen sporting a cheery demeanor as I was cooking breakfast. I was not wearing a shirt, and as he passed me, he grabbed my chest hair "playfully" and yanked. A bolt of pain shot through me, and reflexively—with what must have been a couple of decades of repressed anger—I punched him in the chest. He staggered back, didn't fall. We just stared at each other for a long time. Incredulous, speechless. "That hurt," I finally said. Nothing more passed between us about this event.

I realized later that he'd been angry with me about the therapy session. When he attacked me, though, I'd defended myself. I'd hit him and—my gosh—he didn't go completely blind! I'd unwittingly confronted my worst fear, of expressing my anger with him, and no disaster occurred.

Something began to resolve in me at that point.

"Whew. He's a tough guy," my therapist said when I reported this exchange.

He hesitated. "You've got a really difficult decision to make. Are you going to continue to carry this mountain of grief and sadness on your back so that you can stay in your dad's world—or can you let it go and finally allow yourself to become a real person? Not an easy choice, Rob."

The mountain of grief turned into rivers of tears. I cried long and hard in that session. Afterward, I spoke with a close friend from college who knew my dad. He said about my father, "Yes, true, he's an impressive guy, in his own way. But you don't want to emulate him. You and he are . . ." There was a long pause. "Different." Another pause. Then he added, bluntly, "He's in your way at this point." I appreciated that.

After this, my friendships with other guys began to flourish. I began to open up, not be so hard on myself and others. I found male friends with whom I could be mutually vulnerable. My relationships with women became easier and more satisfying as well.

I kept a distance from my father during this time. Conversations between us during my early to middle thirties were sparse. There were long periods when we didn't talk with each other. Because he had his friends and my mother, I took comfort in knowing that I didn't have to be the person to make things comfortable for him.

This is a period I can look back on and recognize how I introduced a major revision into the Male Code I'd been trying to uphold over the years. The model of parenting that my dad had so heavily relied on—based on emotional restraint, keeping information to himself, showing only strength, wanting to rely solely on himself—no longer worked for me, if it ever had. If I was going to succeed as a real person and have better relationships, including with my own father, I was going to have to start using the intimacy skills I was teaching my patients.

It also occurred to me in my close male friendships that I was finally finding the missing pieces of my relationship with my father—softness and openness *along with* the kind of strength that I so admired in him. Hiking in the mountains with my best friend, Jake, I remember huffing and puffing along a difficult trail while we were talking about how vulnerable we felt when our kids struggled with their own problems. Today, I think how lucky I am to have—*to be able to have*—this kind of friendship.

Turning the Corner

Over time, things softened between my dad and me. I had given up on the notion that I should be able to consistently "rise above the emotional fray." I stopped worrying about whether getting angry (or expressing any vulnerable emotion) would cause my dad to "really" go blind, and I began to relax into being honest with him. We seemed to do better that way.

A few years before he died, while I was visiting him in his house, I called his attention to something he said that I found offensive. He got up and started to walk out of the room.

"Where are you going?" I asked him, surprised.

"I'm angry with you." He turned around, scowling.

"Why?" I asked, amazed that he'd admitted this.

"Because you're angry with *me*," he said. "People who love each other don't get angry with each other."

I was stunned. He'd just articulated the belief that I'd struggled for so many years to come to terms with.

Fortunately, I was now prepared to respond differently.

"No, not at all, Dad," I said gently. "People who love each other get angry with each other *often*—or at least once in a while. It's really OK. It's normal."

He hesitated, and then returned to his chair and sat down. "Well," he said, relaxing, "you ought to know about those things." What I said had put him at ease.

And then we resumed our conversation. We had started to become friends.

FOSTERING FATHERHOOD
IN THE FRIENDSHIP LAB

Men talk about their children and their struggles with parenting quite a bit in our groups. They also talk about how they co-parent with spouses and work out logistical arrangements, as well as their differences in philosophy of child-rearing. There is no doubt that men today take their fathering seriously.

We try to help them identify both their particular strengths and their challenges as parents. As with other issues, we introduce brief exercises and, periodically, mini retreats on fathering.

We first ask men to describe their fathers as parents, how they parented. They share with the other men what they learned about parenting from their dads, what lessons they value, what they try to emulate today, and what they want to change. In this way, they begin to identify a personal "parenting style" based on their experiences and are able to help each other strengthen their relationships with their own kids.

As I described in my story with my father, these men are often able to identify how some perpetuated features of Male Code stand in the way of their having close, positive relationships with their children. This self-evaluation is one you can do by yourself, with a partner or close friend.

Another powerful exercise we do in the group involves asking men to bring in photos and/or objects that their fathers gave them, items that have special meaning to them in their relationship with their dads. Guys have brought in pictures from special trips, baseballs, gloves, cuff links, and ties their fathers gave them, among other things. In this "show and tell," the men share stories, many incredibly touching, about their relationships and their fathers' histories.

Playing to Your Strengths

Ron, a sixty-five-year-old highly successful university official, shared his father's war medals with the group. As he held them up and passed them around, you could see how important they were in his relationship with his dad. "I didn't see much of him as a kid because he traveled a lot, but I remember him telling me how important leadership and courage were when he gave me these." While telling this story, he choked up a little.

Later in the year, Ron was talking with the group about his struggles with his fourteen-year-old son, Brad, who, following a very responsible preadolescence, was now challenging every parental directive and throwing in curse words now and then for effect—all of which drove Ron and his wife crazy. "I've tried to talk with him, see his point of view, connect with him," Ron said, looking really sad. "Nothing is helping. And his mother is restraining herself from going ballistic with him."

Hugh, a fifty-six-year-old sales representative, asked Ron pointedly, "What would *you* do if one of your staff in a meeting said he thought your strategic plan was stupid, refused to take his assignment, and threw in a few expletives for good measure to make his point?"

Ron responded reflexively, "I'd fire him."

"Well, OK, then." Hugh sat back, but then sat up straight again, continuing to shift the frame. "You're saying that you'd at least be willing to send this guy to his room and take away his Xbox." The group cracked up. Ron smiled, too. He got the point.

Hugh added, more seriously, "I was so impressed with your dad's medals. He respected leadership—and that's what you do so well, at least in your work. Maybe Brad needs to see you 'put on' those medals—at least symbolically—the next time you talk to him about his behavior."

Ron completely grasped Hugh's point, and nodded his appreciation.

A Fatherhood Advisory

In raising kids, it's important for men to be able to revise their traditional notions of parenting based on Male Code, and incorporate EI behaviors in their fathering repertoires. This helps guys build stronger, more intimate parenting bonds with their kids.

Here, I'll offer some guidelines that can help you develop a "Fatherhood Advisory," a system for positively sharing information about your kids with your close guy friends.

It doesn't matter if you're a younger or an older father. Expectations have changed for all generations. Young women expect their spouses and partners to participate much more directly with their kids than in the past. Meanwhile, older guys are discovering that parenting responsibilities continue longer today, either with not-quite-launched children who live away from home but aren't financially independent or with those who move back home for a while.

Parenting issues for guys also resurface when they divorce, with their biological children and with stepchildren and with additional offspring if they start new families in later life. In all of these situations, it's good to have male friends, especially if they've had or are having similar experiences, in any life stage of parenting you happen to inhabit.

We've found in our Friendship Labs that fathers repeatedly wrestle with certain themes. You can address these directly with your friends, using the following guidelines:

*1   Begin to Share Your Parenting Experiences with Your Guy
      Friends Early in Fatherhood, and Check in Regularly with
      Each Other About Your Kids.*

Men who parent young children, particularly those who've been
at-home dads, talk enthusiastically about the value of sharing fatherhood tips and events with other guys from the diaper-changing
stage on, and how this has helped them develop their own unique
identities as dads.

Andy, a forty-five-year-old online marketing rep, told me that
when he worked out of his home years ago, he'd functioned as the
primary parent for his toddler kids. During this time, he'd developed "excellent parent networking skills" with some of his
buddies who were then involved in parenting.

"Today, I call and talk with my guy friends about my teenagers, just as much as I do anyone else." He added, "Guess it's
second nature to me by now."

*2   Keep Your Conversations About Your Kids "Real"
      with Your Guy Friends.*

Share with your friends what's going on in your heart, what you're
really feeling about your kids—not just their precocious T-ball
abilities or rate of college acceptances. Remember to ask your guy
friends how they're feeling about what's going on with their own
kids. There are deep opportunities for bonding and support in
these conversations.

One of my patients, David, told me that his best friend Sam's
wife had died of a rapidly spreading form of breast cancer six
months before.

He hadn't heard from Sam for weeks. He'd only seen him

around the neighborhood with his four-year-old daughter, Lisa. David seemed worried about his friend, so I encouraged him to call him and make a date to get together.

"I asked him what was going on," David reported in our next session. "He told me he was worried about Lisa, that she seemed withdrawn, didn't want to eat. Then I asked him how *he* was. He started crying. Actually, we both started crying. He missed his wife terribly. He wondered if he should call a therapist for a consultation for Lisa, maybe for himself as well. I really encouraged him."

3   *Show Your Children Your Own Friendships in Action.*
Letting your children see you with your guy friends (as well as telling them about these friendships) is more heartening for your kids than you might imagine, and encourages them to make good friends of their own. Occasionally inviting your children to join you on special outings with your guy friends—say, for a weekend hiking trip—is not only fun for them but shows them directly how men can connect about parenting.

As I mentioned earlier, I was fascinated by my father's friendships, saw how much he enjoyed these relationships where he got so much support from other men. It encouraged me to want friends of my own as an adult.

My best friend, Jake, and I have shared parenting experiences since our kids were young. We've taken our kids to local parks together, shared Jewish holidays, and enjoyed hiking trips with our families together in the Canadian Rockies. We coached a championship JCC kids' basketball team together with both our sons, Jeremy (his) and Isaac (mine) as starters.

I remember my young daughter, Julie, watching Jake and me at a family event, catching her look of pleasure and admiration as she watched us together. How many times, while talking about her or others' friends, she's said, "She's [or he's] my Jake," referring to a special sense of closeness in the relationship.

When my son, Isaac, was going through a lonely time, he said, "I need a guy friend in my life, like you have in Jake."

"Any candidates?" I asked him. He named a few. "Well, start working on them," I said. "Really good friendships are a project, but you first have to boot them up to get them started." He liked that. All of my kids now have close friendships that they cherish.

4   *Show Interest in and Support Your Kids in Making Strong
      Friendships with Other Children.*

The precious intangible of friendship is its voluntary nature. Kids need to choose their friends, and if these choices are good ones, they will support your child and his or her interests. As a dad, if you're following your child's developing friendships, you may need to take a step back from your own preconceived notions and/or confer with your friends about this. All kids want to belong to and be accepted by their peer group. First, notice how your child is reaching out to others. To what types of people is he drawn? What is she getting from and bringing to her friendships? You will need to inquire and talk to your kids about these important relationships. This is a good way to learn about your child, what her interests and emotional needs are. It's also a way to find out about how healthy their relationships are.

Sometimes, our childhood experience with friendships impinges on our interactions with our children and their friendships. When you sense something is "off" with your child's friendships, or that your judgment might be a little clouded, this can be a good opportunity to confer with a buddy to help get you on track.

John, a forty-eight-year-old health care consultant, was referred to me for problems with his anxiety. He was worried about his twelve-year-old adopted son, Chad, and the friends his son had chosen. After several years of frustrated efforts, John and his committed partner, Andy, had finally been able to adopt Chad, "a beautiful, chocolate-skinned, ten-year-old boy," through a social services agency in Los Angeles. John had gotten my name from his friend Peter, also a gay parent who'd adopted a child.

"The social worker said she felt we'd hit it off," John said proudly. "And that Chad would have a good chance to make it—with a little help from us." A tiny flicker of unease crossed his face. I registered it, with no particular understanding.

Chad was smart and emotionally resilient and had taken strongly to his new parents. His mother, Anna, a kind but unstable drug addict, had been supportive of the adoption. The new family had moved to Philadelphia last year because Andy had been reassigned by his financial services organization.

I felt glad for these guys. Adoption for gay couples remains difficult. Prejudice and suspicion about their "suitability" to parent continues despite the substantial research that shows high levels of adjustment in adopted kids who grow up in gay and lesbian families.

"He sounds like a great kid," I said. "What's the problem with his friends?"

John hesitated, uncomfortable. "They're . . . preppies."

I made a special effort not to smile. John and Andy lived in an upscale section of Center City Philadelphia, and they'd sent Chad to an elite private school on the suburban Main Line.

"Have you talked with your friend Peter about this?" I asked. "He's a gay adoptive dad as well, isn't he?"

He turned red. Clearly, he hadn't.

"Well, that's part of the problem." He hesitated. "It's embarrassing."

I was puzzled.

He continued, "I think you'll get my point. We've made every effort to try to connect Chad with other African American kids, to help him appreciate city culture, his roots. These kids he hangs out with are all white, straight kids. They're all into soccer and lacrosse." He couldn't resist some caustic humor. "They have names like Brock and Chip, and they all go to summer camps on lakes in Maine."

He took a deep breath, looking around, and said quietly, "And their parents are not like our friends. They're Republicans."

I registered his disapproval, but I felt there was something else here that was really bothering John. Chad liked his friends, and they, him. When he'd had the boys over to their house, John said they seemed like "good kids" and they obviously enjoyed playing with each other.

"They know Chad has gay parents?" I asked, assuming this.

"Yes. He says they're cool with it. No big deal."

"So what's really going on for you about all this?" I asked.

He paused, took a deep breath. "I want Chad to feel connected with who he *really is*. Not to have to hide in some mainstream charade. My parents wanted me to be like the other kids, to play sports, be interested in girls, be in clubs. I wanted to be with gay kids, to go to the Getty exhibits, and go to different kinds of clubs. It was horrible." He looked depressed. "I want Chad . . . to be happy." Clearly, John had not been happy as a teenager. I gave his mood a chance to make its point.

"Is he happy?" I asked. Then I stopped myself. I looked at John. "You don't . . . do you think Chad's gay?"

He laughed. "Not if you watch him ogling the older teenage girls when we're walking through Rittenhouse Square. Either that or he's a good actor. No, I think he really *is* happy." He was floating on this thought.

I could have said more but thought it would more useful at this point to urge him to talk with his friend Peter. "My bet is he'll know exactly what you're talking about. Give it a try?" He shuddered slightly, but said OK.

He returned the next week more relaxed. "Well, Peter didn't mince words," he said, looking sheepish but smiling. "'Could it be that Chad's happy *differently* than you think he should be?' he asked me. He pointed out that Chad's friends certainly wouldn't have worked for us. But for Chad, these guys may be just the friends he needs now." John looked up at me. "You can't imagine how relieved I was to hear him say this."

Actually, I could imagine it. I chimed in. "Plus, Chad's not really deprived of exposure to 'life outside the mainstream' or to his own roots, is he?" I smiled at John. "Your son lives with two gay dads—whom he loves—who prefer art galleries to Phillies games, who march with the Rainbow Coalition, and, if I heard correctly, volunteer in the city's Tree Philly program."

John was starting to look more relieved.

"It really helped to talk with Peter. He helped me chill about Chad. He also told me about their older adopted son, Rashid, whom they'd had to get into therapy because—can you believe this?— he'd just been cut from his high school football team!"

He raised his eyebrows. "It's a different world out there for us gay fathers today, isn't it?" We both chuckled.

5   *Recognize That Your Role as a Father Evolves as Your*
     Children Grow Older, and Find Ways to Continue to Mentor
     Them. Again, Compare Notes with Your Buddies.

Fathering is a lifelong experience. If a man is deeply engaged with his children, connected in his heart, he can choose to stay emotionally in touch with them throughout his life; he does this by sharing day-to-day experiences and life challenges with them through conversations.

These conversations are an important part of what I call the *mentoring* role for dads. I think of mentoring as an aspect of parenting that begins when boys and girls are first preparing for independence in late adolescence and remains critical through their early thirties, when many young adults take on the roles of committed partners and parents.

Of course, if we're around long enough as dads, we can mentor our kids in later life stages as well.

Mentoring implies teaching not simply through intellectual or practical instruction but also by eliciting and sharing emotional experience relevant to the person's needs. It's an evolving process that requires balance in addressing a young person's need for both independence and emotional connection.

Male Code has encouraged fathers of past generations to "let the boy or girl swim on their own," usually at the leaving-home stage, somewhere around eighteen. Fathers are often more rigid with their sons about this issue.

Young people need more than "just time," however. Today's fathers, unpracticed in this kind of extended support, often flounder, caught between their Dumbo ("Ignore the kid, he'll get by") and Machismo ("You'd better set him straight") dementors. These extreme attitudes don't translate very well in practice.

The most difficult emotional obstacles for most fathers are usually those associated with feelings of separation and loss, the awkwardness of how to stay connected when the child has left the physical space and is working on becoming independent.

A fifty-five-year-old patient, whose twenty-two-year-old son, Ronnie, was returning from a drug rehabilitation program for a brief stay at home before returning to college, had trouble persuading the young man to follow through on his AA meetings. The man's own father had died during his teenage years, so he'd never had the advantage of "fatherly oversight" when he left for college. A close friend who'd supported his own daughter through rehab sympathized with him. "This must be really hard for you, with Ronnie, because you had no dad around to help you or ask how *you* felt at his age."

My patient told me he took much support from this comment. He pushed forward with his son, driving him to the meetings. On the way, they talked about a lot of things, one being how uncomfortable Ronnie felt about running into people he knew at these meetings. This allowed his dad to suggest, "If that doesn't feel good, let's find some other meetings where you don't know anyone." His son felt incredibly relieved when he heard this.

A year later, when his son was doing well in college, he reminded his dad of how important that exchange was, and how grateful he was to his dad for hanging in there with him through his recovery.

Emotional mentoring should not be confused with the current trend toward "helicopter parenting," or overinvolvement—as with parents who call their children's college professors to complain about their kids' test results. Nor is it the opposite—the rigid advice of an older, "wiser" person who's "been there, done that" but doesn't know how to listen.

What your sons or daughters need from you is for you to stay connected with them. If they're away at school or have moved away from home, remember to keep in contact with them. Initiating occasional visits helps. In these contacts, be sure you ask them what they're feeling and listen for the answer. If they end up soliciting advice, you're better prepared and you know what to do.

Does this remind you of the material I discussed in Chapter 7, "Staying the Course," on how to maintain a friendship? It's supposed to, because when your mentoring works well with your children, these relationships begin to feel like true friendships over the years.

Dads can help each other by reminding one another that your kids need to know you're on their side. You may not have dealt with the kind of issues they're going through, but they should know you're willing to listen and share your experience with them. That's pure gold.

6 *Parenting While Going Through a Divorce Can Be Lonely and Painful. Share This Experience with a Guy Friend Whether You're Offering or Asking for Support from Him.*

Friends especially need help when they're going through a family crisis or divorce. Here, a man is trying to hold things together when they're falling apart. He wants to support and stay connected with his children, while his relationship with his spouse feels bruised and distant.

Family therapists have described divorce as an alternative path in the family life cycle. This is because family structure and emotions change so dramatically. Children, involved in 60 percent of divorces, can move from initial stages of disruption to single-parent situations and, for young ones at least, into a stepfamily situation—all within a small number of years.

Divorce is never pleasant for children, and most dads worry about how they're going to adjust. Kids will differ in how they react at these various stages, but psychologist Connie Ahrons's book *The Good Divorce* is still one of the wisest, most valuable guides for helping divorcing parents establish healthy postdivorce situations for their children. She describes how divorced parents can establish binuclear families (two cooperating households) and "limited partnerships" (parental relationships that positively focus on the children's well-being and don't get distracted by old emotional baggage).

Most kids do eventually recover from their parents' divorce, but this can take time. Fathers are often surprised by their children's reactions when their kids don't react similarly or respond at the same pace as the adults do in adjusting to losses. My own prior research indicated that children in stepfamilies frequently demonstrated delayed loss-related reactions. These included dashed hopes for their biological parents reuniting, losing access to a single parent when a new person comes on the scene, and fears that a remarried parent may get divorced again. Discovering their children's fears stupefied newlywed stepparents!

Fathers who've been through divorce are often surprised that their kids react so strongly when a new partner, particularly one they think might be a "keeper," enters the scene. Professional consultation about kids and divorce can be helpful. It's good, however, to have friends you can speak with, to help you fasten your seat belt if your kids are adolescents and you bring your new girlfriend onto the scene. Here, their experience—and your patience—may help stem the tide of disruption when you, your children, and your new love enter a new family system.

Daniel (whom I mentioned earlier, in Chapter 4) was a fifty-three-year-old divorced businessman and a single parent of two teenagers. He joined our Friendship Lab looking for support about how to handle conflicts with his children that had erupted when he recently announced he'd invited his girlfriend, Kate, to move into their apartment.

The kids said they wouldn't stay with him. Daniel was hurt and enraged, since up to that point, they'd seemed to like Kate. Also, he'd had a civil co-parenting relationship with his ex-wife, Angela, but now she seemed chilly about his decision and was offering little support in handling his problem with the children.

Daniel was livid in the group. He felt undermined, blindsided by his kids' reactions and his wife's ingratitude. "After divorcing me, my continuing to support our family, taking care of the kids—now when some happiness finally comes my way, she—all of them really—can't find it in their hearts to support me."

Ed, a man who had weathered a similar breakup years ago, said to Daniel, trying to comfort him, "I know how you feel. When Sally [his second wife] and I first got together, my kids wouldn't give her the time of day. Now they love her, and we all have a great time together. But these things take time, and you can't make them go faster than they go."

He added, "From what you've said, it took a long time for you and Angela to get divorced, with a lot of pain along the way. Maybe it's worth taking a little more time, to let something really good develop with Kate and your kids." He hesitated. "You need to talk more with them about this."

Daniel took both comfort and direction from Ed's words.

He and Kate decided to hold off on her moving in. Kate was OK with this. Daniel's kids immediately calmed down and returned to his apartment.

"They told me they felt pushed about Kate's moving in," Daniel reported back to the group. "That I'd never told them. Then Andrea [his daughter] told me she was afraid they were going to *lose me* if Kate and I got married." He choked up, shaking his head in disbelief. "Wow, there's a lot we need to talk about."

As Daniel, Kate, and the kids took things more slowly, their relationship progressed. A few months later, over dinner at a local pizzeria, Andrea and her brother, Josh, proposed they all go back to the apartment to watch the Twilight series together. While there, Andrea took Kate around the apartment, asking her, "Where are you going to put your clothes when you move in?"

Daniel conveyed the story in the next group. He was delighted—and much calmer. "I'm coming around to the words of the immortal Mick Jagger: 'Time is on my side,' or it seems to be if I can be patient." A lot of heads nodded affirmatively.

CHAPTER 11

The Executive Committee

Your Guy Friends in the Workplace

For many men, the workplace is still our primary proving ground. It's where we feel most "on the line" as guys, pushed to demonstrate whether we can earn our financial due, provide well for our families, achieve some power, and, if we're really good, win the respect of others. Job success is a direct line to our beliefs about what it means to be a "real man."

Today's workplace is a rapidly changing environment.

The values of old Male Code still prevail in most work settings, which are governed by an atmosphere of privacy protection, emotional restraint, competitiveness, and an emphasis on separating the personal from the professional.

But many employers, as well as researchers, are starting to

advocate for making the workplace a more personal, user-friendly environment. In some cases, this involves encouraging workers to develop close friendships. There may be both psychological and economic advantages to this notion. Christine Riordan at the University of Kentucky writes, "Camaraderie is more than just having fun. . . . It is also about creating a common sense of purpose and the mentality that we are in it together. . . . [It] promotes a group loyalty that results in a shared commitment to and discipline toward the work."

A 2012 Gallup report found that employees who had a best friend at work were five times more likely to feel a strong connection with their company than those who didn't have a best friend. Other studies show that when employees have close friends at work, they are more satisfied and productive and stay longer at their jobs, and the company is better able to attract other good employees. Encouraging a friendship-friendly work setting could be a way that employers help reduce the alarming rise in stress of American workers due to low wages and heavy workloads.

Men are struggling with these changes. They bounce between the rigid pressures of old Male Code at work and new expectations for openness and transparency. If they're to be more expressive of their feelings, how much expression is permissible without being inappropriate? If team cooperation and inclusiveness is in, how much independent action are they allowed to take to move a project forward? If there's a perceived infraction with a coworker or boss, what's the best way to handle it?

DEVELOPING A PERSONAL EXECUTIVE COMMITTEE IN THE WORKPLACE

Historically, guys seeking support with work-related issues have looked to their wives or partners or, in some cases, friends, all of whom have little or no direct knowledge of the situations with which they struggle in their jobs. Just as often, however, they keep their stress inside, leaving themselves susceptible to emotional and physical symptoms.

I've found over the years that it helps to develop a group of close friends that can support you with work issues. I call this a Personal Executive Committee (PEC). This kind of workplace posse may include guys who work along with you in your company or men who are friends outside of work but have knowledge and experience with the kinds of issues you may struggle with on the job.

First and foremost, you want the men in your PEC to be friends, not simply acquaintances. These are guys who truly care about your well-being, beyond what is merely useful for them. They understand the stakes involved in the tough work issues you face. They understand the shame that can accompany unpleasant exposure in the workplace. They provide safety, caring, and good ideas. Our own survey confirmed that closer guy friendships are more likely to provide you with real support in the workplace.

It's not required that you socialize with all the members of your PEC outside of work. In some situations, this group might include a boss, a colleague, an employee, and, of course, women. The important thing is that they are *friends* and that, whatever your positions, your relationship respectfully honors the boundaries in your workplace.

My enthusiasm about developing workplace friendships has evolved over many years, often as a result of difficulties that arose for me in the work setting. When I was a young academic, running a family therapy training program, I ran into problems with students and faculty that I didn't know how to handle. I needed to identify and speak with colleagues whom I trusted, to garner their support, before I could make some difficult decisions as a director.

Later, when I was in private practice, I ran into problems with violent, psychotic, seriously ill, and suicidal patients or others who were litigious. In these situations as well, I gathered together and relied on the support and counsel of my PEC. In each case, trusted friends helped me settle myself down and handle the situations with good judgment. These were situations in which I felt not only out of my depth in experience but also sensitive about bringing my uncertainties to others. In any of these circumstances, it's a man's isolation that makes him most vulnerable, whatever the specific problems that arise.

Activating Your Personal Executive Committee

Let's examine how a PEC might work for you. Below, I give you some tips about assembling members of a trusted work posse— how to identify them, how to keep them posted, on alert about yourself and your work situation, and how to deal with conflict as it might arise between you and any of these guy friends. In addition, I describe and give case examples of common issues that a strong PEC can help you address at work.

1   *Assembling Your Posse*

There is no clear rulebook for identifying the guys who will eventually be in your PEC. As I indicated in chapters 6 and 7, learning who your close friends are or can be takes both attention and intention. First, notice whom you like, whom you feel you can trust, who has the ability to speak from the heart, and, not least of all, who is a good listener.

Second, you need to reach out yourself, to share something personal or ask for help, to be willing to make yourself a little vulnerable. At the same time, offering support, inquiring about the other man if you notice he's down, or if you've heard something important is going on in his life, is also important. Putting your toe in the water to see if you get positive responses from these exchanges is critical. This is how PECs develop. Hopefully, you have the chance to observe and get to know these guys before a crisis comes knocking that forces you to grasp for support.

Sometimes, problems arise at work in completing an expected task or tasks that are especially difficult to resolve. The difficulty may reside within the context of the work setting because of, say, inadequate resources or staff to complete the tasks, or because of an obstructive or critical supervisor.

Alternatively, our own physical or emotional problems, or those of others in our personal lives, can spill into our work lives. These may be associated with feelings of shame, discomfort, or inadequacy, feelings we're reluctant to share at work. Having a PEC available that you can confer with can help save the day for you and get you back on track for managing your responsibilities.

Dennis was a twenty-eight-year-old law student who'd struggled for many years with undiagnosed obsessive-compulsive disorder

(OCD). He was smart, but people assumed he was "quirky and disorganized." During college, he finally got properly diagnosed and started taking medication and receiving therapy.

About to start his first year of law school, he came to me in a panic, fearing he'd never be able to get through the writing assignments in his classes. He was a brilliant logician, a great debater, but became hopelessly mired down when it came to writing papers and reports. His old cognitive behavior therapist in Chicago was furiously sending him articles about how to improve his efficiency in this area. He confessed that he didn't have time to read them.

I asked him if anyone in his program knew about his OCD. Turning bright red, he said he hadn't revealed this to anyone there. He didn't want people to feel sorry for him or think of him as a deficient professional. I told him it was standard practice in training programs in Philadelphia to work out plans with capable graduate professional students like him who had these organizational problems, and that with support, he'd be able to master the writing assignments.

The only thing he had to do, I told him, was to assemble a support group. I explained the concept of a PEC to him to help him with all of this. I told him I'd work with him on it.

He stared at me in terror. Then said, feebly, "When am I going to get the time to call these people?"

I just stared at him blankly. Then, after a long, purposeful pause, I said, "OK, let's do the math. On one hand, you've got to make a few phone calls and have a few meetings to help expedite your progress. On the other hand, you can go it alone—and continue to spend weeks, months, even years in the living hell of shame and avoidance you're already inhabiting. Hmm. What do you think?"

He cracked up, in spite of himself. "You make a strong point," he said, buttoning himself back up.

Over the next couple of weeks, Dennis identified a friend from college, Harris, now a second-year law student who he felt "knew the ropes" of the program. He also identified a law school faculty mentor, Professor Healy, who'd interviewed him and strongly encouraged him to come to the program, and with whom he felt he "had a good vibe." Finally, there was an older family friend, Stewart, who worked in human resources at another university and was one of the few people who knew about his OCD. Dennis was still skeptical about this approach, mostly the part that involved exposing himself to others, but began to make these contacts.

After a month, he was much more enthusiastic. Stewart had confirmed my statement that law schools regularly helped students with these issues. He said he knew of other lawyers who had been assisted in these matters. He'd urged him to speak with Professor Healy about working out a plan for him. Dennis had already made the appointment to see his old mentor.

His friend, Harris, had invited him to stop by and talk about his questions. "I didn't tell him about my OCD diagnosis—yet. Maybe I will," Dennis reflected.

But Harris had turned him on to a note-sharing program that the students had organized themselves for those who wanted to attend classes without having to write notes. He told Dennis how to enroll in the program. He'd smiled and told Dennis, "Something tells me this is going to make your day."

Dennis passed on this smile to me. "He was not wrong." He told me that he and Harris had scheduled to meet up for beers that afternoon.

As a leader or head of an organization, you may feel just as vulnerable, even more so, when personal problems arise and you haven't developed a PEC within your own company.

Ken, a forty-eight-year-old managing director of a venture capital firm reported that he'd had a disturbing blowup that morning in a meeting with his senior managers.

Ken was going through a painful divorce with his wife, Adrienne. He hadn't shared any of the details with his partners at work because, he said, "I have to maintain a position of calm and control to keep us all focused. I don't want these guys to be distracted because of my personal problems." That morning in the meeting, he'd hurled his coffee cup across the room for no apparent reason. He'd been up late arguing with his wife the night before. His partners were stunned by his surprising and unexpected behavior.

"So much for your maintaining calm and control," Ralph, one of the guys in his men's group, said sardonically to Ken. Then he added, supportively, "You're going to need to talk to your partners, at least a few of them, about what's going on—if you don't want things to degenerate at work. Aren't there at least a couple guys you trust?" Ken shook his head affirmatively and mentioned Al, one of his VPs, and Steve, their chief accountant, both guys he liked and trusted. Ralph said, "You'd better make your phone calls to these guys this afternoon."

Ken did so, and felt touched when both men responded to him, asked to meet with him that day to find out how they could support him through this difficult time. Steve shared that he had been through a rough divorce several years earlier: "We're going to need to have some regular lunches over the next six months, my friend," Steve told him.

"Sign me up," Ken responded. He paused, and added, "No more food fights, I promise."

Steve jumped right back at him. "Hold the coffee, right?"

2   Staying in Contact with Your PEC

I discussed the importance of staying in regular contact with your friends in Chapter 7. The same holds for the men in your PEC. Situations can develop rapidly at work, and if you've been in good contact with your work buddies, some of these can be managed skillfully, with ongoing consultation before they develop into full-blown crises.

Inappropriate behavior or boundary violations involving work responsibilities, interpersonal contact with colleagues, staff and/or bosses, or personal attitudes based on family and cultural values can all cause stress. Sexual harassment, physical or mental abuse, and stealing are among the more serious boundary violations you should steer clear of and protect yourself (and others) from. Whether you're on the receiving end or if you sense you may be viewed as a perpetrator, it's good to attend to the cues and discuss this with the guys in your PEC. The sooner the better.

Alex had just been hired as a junior manager for a large insurance company. His wife, Jeannie, was about to deliver their first child. Alex, now forty-two, found himself the sole breadwinner in the family for the first time since they'd married. He was anxious to succeed in his firm.

Things seemed to go well at first between him and his boss, Pam. After a few weeks, however, she was beginning to give him "extra-long looks" at their meetings and was asking him to work late in the office. Alex, a "pleaser," was uncomfortable but didn't say anything. He spoke to his good friend Mark, who worked in another department in their firm, who told him about a rumor that Pam and her husband had recently separated.

Over the next two weeks, Alex tried politely to refuse Pam's requests for him to stay late and discuss "work" issues, which had now expanded into more personal topics. Pam was insistent, however, saying they had to "dig in," that there were important deadlines, and she wanted him to be in "a good position" when discussion of promotions came up.

Alex called his friend Herby, a lawyer, who was alarmed. "This could be a real disaster, pal," Herby said. Herby researched current employment law and urged Alex to begin to takes notes on his exchanges with Pam, and to meet with her only in public places. If her pressuring continued, Herby said, Alex was going to have to confront her, and he referred Alex to literature on how to have these kinds of conversations with a boss.

The following week, Pam asked Alex to stay later one evening. He called her to cancel that afternoon, having forgotten that he and Jeannie were scheduled to go out for an anniversary dinner. She blew up at him, saying he wasn't committed to his job.

Alex called Pam the next morning and asked to meet with her privately in the conference room. He was anxious, but he was prepared after a long phone call with Herby and Mark the evening before.

When they met, he told her in a firm but respectful way that he appreciated working with her, benefited from their collaboration, and enjoyed working in the firm. But, he added, he didn't feel she was respecting his marriage and his family life. She'd been ignoring him when he told her he couldn't work late. He didn't want this to get out of hand and cause problems in their work together.

Pam was quiet while he was talking. Her face gave away no emotion. As Alex spoke, his fingers tapped nervously on a sheaf of papers he had brought with him describing their interactions. He never mentioned these, but Pam glanced down at them intermittently. She seemed to be deliberating, taking in the whole picture. When he finished, she nodded and said she wanted to think about what he said, and that they'd meet to discuss this further the next day.

When they met the next morning, Pam was more formal, but she jumped right in, in a congenial tone. "I've thought this over," she said, "and I think you might be more comfortable working with one of our other senior partners, someone with a different . . . management style." Alex had rehearsed this as a possible response with Herby and Mark the previous evening. He expressed sincere disappointment, and asked her if she was angry with him or dissatisfied with his work in any way. Absolutely not, she said with a smile, and he noticed a slight quiver in her voice.

She agreed to write an evaluation of his work that he could review with his next manager and wished him good luck. As she turned to leave the meeting, Alex had a vague sense that she was also relieved.

He got a call from another senior manager the next day. They met, and things seemed to go well. He heard that week that Pam had decided to take some vacation time away from the office.

When I heard this story from Alex, I thought he was fortunate to get away with such a "soft landing." Things often take a more defensive and retaliatory direction in these workplace situations. We both agreed that the support and preparation he got from Mark and Herby, his PEC, had been a powerful backstop preventing his slide into deeper peril in this work relationship.

3   Managing and Protecting Your PEC

A close-knit friendship posse in your workplace can be a beautiful thing. Conflicts can arise, however, in and about these relationships. Some of the principles I discuss on friendship first aid in Chapter 8 apply with your friends in the workplace. You may want to consider how to apply them when problems arise.

Two typical kinds of situations occur with members of your PEC. When they do, it can be good to confer with "alternates," other friends within the group, to help alleviate or correct these internal rifts.

The first has to do with issues of *favoritism*. It's one thing to want to confer with and spend time with your trusted friends. But when you and another member of your PEC are seen together all the time, particularly if one or both of you is in a position of leadership or authority, jealousy or feelings of exclusion are likely to arise with your coworkers or employees.

As "high school" as this behavior sounds, it's common in workplace settings. A patient told me she wasn't reporting to her supervisor lately because she'd observed him hanging out regularly with a coworker for whom she had an intense dislike. She suspected they gossiped about her.

Awareness of this dynamic can nip these problems in the bud, or at least reduce the odds of their having a destructive impact. Make a point to separate your work-related activities from informal social get-togethers, or hanging out together with PEC buddies on company time.

Second, practice *transparency* and *inclusion* by including other employees and colleagues in everyday meetings, and particularly those that involve important decision making. This allows your PEC to maintain its discreet presence while protecting yourself and these relationships from unnecessary criticism or controversies. Offices work better this way.

More difficult is when you and a member of your PEC become embroiled in a *personal conflict*, a competitive situation at work or a personal argument unrelated to the job. These conflicts have a great potential to spill into your work environment and disrupt operations.

Leo, a fifty-five-year-old executive and owner of a sporting goods company, described a situation of years ago, when he was a young man in Miami just starting out, working in a chain of athletic equipment stores.

"There were two of us, me and Carlos. We were the junior managers, and there was another guy, Javier, a little older, who was the senior manager. We were all good friends who'd known each other since we were kids. They called us the Three Musketeers.

"Carlos and I made the store run. We were constantly pushing each other with ideas and promotions. We had this amazing creative energy, and Javier was always bragging about how our numbers were higher than any of the other stores in Miami. We were having a great time together.

"One spring, a position in the company for senior manager became available and Javier put in both of our names for consideration. Neither I nor Carlos thought we'd get it. So it was a shock when Javier came in one morning, called us both into his office, and told us that Carlos had been chosen for the position. I remember that Javier was excited and uncomfortable at the same time. I tried to act excited but had this nasty rumbling in the pit of my stomach that I wanted to disappear. Carlos smiled gratefully, but he seemed restrained to me.

"When Javier announced the promotion over the loudspeakers

in the store, and our staff was all clapping, I remember feeling a little down.

"The next week, it was like a depression took over. Everyone knew Carlos was going to be transferred, but not when or where. The energy seemed to drain out of our store, and things started to unravel. Customers looked confused, they suddenly didn't know where to find things, and the staff was slow to respond. Orders were getting lost and it seemed communications had broken down.

"I don't think that I realized until then how much our store had run on the energy that the three of us—me, Carlos, and Javier—had generated. And the three of us weren't talking with each other very much that week.

"Finally, one of our employees, Maria, who'd been at the cash register for many years, came up to me and said, 'What happened? Did someone die?'

"Carlos, Javier, and I realized we had to get together and have a heart-to-heart. The whole place was falling apart, and it was because of this promotion. We had to get our—you know what—together!

"When we sat down by ourselves, I spoke first. I admitted that I felt bad. I was proud and happy for Carlos. But I didn't really want him to leave. And OK, I was jealous also. How come he got the promotion and I didn't?

"Carlos, for his part, said he was embarrassed, that he didn't deserve it more than I did. He was thinking of turning it down. He was serious! We both told him he was a jackass.

"Then we turned to Javier, with the question no one wanted to ask. What was his role in this decision? We knew he'd been asked for his input. Where did he come down?

"Javier shrugged. 'I told them it should be both of you. Really,

I couldn't vote. I took myself out of this.' He looked sad. There was a long silence. But the tension that had kept us apart seemed to have dissolved.

"Then Javier looked up at me, with mock seriousness, and said, 'I think they chose him because he's better-looking than you. You might need a little work done on your face . . . you know?' I told him what he could do with that advice. Carlos laughed. We all laughed.

"'OK, Gregory Peck,' I said to him. 'You can buy us all lunch on your new salary.'"

"That's a great story, Leo," I said. "Thanks." I couldn't resist inquiring, "So where is everyone today?"

"They all have their stores in Miami." He sat back, spreading his arms out broadly. "And I guess you can see, I haven't done so badly—after that great disappointment!"

Epilogue

Jake and I are standing on the edge of the ridge of Ha Ling Peak in the Canadian Rockies. The final fifty yards of the ascent on loose scree have left us sweating and gasping. He pulls out his water bottle and offers me a swig.

In front of us is a magnificent view of the front ranges of these mountains. Below us is a three-thousand-foot sheer drop to the town of Canmore.

I hold up the bottle. "A toast!"

"To friendship," he responds.

A wind is picking up as we're waiting for our heart rates to settle down. I'm studying the water bottle.

"So if you could bottle friendship, put all the ingredients— trust, openness, loyalty, pleasure, all of that—into a bottle, and every man on the planet could drink from this, how do you think that would change our world?"

It's a credit to our friendship that Jake doesn't roll his eyes when I ask rangy questions like this one. He usually takes them seriously.

"Well, you have the data. More guys would be healthy, they'd have better relationships with their partners and kids, and get along better at work, right?"

"Yeah, but what about the big-ticket items—war, poverty, responsible politics, violence against women—those things?"

He takes a deep breath, trying to wrap his head around the question. "I don't know about those things. But I think men would feel safer, could relax more, and wouldn't have to work so hard to prove themselves. I think more men would have happier lives." He shrugs.

That small movement causes him to temporarily lose his balance. He starts to slide on the rocks. Our eyes lock as I grab his arm to steady him.

As our breath returns, I add, for comic relief, "And live longer?"

"That, too," he agrees heartily.

THE MALE FRIENDSHIP AND EMOTIONAL INTIMACY (MFEI) SURVEY

AN INITIAL REPORT

The following is the first published report of a national survey on men's friendships and emotional intimacy. The report was written by Robert Heasley, PhD, Robert Garfield, MD, and John Anderson, PhD. Other investigators involved in the survey are Isaac Garfield, MSS, LCSW, Jacob Kriger, MSS, and Suzanne McMurphy, PhD.

BACKGROUND

Introduction to the Study

The Men's Friendship and Emotional Intimacy (MFEI) Survey was designed to understand how males experience their closest male friendships. Specifically, we were interested in the extent to which males eighteen and older experience emotionally close same-sex friendships and the extent of interaction that men have with those friends. We were also interested in how men experience those relationships, how they interact with their closest male friends, and in what context. Is it through shared interests in sports, for instance, or through an intention to have someone in their lives to talk with about problems and challenges they are facing? When and how men stay in contact with their closest friends were among the questions included in the survey, as were questions about how these friendships influenced the quality of men's lives overall.

The Research Team

The study was initiated through the leadership of psychiatrist Robert Garfield, MD, and his son, Isaac Garfield, MSS, LCSW, based on their interests as clinicians in gaining an understanding of the friendships in men's lives. The research team included Jake Kriger, MSS, a therapist who primarily sees male clients, Robert Heasley, PhD, and John Anderson, PhD, both professors of sociology at Indiana University of Pennsylvania (IUP). Heasley is also a marriage and family therapist, and Anderson is director, Administration and Leadership Studies Research and Training Center at IUP. Suzanne McMurphy, PhD, assistant professor in the School of Social Work at the University of Windsor in Windsor, Ontario, Canada, also contributed to development of the survey questions.

The study was conducted with the support of Indiana University of Pennsylvania, which granted approval through their Institutional Review Board (IRB) for the Protection of Human Subjects. John Anderson performed the primary data analysis.

Research Design

The research was conducted via an online survey developed through SurveyMonkey. Survey respondents were males over eighteen years of age randomly selected through SurveyMonkey's panel database. The respondent pool was selected with the intention of gaining a representative sample of males with a range of backgrounds in age, race, and income and education levels of the national population. Respondents were asked to complete the survey online. Of the 400 responses, a total of 381 surveys were completed adequately for analysis.

About the Respondents

The men who completed the survey ranged in age from 18 to 87, with an average age of 36.5. While the majority of respondents were white, nearly 9% identified as Hispanic/Latino, 8% as Black/African American, 2.5% as Asian, 2% as Biracial, 1.3% as American Indian, less than 1% as Middle Eastern, and less than 1% as Native Hawaiian/Pacific Islander.

Slightly over 90% of respondents identified as heterosexual, while 8% identified as homosexual or bisexual. Those identifying as "questioning" their sexual orientation, or as "other," and those identifying as "asexual" were less than 1% in each category.

Slightly more men identified as single (42.5%) than those who indicated they were married (41.5%). Other respondents indicated they were in a committed relationship (7.5%), divorced or separated (8%), or had a civil union (1%). Less than 1% indicated they were widowed.

The income of these men covered a broad range, with 16.5% indicating their income category to be $0 to $20,000, and close to 24% as between $21,000 and $40,000. Approximately 28% of the men had incomes between $41,000 and $75,000, and 24% had incomes between $76,000 and $125,000. An additional 6% of the men had incomes between $126,000 and $200,000 while a few, just 2%, had incomes over $200,000.

Nearly 28% of respondents were college graduates, while an additional 11% had a postgraduate degree. Those with some college or technical school in their background represented 42.9% of respondents, and 17.3% completed high school without having post–high school education. A small portion, 1.6%, had some or less than some high school education, but did not graduate.

The majority of our respondents identified with having some religious identity, with a little over 26% indicating they were Catholic and 25% saying they were Protestant; 23% indicated "other" when asked about what category of religion best represented them, nearly 10% indicated they were atheist, 8.5% said they were agnostic, and 4% identified as Jewish. Muslim, Buddhist, and Hindu were each 1% or less of those responding.

What Men Said About Their Friendships

The survey asked men questions about their closest male friendships. We started by asking them to list their three closest friends. All but one of the men taking the survey indicated they had at least one close male friend. However, fewer (85%) indicated they had at least two close male friends, and 78% said they had at least three close male friends. Another way to look at this data is to realize that nearly 25% of men have only one or two close friends— suggesting both the limited numbers of close friends in men's lives and the importance these friendships may have.

We asked men to think about these particular friendships when answering the survey questions. For instance, we asked how much contact they had with each of these friends and what they talked about or activities they did together. The survey also asked how relations with these three best friends changed over time due to such transitions as moving, changes in jobs, or getting married and having children.

Next, the respondents were asked to share what value they placed on these friendships. For instance, we asked each what impact these relationships had on their lives and whether respondents had a desire for more close friendships, or a desire to get closer to the friends they reported having. Along with these questions, we asked about the respondents' perceptions about the quality of their fathers' friendships with other men, and the relationship respondents had in terms of emotional closeness with their father or significant male figure. Some of what we learned is reported below.

Extent of Emotional Intimacy

The study used seven criteria as indicators of emotional intimacy. These were:

1   *Emotional expressiveness*—sharing personal feelings such as contentment, happiness, sadness, frustration, or fear

2   *Self-disclosure*—whether men revealed intimate details about themselves or about their relationships

3   *Vulnerability*—the likelihood that the respondents could or would be willing to share their weaknesses with their closest male friends

4   *Giving and getting emotional support*—whether there was a sense of mutual exchange

5   *Cooperation*—whether men felt there was a willingness between them and their close friends to compromise and work toward common goals

6   *Reciprocity*—whether men felt there was a balance of giving and taking in the relationship

7   *Physical affection*—such behaviors as hugging or comforting each other in some way that included physical touch

Respondents told us whether these qualities were part of their closest friendships, using a scale of 1 (not a significant part of the relationship) to 5 (a strong part of the relationship). When we combined the scores for men's responses to all seven categories, we found that 43% of men had at least a medium level of these qualities in their relationships, meaning they were likely to have a combined score at the medium range (3) on the 5-point scale.

An additional 20% of males had combined scores suggesting they had what we saw as medium-high levels of intimacy, and another 12% experienced high levels of qualities associated with emotional intimacy in their friendships—having a combined score of 4 or 5 on the scale. This group, which totaled 32% of those taking the survey, was most likely to share intimate feelings and experiences with their closest male friends. Their friendships were more than just being "buddies"—guys who get together for activities such as work or play. Rather, these relationships reflected what we think of as being emotionally intimate. Such relationships allow males to express personal aspects of their lives that might be difficult to share with most others.

At the lower end of responses, 13% of males scored at the low-medium level, and an additional 12% had combined scores that indicated a very low level of emotional intimacy in their friendships. This suggests that a quarter (25%) of the men participating in the survey have little experience of emotional intimacy in their close friendships.

What Men Say About Their Experience

The men with close male friendships valued their experience. Just over 25% said their close male friendships were more important to them than other close relationships, for instance with family members, while 40% of the men indicated that their closest male friends provided support and helped them in their current or recent romantic relationships. We also found that the more emotional closeness men had with their male friends, the more they desired to both increase their number of male friends and deepen the emotional intimacy with male friends they currently have. Slightly over 60% of the men said they wanted greater emotional closeness in their same-sex friendships. When we asked about what specifically men wanted, 33% said they wanted to give and get more support from their closest male friends, while 18% indicated they wanted a greater level of vulnerability. We saw the same types of responses from men regardless of their age; thus young, middle-aged, and older males appear to share the desire for close friendships.

How Males Rely on Male Friends

When it comes to emotionally close friendships, we found that as the level of emotional intimacy with male friends increases, the odds of getting help on a number of levels increases.

This in itself is not a surprise, perhaps, but is important when it comes to appreciating the benefits of seeking out and maintaining emotionally close relationships.

We asked men to respond to questions about times when they feel they have support in a number of areas, from work issues to concerns about relationships and sexuality. Consistently, males with greater intimacy in their male friendships had higher levels of support, regardless of other differences among those responding to the survey, such as age, race, or social class background.

For instance, in the area of romance, males with the greatest emotional intimacy in their male friendships indicated they were likely to have had help from male friends. These men responded "yes" to experiences listed in the survey that included "Male friends listen to me vent my feelings about the relationship (which may include fear, joy, sadness, anger, happiness or jealousy)." It also meant male friends were likely to give suggestions or help men "take their mind off of the relationship" when things were not going well, and were likely to provide suggestions about what to do.

Respondents also answered "yes" to the item "I have a better sex life because I follow or have followed suggestions from friends (for example, to increase sexual pleasure and intimacy)." They also indicated male friends helped them with workplace situations, answering "yes" when asked if friends "help me better deal with work relationships."

Those respondents with a high degree of emotionally intimate male friends were also more likely than those with low levels of emotional intimacy to respond "yes" to the statement "My male friends help me maintain or improve my physical health and . . . encourage me to attend to my medical needs." The message from these men is clear: The higher the level of emotional intimacy in men's friendships, the greater the odds of experiencing help from male friends in some of the most intimate and important areas of men's lives—relationships, parenting, sex, health, and work.

Differences in Relating to Female Compared to Male Friends

When we asked about whether there is a difference in men's expression of emotions with close male friends and with close female friends, we found that men were slightly more emotionally expressive with other men than with women. While 27% said they lean more toward women in sharing emotions, 33% responded that they were more expressive with men. The remaining 40% said they were equally expressive with men and women.

Tensions in Men's Friendships

Given that even the closest friendships may experience some difficulty, we asked men what they do when feelings are hurt or they are upset by something that occurs with their close male friends. Nearly half of the men in the survey (46%) indicated they were likely to talk or take steps to resolve the problem. This implies that some type of processing of their experience with their friend is likely to take place. For other men, there is a tendency to make light of the matter through joking (17%) or simply ignoring (20%) the problem or issues that created the difficulty. A smaller proportion of respondents indicated they were likely to "take a break" from the friendship itself, while a very small number (less than 1%) said they were likely to end the relationship.

Influence of Social Stigma

One of the interests we had in preparing survey questions was the extent to which men might hold back from expressing themselves and their feelings for male friends through displays of physical or emotional closeness. Essentially, we wanted to know if men hesitate in their physical or emotional expression for fear of how others might interpret their actions. We asked: *How much do your concerns about how other people might respond interfere with how you express yourself physically and emotionally with your close male friends?*

For many men in our survey, the concern about other people's judgment did interfere with how they express themselves physically with their closest male friends. Such behaviors might include extending a hug, touching while in conversation, or even standing or sitting in close proximity. Only 12% of the respondents indicated that concern about others' judgment interfered frequently or all the time in their relationships. For 42% of our respondents, however, there is at least some degree of concern that might cause them to hesitate in displaying physical expression of their friendship. For a large percentage of our respondents, 46% overall, concern about others' judgment does not have an influence on their physical expression with their male friends.

When it comes to emotional expression—expressing excitement, sadness, joy, or hurt to their closest male friends—roughly 14% of our respondents indicated they hold back due to concerns about others' perceptions. Similar to comfort with physical expression, nearly 42% said they had some concern, but their responses suggest they are still likely to display emotions. For the remaining 44% of men taking the survey, concern with others' judgment does not interfere with their emotional expression.

Changes in Friendships over Time

We asked men to share how they experienced changes in their friendships that resulted from changes in their personal life. The changes we asked about included moving away from home, starting work full-time, entering a serious romantic relationship, moving in with a romantic partner, moving to another city, becoming a parent. With one exception, between 60% and 75% of our respondents indicated the number of close male friendships remained about the same, as did the level of intimacy and time spent in those relationships, regardless of personal changes they were experiencing. This response suggests that for many males, having close male friendships is a constant—once established, males are likely to continue to have such friendships at about the same level and with a similar degree of closeness, over time.

The most frequent shift in numbers of friends as a result of a personal life change came when men moved away from the family home. Twenty-seven percent of men reported they increased the number of friendships when they moved from home, and 23% indicated the number decreased. For 26% of our respondents there was an increase in the amount of time spent with friends after moving away from the family home, while 30% indicated the time together had decreased after moving.

At the same time, the emotional intimacy of their friendships dropped most significantly during this phase. This could be interpreted that having more friends also means having more caution about how open young men are willing to be at this stage of leaving home.

In all other areas we asked about—from job changes to parenting—between 15% and 30% of men indicated there was a shift in the quality of their friendships.

For most of the respondents with higher-level EI friendships, there was a significant drop-off in time spent with friends, though not in the number or the degree of intimacy with friends. When the men became parents, however, both number of friends and time spent with friends were significantly reduced. It's important to consider how these drop-offs in intimacy, as well as in numbers and time spent with friends, translate into the need for more support during these critical life stages.

The Influence of Father-Son Relationships

Males who grow up with emotionally close relationships with their own fathers, or a significant adult male figure, are more likely than other men to have emotionally close male friendships. This was true as well for males who were aware of their own fathers having emotionally close friendships. There was a 95% correlation between males having had emotionally close relationships with their father, or significant adult male figure, and the likelihood they had emotionally close male friendships themselves. A similar correlation was evident for those males who felt their own fathers had emotionally close male friendships. Additionally, a positive correlation exists between these respondents' desire for more close friendships and their desire for deepening the intimacy in their existing male friendships.

The absence of close father-son relationships appears to reduce the likelihood that males will have as many emotionally close male friends. Men taking the survey who indicated they had fewer than three close friends, or indicated they had little emotional closeness in their same-sex friendships, were also less likely than other males to have had emotionally close relationships with their fathers.

Friendships Matter—and Close,
Intimate Male Friendships Matter Greatly

Based on survey findings, it is clear that male friendships matter. For many men, they are a significant source of emotional intimacy. Such friendships are likely to be as important as or more important than men's close friendships with women in their lives. Some men will hold back displays of closeness, physical or emotional, out of concern about the stigma attached to such displays. For a small number of our respondents, those with little exposure to same-sex emotionally close friendships, there is little desire to pursue such relationships. Experience matters. The more males are exposed to emotionally close relationships with other males—and notably, the experience of having an emotionally close relationship with their father or father figure—the greater men's desire for such relationships throughout their lives. The findings suggest that it is important for boys to experience emotionally close relationships with their fathers or adult male figures, and for men of all ages and backgrounds to pursue such relationships throughout their lives.

NOTES

CHAPTER 1 | MEN IN TRANSITION

7 **because they do not yet need to."** Harriet Lerner, *The Dance of Intimacy: A Woman's Guide to Courageous Acts of Change in Key Relationships* (New York: Harper & Row, 1989), 7.

8 **40–60 percent for women.** Kim Parker and Wendy Wang, "Modern Parenthood: Roles of Moms and Dads Converge as They Balance Work and Family," Pew Research Social & Demographic Trends, March 14, 2013.

9 **than those who have close relationships.** E. H. Nasser and J. C. Overholser, "Recovery from Major Depression: The Role of Support from Family, Friends and Spiritual Beliefs," *Acta Psychiatrica Scandinavica* 111, no. 2 (February 2005): 125–132.

9 **depression and suicide.** Niobe Way, "What Boys *Really* Want from Their Fathers," *Huffington Post*, June 17, 2011.

9 **two out of every three divorces today.** Vicki Larson, "Why Women Walk Out More Than Men," *Huffington Post*, May 25, 2011. Larson cites a report from the National Marriage Project, University of Virginia.

9 **survival rates compared with those who do.** Chris Woolston, "Health Benefits of Friendship," *HealthDay*, March 11, 2014, a review of medical research on friendship and heart health.

10 **in *The Feminine Mystique*.** Betty Friedan, *The Feminine Mystique* (New York: W. W. Norton, 1997). Originally published in 1963.

11 **gays and lesbians, and Native Americans.** See Michael Kimmel, *Manhood in America: A Cultural History* (New York: Free Press, 1996). Also see Michael A. Messner, *Politics of Masculinities: Men in Movements* (Lanham, MD: Rowman & Littlefield, 1997) for a history and analysis of men's movements in the United States.

11 **the "mythopoetic men's movement."** Robert Bly, *Iron John: A Book About Men* (Reading, MA: Addison-Wesley, 1990).

11 **relating in openhearted and humane ways.** Authors include Terrence Real, *I Don't Want to Talk About It: Overcoming the Secret Legacy of Male Depression* (New York: Simon & Schuster, 1997); Samuel Osherson, *Finding Our Fathers: How a Man's Life Is Shaped by His Relationship with His Father* (New York: Ballantine, 1986); and Michael Kimmel, *Guyland: The Perilous World Where Boys Become Men* (New York: HarperCollins, 2008).

14 **called relational power.** Priscilla W. Blanton and Maria Vandergriff-Avery, "Marital Therapy and Marital Power: Constructing Narratives of Sharing Relational and Positional Power," *Contemporary Family Therapy* 23, no. 3 (September 2001): 295–308.

15 **maleness or femaleness its own unique character.** Harry Brod, "The Case for Men's Studies," in *The Making of Masculinities: The New Men's Studies,* ed. Harry Brod (Winchester, MA: Allen & Unwin, 1987), 39–62. Also see R. W. Connell, *Masculinities* (Berkeley: University of California Press, 1995).

16 **resistances about which I spoke earlier.** Richard L. Meth and Robert S. Pasick, *Men in Therapy: The Challenge of Change* (New York: Guilford Press, 1990).

17 **support groups in the 1970s and 1980s.** See Warren Farrell, *The Liberated Man: Beyond Masculinity; Freeing Men and Their Relationships with Women* (New York: Random House, 1974). Also see Herb Goldberg, *The Hazards of Being Male: Surviving the Myth of Masculine Privilege* (New York: Nash, 1976).

18 **local and national workshops and conferences.** Robert Garfield, "Male Emotional Intimacy: How Therapeutic Men's Groups Can

Enhance Couples Therapy," *Family Process* 49, no. 1 (March 2010): 109–122, and "Using Men's Groups to Enhance Couples Therapy: Men Helping Men," *Psychotherapy Networker* 36, no. 3 (May/June 2012).

18   **after they leave the group.** Contrast with other group models as described in Irvin D. Yalom and Molyn Leszcz, *The Theory and Practice of Group Psychotherapy* (New York: Basic Books, 2005).

21   **emotionally intimate exchanges with other men.** For good summaries of friendship research, including male friendship, see Beverley Fehr, *Friendship Processes* (Thousand Oaks, CA: Sage Publications, 1995), and R. Blieszner and R. Adams, *Adult Friendship* (Newbury Park, CA: Sage Publications, 1992).

21   **primarily on trust and emotional intimacy.** Ray Pahl, *On Friendship* (Cambridge, UK: Polity, 2000).

21   **while *complaining about this situation at the same time.*** Beverley Fehr, *Friendship Processes* (Thousand Oaks, CA: Sage Publications, 1995) 41, describes controversial findings in research about men's desire for and ability to have intimate conversations in male friendships.

CHAPTER 2 | BREAKING THE MALE CODE

29   **their emotional, expressive natures.** William Pollack, *Real Boys: Rescuing Our Sons from the Myths of Boyhood* (New York: Random House, 1998).

29   **that reinforce these behaviors.** Michael Kimmel, *Guyland: The Perilous World Where Boys Become Men* (New York: HarperCollins, 2008), 42–64.

30   **health and relationships with others.** Traditional behaviors associated with Male Code recur in the literature on men's difficulties with emotional adjustment. They are used in this book to contrast with emotional intimacy behaviors (also described in the literature). We used the latter as baseline behaviors we measure in our survey.

30 **chastity, fearlessness, and patriotism.** George L. Mosse, *The Image of Man: The Creation of Modern Masculinity* (New York: Oxford University Press, 1996), Chapters 1 and 2.

30 **personal sphere of home and women.** Michael Kimmel, *Manhood in America: A Cultural History* (New York: Free Press, 1996).

30 **expects from men over the past century.** Robert Brannon, "The Male Sex Role and What It's Done for Us Lately," in *The Forty-Nine Percent Majority: The Male Sex Role*, eds. Deborah S. David and Robert Brannon (Reading, MA: Addison-Wesley, 1976).

31 **guys are acting "up to code."** Kimmel, *Guyland*.

32 **Gay beatings and school shootings are examples.** Lila Shapiro, "Highest Number of Anti-Gay Murders Ever Reported in 2011: The National Coalition of Antiviolence Programs," *Huffington Post*, June 2, 2012. Also see Centers for Disease Control and Prevention's "Youth Risk Behavior Surveillance—United States 2013," *Surveillance Summaries* 63, no. 4 (June 2014).

32 **called for a return to militant masculinity."** See Joanna Bourke's review of George Mosse's *The Image of Man* in *Reviews in History* (review no. 23), February 1997.

33 **problems for men's health and their relationships.** Joseph H. Pleck, "The Gender Role Strain Paradigm: An Update," in *A New Psychology of Men*, eds. Robert F. Levant and William S. Pollack (New York: Basic Books, 1995), 11–32.

34 **health visits are not worth the time or cost.** P. M. Galdas, F. Cheater, and P. Marshall, "Men and Health Help-Seeking Behavior: Literature Review," *Journal of Advanced Nursing* 49, no. 6 (March 2005): 616–623.

34 **because of their higher-risk driving behavior.** Johns Hopkins School of Public Health, "Women Not Necessarily Better Drivers Than Men," *ScienceDaily*, June 18, 1988. Also see Ezio C. Cerrelli, "Crash Data and Rates for Age-Sex Groups of Drivers, 1996," NHTSA Research Note, January 1998.

40 **gay sex punishable by death.** Terri Rupar points out that ten countries—Yemen, Iran, Iraq, Mauritania, Nigeria, Qatar, Saudi Arabia, Somalia, Sudan, and the United Arab Emirates (possibly)—call for the death penalty for homosexual acts. Rupar, "Here Are the 10 Countries Where Homosexuality May Be Punished by Death," *Washington Post*, February 24, 2014.

42 **our abilities to process and communicate emotions.** Anne Fausto-Sterling, *Sexing the Body: Gender Politics and the Construction of Sexuality* (New York: Basic Books, 2000). See also Cordelia Fine, *Delusions of Gender: How Our Minds, Society, and Neurosexism Create Difference* (New York: W. W. Norton, 2010).

43 **each sex is able to listen in conversations!** Ashley Black, "Differences in Listening between a Man and a Woman," *eHow* (online), June 3, 2014. Lateralization differences of brain functioning in men and women, however, are still being debated in research studies. See Larry Barker and Kittie Watson, *Listen Up* (New York: St. Martin's Press, 2000).

43 **cognitive behavior therapy (CBT) and meditation.** Sharon Begley, "How Thinking Can Change the Brain," *Wall Street Journal*, January 19, 2007. Also see Fadel Zeidan et al., "Neural Correlates of Mindfulness Meditation-Related Anxiety Relief," *Social Cognitive and Affective Neuroscience* 9, no. 6 (June 2013): 751–759.

CHAPTER 3 | A BRIEF HISTORY OF MALE FRIENDSHIP

52 **intimacy closed only with his life."** Richard Behn, "The Boys" (see section on Joshua F. Speed [1814–1882]), in *Mr. Lincoln & Friends*, an educational website supported by the Lincoln Institute. Dr. Behn is director of research. www.mrlincolnandfriends.org.

52 **with a fervor and openness."** Caleb Crain, *American Sympathy: Men, Friendship, and Literature in the New Nation* (New Haven, CT: Yale University Press, 2001).

53 **degrees hitherto unknown."** Walt Whitman, *Democratic Vistas* (1871) (Amazon Digital Services, 2014).

54   **uniting for each other's benefit.** Aristotle's ideas about friendship are written in his *Nichomachean Ethics*, trans. and with notes by Terence Irwin (Indianapolis: Hackett Publishing, 1999). Cicero's ideas are written in *De Amicitia* (Amazon Digital Services, 2012).

54   **but the image of mine for thee?"** Walter Fröhlich (trans.), *The Letters of Saint Anselm of Canterbury*, Vol. 3 (Collegeville, MN: Cistercian Publications, 1994).

55   **examples in literature of this trend.** Leslie A. Fiedler, *Love and Death in the American Novel* (New York: Criterion, 1960).

55   **during the nineteenth century in Europe.** On romantic friendship, see E. Anthony Rotundo, "Romantic Friendship," *Journal of the History of Sexuality* 23 (1989):1–25. Also see Robert Brain, *Friends and Lovers* (New York: Basic Books, 1976). And see Lillian Faderman, *Surpassing the Love of Men: Romantic Friendship and Love Between Women from the Renaissance to the Present* (New York: William Morrow, 1981).

55   **defining guidelines for men and women in Europe and America.** For the Victorian influence on separate spheres, see Alexis de Tocqueville, *Democracy in America* (London: Saunders and Otley, 1840), Chapter XII: "How the Americans Understand the Equality of the Sexes," 101. Also see Charles E. Rosenberg, "Sexuality, Class and Role in 19th-Century America," *American Quarterly* 25, no. 2 (May 1973): 131–153. Finally, John Ruskin, *Sesame and Lilies* (1865), from Lecture 11—"Lilies," at Town Hall, Manchester, UK (Amazon Digital Services, 2011).

56   **support for their families and their marriages.** On the "companionate marriage," see Stacey J. Oliker, *Best Friends and Marriage: Exchange Among Women* (Berkeley: University of California Press, 1989), 4–14.

56   **same-sex friends well into the twenty-first century.** Drury Sherrod, "The Bonds of Men: Problems and Possibilities in Close Male Relationships," in *The Making of Masculinities: The New Men's Studies*, ed. Harry Brod (Winchester, MA: Allen and Unwin, 1987), 213–241.

59 **Geoff Greif describes as shoulder-to-shoulder style.** Geoffrey L.
    Greif, *Buddy System: Understanding Male Friendships* (New York:
    Oxford University Press, 2008), 66.

63 **what psychologist Pauline Boss calls ambiguous loss.** Pauline
    Boss, *Ambiguous Loss: Learning to Live with Unresolved Grief*
    (Cambridge, MA: Harvard University Press, 2000).

64 **what we can learn from these differences.** Hank Mandel (dir.),
    Five Friends documentary film, 2011, produced by Mandel and Erik
    Santiago, 70 min.

65 **to demonstrate his commitment to a friend.** Jan Yager,
    Friendshifts: The Power of Friendship and How It Shapes Our Lives,
    2nd ed. (Stamford, CT: Hannacroix Creek Books, 1999), 25–39.

66 **their middle-class counterparts.** Theodore F. Cohen, "Men's
    Families, Men's Friends: A Structural Analysis of Constraints on Men's
    Social Ties," in *Men's Friendships*, ed. Peter M. Nardi (Newbury Park,
    CA: Sage Publications, 1992), 115–131. Also see Clyde W. Franklin II,
    "Hey, Home—Yo, Bro," in Nardi, 201–214.

67 **continue them as emotionally intimate friendships.** Peter M. Nardi,
    "Sex, Friendship, and Gender Roles among Gay Men," in *Men's
    Friendships*, ed. Peter M. Nardi (Newbury Park, CA: Sage Publications,
    1992), 173–185.

67 **with other men because of this concern.** Louis Crompton,
    Homosexuality and Civilization (Cambridge, MA: Belknap Press of
    Harvard University Press, 2003). Also see Stephen O. Murray,
    Homosexualities (Chicago: University of Chicago Press, 2000).

68 **for an intimate discussion is a woman."** Sociologist Harry Reis,
    reported in Beverley Fehr, *Friendship Processes* (Thousand Oaks, CA:
    Sage Publications, 1996), 130.

69 **in the face of stressful stimuli.** Shelley E. Taylor et al.,
    "Biobehavioral Responses to Stress in Females: Tend-and-Befriend,
    Not Fight-or-Flight," *Psychological Review* 107, no. 3 (2000):
    411–429.

CHAPTER 4 | **THE SEASONS OF A MAN'S FRIENDSHIPS**

73 **age-related challenges in order to feel fulfilled.** Erik H. Erikson,
Childhood and Society (New York: W. W. Norton, 2013); originally
published 1950. Also see Daniel J. Levinson, *The Seasons of a Man's
Life* (New York: Knopf, 1978).

73 **how they will fare in future adult relationships.** William M. Bukowski,
Andrew F. Newcomb, and Willard W. Hartup, eds., *The Company
They Keep: Friendship in Childhood and Adolescence* (Cambridge, UK:
Cambridge University Press, 1996). Also see Thomas J. Berndt,
"Children's Friendships: Shifts over a Half-Century in Perspectives
on Their Development and Their Effects," *Merrill-Palmer Quarterly*
50, no. 3 (July 2004): 206–223.

73–74 **friendships earlier than we might think.** Michael Thompson and
Catherine O'Neill Grace, *Best Friends, Worst Enemies: Understanding the
Social Lives of Children* (New York: Ballantine Books, 2001), Chapter 3.

74 **Harry Stack Sullivan called chumships.** F. Barton Evans III,
Harry Stack Sullivan: Interpersonal Theory and Psychotherapy (London:
Taylor & Francis e-library, 2005). Originally published 1996.

75 **less than girls in their early years.** Lloyd deMause, "Why Men
Are More Violent," in *The Origins of War in Child Abuse*, printed in
the *Journal of Psychohistory*, 2010. Also see Robert Heasley, "Where
the Boys Are: And Where They Can Be If We Help," *Ithaca Child* 9,
no. 2 (Spring 1999).

75 **linked to 75 percent of school shooting incidents.** Centers for
Disease Control and Prevention's "Youth Risk Behavior
Surveillance—United States 2013," *Surveillance Summaries* 63, no. 4
(June 2014).

78 **when they are feeling vulnerable."** Niobe Way, *Deep Secrets: Boys'
Friendships and the Crisis of Connection* (Cambridge, MA: Harvard
University Press, 2011).

78 **a matter of manliness, maturity or sexuality."** Niobe Way, "What
Boys *Really* Want from Their Fathers," *Huffington Post*, June 17, 2011.

79 **and a family in the future.** Paul Taylor, "Young, Underemployed and Optimistic: Coming of Age, Slowly, in a Tough Economy," Pew Research Social & Demographic Trends, February 9, 2012.

80 **didn't work out as planned.** Michael Kimmel, keynote address, American Men's Study Association (AMSA) annual conference, Kansas City, April 2, 2011.

86 **it's not enough and feel bad about this.** Kim Parker and Wendy Wang, "Modern Parenthood: Roles of Moms and Dads Converge as They Balance Work and Family," Pew Research Social & Demographic Trends, March 14, 2013.

86 **than any other stage in the life cycle for *both men and women.*** Tim Walker and Alia McKee, "The State of Friendship in America 2013: A Crisis of Confidence," May 21, 2013. Self-published online survey by Lifeboat: Friends at Their Best, an organization concerned with the status of friendship in the United States.

86 **after their children were born.** See Appendix, "MFEI Survey," section "Changes in Friendships Over Time," pp. 274–276.

90 ***more stressed out* (uncertain of their futures).** Julian Hooks, "Baby Boomers More Stressed, More Satisfied Than Other Generations," *Business Administration Information*, November 1, 2013. A report of a study from PayScale.

90 **that figure rose to one in four.** Susan L. Brown and I-Fen Lin, "The Gray Divorce Revolution: Rising Divorce Among Middle-Aged and Older Adults, 1990–2010," *Journal of Gerontology: Social Sciences* 67, no. 6 (November 2012): 274–276.

90 **disappointed with the quality of their friendships.** See Tim Walker and Alia McKee, "The State of Friendship," 85.

CHAPTER 5 | AT THE STARTING GATE

99 **is profound and moving.** Stuart Miller, *Men and Friendship* (New York: Houghton Mifflin, 1983).

110   **Today, membership stands at 7 percent.** James B. Twitchell, *Where Men Hide* (New York: Columbia University Press, 2006), Chapter 3, "The Fraternal Lodge."

CHAPTER 6 | CONVERSATIONS FROM THE HEART

121   **whether they already had some or not.** See Appendix, "MFEI Survey," section "What Men Say About Their Experience," p. 271.

127   **what it means to be a man."** Terrence Real, *I Don't Want to Talk About It: Overcoming the Secret Legacy of Male Depression* (New York: Scribner, 1997), 125–127.

130   **all can make us feel vulnerable.** Brené Brown, *Daring Greatly: How the Courage to Be Vulnerable Transforms the Way We Live, Love, Parent, and Lead* (New York: Gotham, 2012).

134   **to easily manage complex emotional communication.** Simon Baron-Cohen, *The Essential Difference: Men, Women and the Extreme Male Brain* (New York: Penguin, 2004).

134   **demonstrated by both men and women.** Daphna Joel, "Male or Female? Brains Are Intersex," *Frontiers in Integrative Neuroscience 5*, no. 57 (September 2011). Also see Daphna Joel, TED Talk, "Are Brains Male or Female?" October 8, 2012.

135   **close male friendships.** See Appendix, "MFEI Survey," section "Extent of Emotional Intimacy," p. 270.

135   **attempts to form intimate friendships.** Barbara J. Bank and Suzanne L. Hansford, "Gender and Friendship: Why Are Men's Best Same-Sex Friendships Less Intimate and Supportive?" *Personal Relationships* 7, no. 1 (March 2000): 63–78.

137   **thoughts that come up along the way.** Jon Kabat-Zinn, *Wherever You Go, There You Are: Mindfulness Meditation for Everyday Life* (London: Piatkus/Little, Brown, 2004).

139 **words that describe their feelings.** The Feelings Wheel was developed by Gloria Willcox for use with adults and children to make connections with their feelings in a variety of therapy settings.

146 **not interested or not paying attention.** See Larry Barker and Kittie Watson, *Listen Up* (New York: St. Martin's Press, 2000).

147 **feed back our experience to him.** Vilayanur Ramachandran, "Self Awareness: The Last Frontier," Edge Foundation website, January 1, 2009. Accessed October 19, 2011.

147 **textbook written in the past twenty years.** Harville Hendrix, *Getting the Love You Want: A Guide for Couples* (New York: Henry Holt, 1988).

CHAPTER 7 | STAYING THE COURSE

157 **how satisfied they feel with their friendships.** See Tim Walker and Alia McKee, "The State of Friendship in America 2013: A Crisis of Confidence," May 21, 2013, Chapter 5, "Where Does Social Media Fit In?"

165 **their spouse, their children, and their parents.** See Appendix, "MFEI Survey," section "What Men Say About Their Experience," p. 271. This finding is also reported in Beverley Fehr, *Friendship Processes* (Thousand Oaks, CA: Sage Publications, 1996), 2.

CHAPTER 8 | FRIENDSHIP FIRST AID

174 **or taking a break to de-escalate tension.** See Appendix, "MFEI Survey," section "Tensions in Men's Friendships," p. 273.

188 **before it is entitled to the appellation."** George Washington in *Maxims of George Washington: Political, Military, Social, Moral and Religious* (Mount Vernon, VA: Mount Vernon Ladies' Association, 1953).

CHAPTER 9 | THE MEN BEHIND YOUR MARRIAGE

196 **contribute to problems within marriages.** Stephanie Coontz, "The Family Revolution," *Greater Good: The Science of a Meaningful Life* (online), September 1, 2007.

196 **lack of friendship that makes unhappy marriages.** Friedrich Nietzsche, *Thus Spoke Zarathustra* (originally published 1883–85), trans. R. J. Hollingdale (London: Penguin, 1969).

196 **when they spoke with close guy friends.** See Appendix, "MFEI Survey," section "How Males Rely on Male Friends," pp. 271–272.

207 **better deal with their relationships.** Michael P. Nichols and Richard C. Schwartz, *Family Therapy: Concepts and Methods* (Boston: Allyn & Bacon, 2004). See Introduction, material on triangles. For conceptual support, see Stacey J. Oliker, *Best Friends and Marriage: Exchange Among Women* (Berkeley: University of California Press, 1989), Chapter 1, "The Modernization of Friendship and Marriage," 1–32.

211 **infractions, possibly couples counseling.** Janis Abrahms Spring, *After the Affair: Healing the Pain and Rebuilding Trust When a Partner Has Been Unfaithful* (New York: HarperCollins, 1996). For clinicians, Gerald R. Weeks, Nancy Gambescia, and Robert Jenkins, *Treating Infidelity: Therapeutic Dilemmas and Effective Strategies* (New York: W. W. Norton, 2003).

213 **talk to your friend about his marriage.** Shirley P. Glass, *Not "Just Friends": Protect Your Relationship from Infidelity and Heal the Trauma of Betrayal* (New York: Free Press, 2003). Contains updated material on "the new infidelity," the workplace as the danger zone.

CHAPTER 10 | THE FATHER'S CLUB

220 **who received help in parenting their children.** See Appendix, "MFEI Survey," section "How Males Rely on Male Friends," pp. 271–272.

221 **their fathers or other important men during childhood.** See Appendix, "MFEI Survey," section "The Influence of Father-Son Relationships," p. 276.

221 **sons having their own close male bonds.** See Barbara J. Bank and Suzanne L. Hansford, "Gender and Friendship: Why Are Men's Best Same-Sex Friendships Less Intimate and Supportive?" *Personal Relationships* 7, no. 1 (March 2000): 63–78.

237 **adopted kids who grow up in gay and lesbian families.** Rachel H. Farr and Charlotte J. Patterson, "Coparenting among Lesbian, Gay, and Heterosexual Couples: Associations with Adopted Children's Outcomes," *Child Development* 84, no. 4 (July/August 2013): 1226–1240.

240 **the *mentoring* role for dads.** A model for *emotional* mentoring, presented in Lawrence Agresto, *A Father's New Beginning* (Amazon Digital Services, Motivational Press, 2014).

241 **call their children's college professors to complain about their kids' test results.** Neil M. Montgomery, "The Negative Impact of Helicopter Parenting on Personality," Research (poster session X) presented at 22nd annual convention of Association for Psychological Science, Boston, May 29, 2010.

243 **all within a small number of years.** Monica McGoldrick, Betty Carter, and Nydia Garcia Preto, *The Expanded Family Life Cycle: Individual, Family, and Social Perspectives* (New York: Allyn & Bacon, 2010).

243 **don't get distracted by old emotional baggage).** Constance Ahrons, *The Good Divorce: Keeping Your Family Together When Your Marriage Comes Apart* (New York: HarperCollins, 1994).

243 **children's fears stupefied newlywed stepparents!** Robert Garfield and Linda Schwoeri, unpublished findings from pilot study "Working with Stepfamilies," supported by Hahnemann Medical University, Department of Mental Health Sciences, 1982.

243 **consultation about kids and divorce can be helpful.** Patricia L. Papernow, *Surviving and Thriving in Stepfamily Relationships: What Works and What Doesn't* (New York: Routledge, 2013).

CHAPTER 11 | THE EXECUTIVE COMMITTEE

248 **encouraging workers to develop close friendships.** Dorie Clark,
"Debunking the 'No Friends at Work' Rule: Why Friend-Friendly
Workplaces Are the Future," interview of Alia McKee and Tim
Walker, cofounders of Lifeboat, *Forbes* (online), May 21, 2013.

248 **results in a shared commitment to and discipline toward the
work."** Christine M. Riordan, "We All Need Friends at Work,"
Harvard Business Review, July 3, 2013. Riordan cites a 2012 Gallup
report that found that 50 percent of employees with a best friend at
work reported that they feel a strong connection with their company,
compared to just 10 percent of employees without a best friend at work.

248 **better able to attract other good employees.** Jim Meyerle, "The
Friendship Effect," *Huffington Post*, December 20, 2012. This is a report
of a series of studies by the same name on the effect of friendship in
the workplace. Meyerle's workforce intelligence company, Evolv,
reports that employees referred by their friends are less likely to quit
and are more productive.

255 **steer clear of and protect yourself (and others) from.** Richard G.
Weaver and John D. Farrell, *Managers as Facilitators: A Practical
Guide to Getting Work Done in a Changing Workplace* (Oakland:
Berrett-Koehler, 1997), Chapter 9, "Facilitation Is Boundary
Management," 147–173.

259 **spill into your work environment and disrupt operations.** Abbi
Perets, "Who's the Boss? Tips for Managing Friends and Former
Peers," *TechRepublic*, September 30, 2002.

ACKNOWLEDGMENTS

This book is my first one, and as many people warned me, writing a book is not an easy task. It required discipline, time alone, and getting a lot of support—three things I learned I wasn't as good at as I needed to be.

Help came in many forms: inspiration, encouragement, as well as much-needed hands-on guidance.

Influences

I've been blessed with wonderful mentors. Carl Whitaker taught me about the power of emotional intimacy in healing. An early therapist, Warren Hampe, allowed me to help him, and by doing so helped me gain confidence in myself. Israel Zwerling, my first boss in Philadelphia, was tough and pushed me hard to become a competent psychiatrist and academic. These men, all different personalities, cared about me in their own ways. They were father figures who helped me grow up, personally and professionally.

Three women, Marianne Walters, Peggy Papp, and Olga Silverstein, were also influences. I didn't have as much contact with Marianne as I'd have liked because she passed away too soon. They all helped me appreciate how gender inequality not only limited women's opportunities but also limits men's abilities to connect with others and to care for ourselves.

I've worked with my longtime professional partner, Ellen

Berman, and our practice group, Bala Psychological Resources, collaborating on cases and supporting one another for twenty-five years. My clinical work with men and women, individually and together, has developed and matured within this group.

The American Family Therapy Academy has been a professional extended family for me since 1980. I've never quite believed my good fortune to have this creative group of individuals as colleagues. They are leaders in the field of family systems theory and therapy, as well as in integrating issues of gender and culture into clinical practice. Many of their ideas are fundamental to this book. Thank you, Connie Ahrons, Evan Imber-Black, Pauline Boss, Larry Levner, Marilyn Mason, Monica McGoldrick, Patricia Papernow, and David Wohlsifer. The AFTA Men's Institute, now organized by Roger Lake and Jim Verser, has long supported deeper connections between the men in our organization.

My more recent friendship and collaboration with Robert Heasley, former president of the American Men's Studies Association, has deepened my thinking about men and masculinity in society. Through AMSA I've met and have been enriched by the work of the brilliant Michael Kimmel, a man who understands the dilemmas faced by men in this country as well as anyone. Meeting and working with therapist and film producer Hank Mandel (*Five Friends*) has been another important connection for me.

Together, Robert and I developed and launched a survey on men's friendships and emotional intimacy ("MFEI Survey," 2012). I want to thank our research team, which includes my son, Isaac Garfield; Jake Kriger; and two exceptional research colleagues, John Anderson at Indiana University of Pennsylvania and Suzanne McMurphy at the University of Windsor.

The Writing

My "home" editor, Marian Sandmaier, has been involved with the book from the beginning. Marian is a gifted writer and editor, and she helped me write the book I wanted to write, one that's accessible, written in what she calls "kitchen table" language. I can't describe the pleasure I've had in working with her, delighting in her delight over what I was writing, laughing about my stories, and tossing around different ways of saying things. Her observations and suggestions have been the equivalent of being in a writer's program. I've grown so much from working with you, Marian.

If agents can be guardian angels, Joelle Delbourgo is one. She's an author's dream agent, smart and experienced. Joelle has an intuitive grasp of psychology. I'll never forget her looking at me at lunch, after I'd insisted on driving three hours to Montclair, New Jersey, to meet her before signing a contract. With some amusement, she said, "I guess you're a therapist, and you really want to know who you're working with, right?" She "got" the book and in short order got us to Gotham/Penguin, where the book found its home.

Joelle offered me an impressive tutorial on how things "really" work in today's publishing world. "Chill, it'll be OK," was her favorite line. She was right.

Lauren Marino, the editorial director at Gotham, acquired the book and pushed me from the beginning to make it bigger. Over time I saw her point. As a result, I believe that the book is far better, a more powerful book. Brooke Carey line edited the entire manuscript and helped me reshape the initial chapters. Brooke is smart, enthusiastic, and has breezily walked me through all the numerous steps necessary to get the book into production. She and

Lauren's assistant, Emily Wunderlich, have made this complicated process go much easier. Thanks to all of you.

Many other people helped in the reading of chapters and early drafts, as well as proving advice about the publishing process. My wife, Sandy, made useful suggestions about the clarity of my ideas and what material did or didn't engage the reader. Ellen Berman was helpful around what issues should be included, left out, or altered, especially in the early drafts. Jake Kriger provided clinical insights around the cases I described from our Friendship Labs. My brother, David Garfield; Nancy Gambescia; and Arlene Goldman all gave me helpful insights about what to expect in the process of writing the book.

Personal Support

My close guy friends have supported me over my lifetime. I've included our stories in the book. In the process of writing, I've reconnected with some along the way, rebooting these relationships while deepening others that are more current. There's not room here to name all your names, but thank you especially, Doug, Larry, Michael, David, Rich, most of the Geezers (identified in the book), Anson, and the guys from my college singing group, the Footnotes, and finally, my movie club guys, Reel Men.

Special thanks to my best friend, Jake Kriger, whose multiple roles in my life and whose spirit permeate this book, for listening, and patiently supporting my writing for the past two years. You taught me how to become a good best friend.

I want to thank the men I've worked with individually, as well as those who've been part of our Friendship Labs. In opening your hearts, sharing your stories with us, and helping one another become stronger and more compassionate human beings, you've incredibly enriched my life by allowing me to witness and have the opportunity to facilitate this process.

Sandy, my wife, has been my best friend and support throughout the writing. Her willingness to allow me the time and leeway, to serve as an auxiliary brain around tasks that I handled better when I wasn't so preoccupied, is immensely appreciated. At a point of overwhelm when I felt I wouldn't be able to meet the writing deadline and should resign from the project, she took my head in her hands, looked into my eyes, smiled, and said, "Yeah, right." I came to my senses. Thanks, honey.

My brother and sister, Deborah and David, and I have been best friends since childhood. Deborah has encouraged this book from the start. David, an academic psychiatrist and author of several books, provided great suggestions for the organization of the initial chapters and invaluable advice and wisdom on the publication process. Thanks, Ds.

My children, Isaac, Julie, and Beki, have all been cheerleaders. My son Isaac, a therapist, has been a staunch supporter and a direct contributor himself with his key role in organizing the survey. It's been exhilarating and a great source of pride to me to work with him. My daughters, Julie and Beki, have also weighed in on the project with their marketing and design ideas.

And thanks, finally, to my parents, Milt and Harriet. Your imprint is all over this book, especially your rock-solid support of friendships—your own, mine, and those I've seen my children develop.

INDEX